To Right Historical Wrongs

Law and Society Series
W. Wesley Pue, General Editor

The Law and Society Series explores law as a socially embedded phenomenon. It is premised on the understanding that the conventional
division of law from society creates false dichotomies in thinking, scholarship, educational practice, and social life. Books in the series treat law
and society as mutually constitutive and seek to bridge scholarship
emerging from interdisciplinary engagement of law with disciplines
such as politics, social theory, history, political economy, and gender
studies.

A list of titles in the series appears at the end of the book.

To Right Historical Wrongs

Race, Gender, and Sentencing in Canada

CARMELA MURDOCCA

UBCPress · Vancouver · Toronto

21 20 19 18 17 16 15 14 13   5 4 3 2 1

Printed in Canada on FSC-certified ancient-forest-free paper
(100% post-consumer recycled) that is processed chlorine- and acid-free.

_____

Library and Archives Canada Cataloguing in Publication

Murdocca, Carmela, author
     To right historical wrongs : race, gender, and sentencing in Canada /
Carmela Murdocca.

(Law and society, 1496-4953)
Parts of this book were previously published in journals.
Includes bibliographical references and index.
Issued in print and electronic formats.

ISBN 978-0-7748-2497-2 (bound); ISBN 978-0-7748-2499-6 (pdf)

     1. Discrimination in criminal justice administration – Canada. 2. Prison sentences – Canada. 3. Native peoples – Legal status, laws, etc. – Canada. 4. Minorities – Legal status, laws, etc. – Canada. 5. Reparations for historical injustices – Canada. 6. Race discrimination – Canada. 7. Canada – Race relations. I. Title. II. Series: Law and society series (Vancouver, B.C.)

HV9960.C2M87 2013   364.971   C2013-905267-4
                                                        C2013-905268-2

_____

Canadä

UBC Press gratefully acknowledges the financial support for our publishing program of the Government of Canada (through the Canada Book Fund), the Canada Council for the Arts, and the British Columbia Arts Council.

This book has been published with the help of a grant from the Canadian Federation for the Humanities and Social Sciences, through the Awards to Scholarly Publications Program, using funds provided by the Social Sciences and Humanities Research Council of Canada.

UBC Press
The University of British Columbia
2029 West Mall
Vancouver, BC V6T 1Z2
www.ubcpress.ca

Contents

Preface and Acknowledgments

Section 718.2(e) of the *Criminal Code* of Canada is a sentencing provision designed to address the overrepresentation of Aboriginal people in Canadian prisons.[1] This section was most recently considered by the Supreme Court of Canada in the 2012 decision of *R. v Ipeelee*, in which the Court stated: "When sentencing an aboriginal offender, courts must take judicial notice of such matters as the history of colonialism, displacement, and residential schools and how that history continues to translate into lower educational attainment, lower incomes, higher unemployment, higher rates of substance abuse and suicide, and, of course, higher levels of incarceration for aboriginal peoples."[2] *Ipeelee* identifies the necessity of connecting past injustice to present-day realities for all offenders, with a particular emphasis on the unique experiences of indigenous people. This book examines how such matters of historical injustice and contemporary forms of marginalization are taken into account in criminal sentencing in Canada. I examine several legal cases, parliamentary debates, government reports, media commentary, and community sources in order to show how the interaction between narratives about past injustices and contemporary discrimination are given new meaning in Canada's sentencing regime. To highlight my specific interest in exploring how a concern with the past is used in sentencing,

I examine the racial and gendered implications for indigenous men and women and black women when considerations of historical injustice are at stake in the law.

There are more indigenous and racialized people incarcerated today than at any time in Canadian history.[3] The absence of a public conversation about the racial dimensions of imprisonment is consistent with the moral and ethical concerns that have constituted the Canadian state since early settler colonialism. As many prison activists suggest, the people who experience forms of punishment at increased rates come to symbolize the essence and intent of the moral and social ideas and ideals that form the basis of any nation. Canada is not unique in its practices of incarcerating indigenous and racialized people. The United Nations has drawn attention to the fact that in the last forty years incarceration rates for indigenous and racialized people across liberal settler states, including Canada, the United States, Australia, and New Zealand, is an international crisis. Neither is Canada unique in signifying a willingness to ameliorate conditions for indigenous people. In the post–Second World War period, scholars have noted a trend towards amending historical injustices through practices of reparative justice and reconciliation in liberal multicultural states.[4] Interest in historical forms of injustice is at the centre of global politics and international morality. In recent years, the Canadian state has engaged in an array of reparative practices that address historical forms of injustice towards indigenous peoples, including apologies, a royal commission, public inquiries, and a truth and reconciliation commission. This new emphasis on moral issues, domestically and internationally, "has been characterized not only by accusing other countries of human rights abuses but also by self-examination," and it has been described as the "new guilt of nations."[5]

At its core, this book is motivated by an attempt to examine two contemporary social and political practices: the mass incarceration of indigenous and racialized people and the post–Second World War trend of amending historical injustices in liberal nation-states. In so doing, I explore a criminal justice reform project as a launching point with which to examine these social and political trends. In 1996, significant amendments were made to the *Criminal Code*. Of the many amendments, section 718.2(e) was added to the principles of sentencing, and it states: "A court that imposes a sentence shall take into consideration the following principles: ... (e) all available sanctions other than imprisonment that are reasonable in the circumstances should be considered for all offenders, with particular attention to the circumstances of aboriginal offenders."[6] This reform project was a contested exercise when amendments to the *Criminal Code* were under consideration. When I began the research for this project, I mainly encountered formal legal observations of the potentials and pitfalls of such a reform project, and this body of literature has been central to my thinking as well as to the substantive legal and sociological considerations of the provisions that I consider in the *Criminal Code*.

This work then encouraged me to pursue an analysis of what is at the core of this legal provision – namely a project of reparative justice that illuminates the relationships between histories of colonization, contemporary racisms, and reparative justice in liberal multicultural states. It is indeed a judicial quagmire to consider historical injustice at the moment of sentencing – to bind retribution with reparation. Concerning reparations for slavery, Stephen Best and Saidiya Hartman ask, "why is the appeal for redress one that seems always to arrive too late, and to be marked by a note of belatedness and insufficiency?"[7] What, then, can we make of this appeal for redress in Canada at the moment when a person is confronting imprisonment and confinement? While a sentencing hearing may be an unusual point in the criminal justice process to link the present and the past in this manner, it is nevertheless a moment that is remarkably rich for considering the ethical grounds of race, gender, reparations, and nationalism. It is also, I would add, idiosyncratically Canadian in its seemingly contradictory aspirations.

There is a grave social and ethical crisis at the heart of this book – one that destroys lives and entire communities. Indigenous overrepresentation in prisons continues to increase, and Aboriginal women are currently being incarcerated at even more alarming rates than ever before. These rates occur even though formal amendments to sentencing were made in the mid-1990s, with the stated intent to take national responsibility for the disproportionate incarceration of indigenous peoples. There is no question that Canada has attempted to be creative in sentencing. However, regional variations show that certain racialized groups are targeted for crimes even in the face of ameliorative sentencing regimes. Today, Canada is proceeding with the institutionalized practices of reconciliation, commemoration, and reparation at the same time that mass incarceration and other forms of destruction and degradation destroy indigenous and racialized communities. These parallel realities require our critical attention, for they reveal much about the interdependence between violence, marginalization, and progress in liberal and multicultural societies.

This book would not have been written without the early support of Sherene Razack, Kari Dehli, D. Alissa Trotz, and Jonathan Goldberg-Hiller. I am indebted to Sherene Razack's intellectual work, and I am grateful for her continuing guidance. A number of institutions provided financial support for this project. This book has been published with the support of the Canadian Federation for the Humanities and Social Sciences, through the Awards to Scholarly Publications Program, using funds provided by the Social Science and Humanities Research Council of Canada. I wrote early drafts of this book while holding a Fulbright Fellowship at Columbia University, and I thank the Canada-US Fulbright Program, the Center for the Study of Law and Culture at Columbia Law School, and especially Katherine Franke and Elizabeth Povinelli, for supporting the project.

I have learned that graduate students renew the life of earlier projects. In my case, graduate students in sociology, socio-legal studies, and social and political thought at York University, in particular, Fenn Stewart and Shaira Vadasaria, helped me to find new ways into this work. Kristin Ciupa provided invaluable legal research assistance. Fenn Stewart's steadfast engagement and research assistance immeasurably improved the book. Randy Schmidt at UBC Press devoted his time to support this book, and the anonymous reviewers generously and substantively improved the book. Over the years, I have also benefited from the support and engagement of colleagues from the Law and Society Association and the Canadian Law and Society Association. I thank Christine Jonathan, Natasha Bakht, and Carla Mancini for being stalwart advisors and supporters. Last, but certainly not least, I thank my mother and father.

Parts of the book were published in earlier forms in the following publications and are reprinted with permission: C. Murdocca, "From Incarceration to Restoration: National Responsibility, Gender and the Production of Difference," *Social and Legal Studies* 18, no. 1 (2009): 23-45 and C. Murdocca, "National Responsibility and Systemic Racism in Criminal Sentencing: The Case of *R. v. Hamilton,*" in Nicholas Blomley and Sean Robertson, eds., *The Place of Justice* (Vancouver: Fernwood Publishing, 2006) 67-94.

To Right Historical Wrongs

Introduction

On 28 February 1995 in Ottawa, Martha Flaherty, president of Pauktuutit (the Inuit women's association of Canada), presented a submission to the Standing Committee on Justice and Legal Affairs concerning a proposal to overhaul the sentencing guidelines in the *Criminal Code* of Canada.[1] Much like today, the incarceration of indigenous peoples in 1995 had reached record levels, and many justice and public inquiries were pointing to the need to address the problem. Bill C-41 contained proposals to amend the *Criminal Code* in order to encourage judges to consider historical and systemic issues when sentencing Aboriginal and Inuit offenders. The amendments were intended to also incorporate restorative justice principles in the sentencing process that would help to address the problem of overincarceration of Aboriginal peoples in Canadian prisons and detention centres.[2] Flaherty and Pauktuutit were most troubled by the proposed changes to the principles of sentencing that would instruct judges to offer alternative sanctions to imprisonment for all offenders, while encouraging judges to pay particular attention to the historical and contemporary circumstances of Aboriginal offenders.[3] In her oral submission to the committee, Flaherty recounted the ways in which Canada's criminal justice system had failed the women of her community, who experience ongoing colonialism and violence in every aspect of their lives. "Without sounding like a broken record," Flaherty explained to the committee, "women and children are not safe from abuse and assault. To suggest the purpose of sentencing is to maintain the safe society we live in ignores this reality."[4] Flaherty was concerned that the proposed changes would not address the very real issues of violence and marginalization in the lives of the women she represents.

Pauktuutit demonstrated that when issues of violence are at stake in law notions of indigenous culture have often been distorted, with effects that put Inuit women at increased risk of violence. As Flaherty explained,

> when non-Inuit judges take into account mitigating factors that are based on cultural issues, such as the man being a good hunter and providing for his family, not knowing that what he did was not acceptable in the law since it is acceptable in Inuit culture, and failing to fully understand the extent of the harm and violence of sexual assault as a violent act, not just a matter of sex without affection – we believe this is a violation of our rights. We fear that Bill C-41 will not address the injustice of the current system, but instead will result in greater violations and inequities for Inuit women.[5]

In directly addressing the proposed amendments to the *Criminal Code*, Flaherty's submission was underpinned by the following questions. If amendments to sentencing will not benefit Aboriginal and Inuit communities, and women in particular, then who will be the beneficiary of this amendment? What is its intended purpose? Indeed, a new approach to sentencing has been part of a much longer history of Aboriginal and Inuit negotiations with the Canadian government, in which notions of cultural distinctiveness and cultural difference have been central. The unease that Pauktuutit identified regarding the new sentencing guidelines suggested that these proposals would continue the history of the legal system appropriating the notion of culture in perilous ways. In expressing the anxieties of her organization regarding the proposed bill, Flaherty asked: "What do we have to give up to get what the government is offering us through this bill?" "For some Inuit Women," Flaherty insisted, "the effectiveness of any new approach to dealing with accused offenders could be a matter of life and death."[6] Pauktuutit's concerns notwithstanding, the amendment was proclaimed as law a year later.

The *Criminal Code* now contains a unique sentencing provision aimed at offering alternatives to incarceration for Aboriginal peoples. Section 718.2(e) of the *Criminal Code* states: "A court that imposes a sentence shall take into consideration the following principles: ... (e) all available sanctions other than imprisonment that are reasonable in the circumstances should be considered for all offenders, with particular attention to the circumstances of aboriginal offenders."[7] This provision was developed by the Canadian government in order to address the overincarceration rates of indigenous people in Canadian prisons. The aspiration (on the part of the government) was to recognize the history of colonization (as well as the historical circumstances and experiences of indigenous peoples that may bring them into more frequent contact with the criminal justice system) and to take national responsibility for the egregious numbers of incarcerated indigenous people. Since the amendment, sentencing decisions have also considered the application of section 718.2(e) to the sentencing of black Canadian women, who experience systemic racism in the criminal justice system.

This book traces the emergence, implications, and application of section 718.2(e) of the *Criminal Code*, as it pertains to the legal production of indigenous and racialized subjects in the context of considerations of the relationship between criminalization and historical forms of injustice. Since section 718.2(e) of the *Criminal Code* is oriented towards a concern about the injustices of the past and the relationship of these injustices to the present, I suggest that this sentencing provision requires that we think critically about how ideas concerning reparative justice are pursued in law. In this book, I trace three aspects of section 718.2(e): (1) the racial and gendered implications of section 718.2(e) for indigenous and other racialized groups; (2) the generative function of appeals to historical injustice in sentencing decisions; and (3) the contestations that result from negotiating ideas about reparative justice in law. I argue that restorative approaches in sentencing entrench rather than alleviate certain forms of racism and sexism when they are structured as appeals to cultural difference. This book is informed by socio-legal, post-colonial, anthropological, and critical race scholarship.

Given the many interactions and contestations between indigenous communities and federal and provincial governments in Canada, Pauktuutit's submission to the Standing Committee on Justice and Legal Affairs is a familiar historical moment in the context of Aboriginal, Métis, and Inuit peoples' dissatisfaction with attempts by the Canadian government to develop policy incentives that aim to benefit indigenous communities. A parliamentary committee is one of the many sites where indigenous people articulate their dissatisfaction with experiences of government regulation. This archive of official interaction with the state shows that such exchanges do not amount to simple appeals for indigenous agency but, rather, show the density of indigenous political subjectivity when operative in the official legal and public domain. Pauktuutit's submission highlights the many ways in which contestations around the government regulation of "indigenous affairs" reveal that particular ideas about cultural difference are central to the production of gendered and racial knowledge about indigenous peoples. As Pauktuutit points out, cultural approaches to understanding indigenous communities often saturate the legal process for indigenous peoples.

This book pursues an analysis of section 718.2(e) beyond the context of its legal machinations in order to examine the ways in which ideas about reparation and reconciliation are intertwined and emerge out of processes of criminalization. Indeed, the links between criminalization and reparation have been established by appeals to truth and reconciliation and are often motivated by the experience and evidence of extreme forms of violence and criminalization. Criminality is often and increasingly the ground upon which questions of justice, moral responsibility, and the ethical responses of states are opened up to contestation and consideration. While these considerations frequently take place in the context of mass atrocities and extreme forms of violence and degradation, and are often motivated by appeals to a global community, this book urges us to consider these questions as also and equally emerging from (and being constituted by) distinctly national provisions that are ultimately manifest in the everyday workings of the criminal justice system.

An analysis of section 718.2(e) allows us to think through the many ways in which forms of racial governance occasion, and are occasioned by, a system of regulation that is at once national and global.[8] This sentencing provision, I argue, can be considered a practice of reparative justice because it bears the traces of an approach to ameliorating the overincarceration of Aboriginal peoples that is inflected with a reconciliatory and reparative framework. This sentencing provision demands and compels an engagement with the past in its assessment of the present realities of Aboriginal offenders. It is in this sense that I suggest that section 718.2(e) is a practice of reparative justice. "Reparative justice" is a broad phrase that refers to the social, political, artistic, and legal practices that orient to the past in considering the present (a broader analysis of the definitional contours of reparative and restorative justice is contained in Chapter 1).

Mark D. Walters suggests that Canadian law is unique to the extent that an idea of reconciliation is embedded in forms of legality concerning indigenous peoples.[9] Walters canvasses Aboriginal rights cases and suggests that a "jurisprudence of reconciliation" permeates much of the legal discourse concerning indigenous peoples in Canada.[10] While the proposed sentencing amendments explicitly invoke the idea that the government should take national responsibility for disproportionate incarceration, as I show in subsequent chapters, the amendments also provide the ground upon which to consider the epistemological basis of racial and gendered subjectivities in the context of legal considerations of historical injustice. It is indeed a unique practice to consider historical experiences of injustice at the moment of sentencing, and this book reveals that it may be a pernicious practice, not least because this provision invokes notions of cultural difference in the context of systemic injustice. The use of section 718.2(e) in sentencing decisions highlights the different and often paradoxical meanings that culture acquires in law.

Although there has been considerable academic interest in this sentencing provision in Canada, much of it has been focused primarily on a strict reading of its legal implications and its effect within the criminal justice domain.[11] Other scholars have shown the ways in which this legal provision has had varied effects and limited success concerning the overincarceration of Aboriginal peoples.[12] Scholars also examine the ways in which this legal provision involves issues concerning restorative justice.[13] This research points also to the limits of sentencing as a criminal justice practice to respond to systemic issues in the criminal justice system. A practice embedded at the end of the criminal justice process cannot alone undo the social, political, and economic forms of marginalization that result in indigenous and racialized people having more frequent contact with the criminal justice system. For example, sentencing as a response to overincarceration does not address the broader processes of criminalization that include how crimes are identified and constructed, the historical specificity of sentences, and how sentences relate to practices of police discretion.[14] In this regard, the limits of the role of sentencing judges in addressing systemic issues and the nature and practice of individualized sentencing (that is, sentences that are tailored to the specific offence and specific offender as revealed by the evidentiary facts of a case) have also formed the basis of scholarship pertaining to section 718.2(e).[15]

To date, little of this literature locates this legal provision within the broader context of examining the production of racial knowledge through the notion of cultural difference, gendered forms of racism and violence, and legal subjectivity for racialized peoples (indigenous and non-indigenous) when invocations of historical injustice are at stake. This book examines the practical and ontological barriers of addressing questions of historical injustice in the sentencing process for both indigenous and other racialized Canadians. Arguably, as I will assess in subsequent chapters, these barriers emerge through a "jurisprudence of reconciliation."[16] This book examines section 718.2(e) of the *Criminal Code* for what it reveals about the ways in which liberal considerations of historical injustice produce indigenous and racialized subjects through reparative sentencing mechanisms. My aim is to show how the production of particular modes of racial governance is central to the current and robust interest in issues of historical injustice, reparations, and multiculturalism in Canada. This book develops and advances a framework for understanding the contemporary production of indigenous and racialized subjects in the context of reparative justice projects.

The title of the book is derived from a significant case (examined in Chapter 4) concerning two black women charged with the crime of cocaine importation where the Ontario Court of Appeal reasoned that sentencing was not the place *"to right perceived societal wrongs ... or 'make up' for perceived social injustices."*[17] Although the court suggested that sentencing was not the place to right historical wrongs, the emergence and contingence of the statement suggests that forms of criminalization and incarceration are tethered to ethical and moral imperatives concerning temporalities that link past and present injustices. Pursuing these linkages motivates the questions that guide this book. How does race-based sentencing offer us a way to consider the connections between historical injustices and contemporary racisms? How do different racialized communities make similar and different claims to the legal notions of historical disadvantage and systemic racism? How is responsibility articulated as a national interest in criminal sentencing? What kinds of national subjects are produced because of, and despite, these claims?

Some Background

In 1994, a comprehensive sentencing reform bill, Bill C-41, was introduced in the Parliament of Canada. Bill C-41 eventually led to an overhaul of the *Criminal Code* and, specifically, to the addition of section 718.2(e) in 1996. Legal scholars have suggested that the 1996 overhaul of the *Criminal Code* began in 1979, when the federal government unanimously decided that a comprehensive review of the *Criminal Code* was needed, owing to a number of concerns pertaining to punishment and incarceration. These concerns included, as Toni Williams notes, "three main concerns about established practices: the broad scope of judicial discretion at sentencing; general over-use of incarceration in penal sanctions; and the disproportionate representation of Aboriginal people in Canadian prisons."[18] There is evidence to suggest that section 718.2(e) in particular was the direct result of much government attention in the form of public inquiries, the Royal Commission on Aboriginal

Peoples, community legal pressure, and other reports regarding the need to take national responsibility for addressing the disproportionate representation of Aboriginal peoples in the criminal justice system.[19] Williams suggests that sentencing reform needs to be understood within the broader context of industrialized and democratic nations that have sought in the last twenty-five years to "restructure aspects of criminalization and crime control practice," including "decisions about punishment – what kind, how much, and under what conditions."[20] These preoccupations and new policy strategies took place in Canada in the context of "an increase in imprisonment that had occurred in the 1980s and early 1990s."[21] It was not until 1999, when the Supreme Court of Canada released *R. v Gladue,* that the meaning of section 718.2(e) was interpreted judicially and thus acquired the status of a significant legal precedent.[22] In this case, the Court reasoned (following Parliament's lead) that Canadian judges who sentence Aboriginal offenders must consider the historical and systemic disadvantage that First Nations people and communities have endured and must contemplate creative, remedial, or restorative justice principles in the application of alternative sentencing in order to address and reduce the number of indigenous people who are incarcerated.

The aspirations for section 718.2(e) have not yet been realized, even though the impact of the *Gladue* decision has led to a significant shift in criminal justice practices, including the institutionalized development of Aboriginal courts in Canada, the addition of *Gladue* principles in the 2002 *Youth Criminal Justice Act,* and the fact that in Ontario *Gladue* "now applies throughout the court process whenever the liberty of an Aboriginal person is at stake," including bail hearings,[23] parole eligibility, dangerous offender applications, and consideration in the civil contempt of court cases and disposition hearings at the Ontario Review Board.[24] While *Gladue* has become an important catalyst for a range of new institutional practices and procedures, we must temper our heralding of *Gladue* as a "signpost of social change" or the changes it has ushered as "totemic markers of irrevocable social change."[25] One legal decision does not change historical and systemic challenges.

As a number of scholars and government reports note, Aboriginal overrepresentation has continued to increase since the introduction of section 718.2(e).[26] Notably, although there has been a decline in Canada's total incarceration rates, "analysis shows significant and troubling variations among different populations, with Aboriginal women being imprisoned disproportionately and at higher rates than in the past."[27] A Statistics Canada reports show that,

> from 1998/1999 to 2007/2008, there has been a slower decrease in the number of Aboriginal people admitted to provincial and territorial sentenced custody compared to non-Aboriginal persons ... Consequently, their proportion increased from 13% to 18%. Among females, this increase in representation was even greater, moving from 17% to 24%.[28]

Significantly, since section 718.2(e) was implemented, the following statistics reflect the number of Aboriginal women who have been incarcerated in federal institutions:

> The Aboriginal female population has doubled, (from 64 women in 1996 to 128 women in 2006), since 1996, whereas the non-Aboriginal female population has increased by 14%, (from 244 women to 280 women). As a result of this difference, Aboriginal women represented close to one in three (31%) federal female prisoners in 2006, up from one in five (21%) in 1996.[29]

These numbers represent those who are federally incarcerated. It should be noted that in "2007/2008, there were about 369,200 admissions to corrections services (and an increase of 3,464 from 2006/2007) of Aboriginal peoples."[30]

These admissions include a range of criminal justice practices, including remand, custody, probation, provincial parole, conditional sentences, and community releases. These increases are due to a number of issues that have worked against the aspirations of section 718.2(e), including the increase of mandatory minimum sentences, discretion by police and Crown attorneys to charge defendants with indictable or summary offences, and the continuing racialization of violent and serious crime.[31] These factors will be revisited in Chapter 3. Sentencing decisions have also considered the impact of systemic racism against the black community in Canada by invoking the possible use of section 718.2(e). Judges have attempted to reduce sentences for black offenders, recognizing how structural disadvantage and systemic racism have affected their lives and their crimes. These sentencing cases mark the first decisions that have attempted to extend the provisions set out in the *Criminal Code* by applying them to a racialized community other than Aboriginal peoples. These cases are examined in Chapter 4.

The chapters that follow are dedicated to examining particular forms of racial and gendered governance, the knowledge that is produced through notions of cultural difference, the political rationalities that underpin legal responses to historical injustices, and the contestations and contradictions that inhere and cohere legal subjectivity for marginalized peoples. In grounding these motivations, I turn to a brief sketch of the analytic fields that coalesce, converge, and produce the questions that guide this inquiry.

Reparative Justice in White Settler Societies

In this book, I use the phrase "reparative justice" to refer to a range of practices concerning invocations of historical and ongoing injustice in the present, including restorative justice approaches in sentencing. "Reparative justice," therefore, is a catch-all phrase to include social, political, representational, artistic, and legal practices that orient to the past in considering the present. Scholars of reparations often frame reparation politics as a "field of related activities" that range from transitional justice, reparations, apologies, and also "communicative histories," which include memory, memorials, and historical consciousness, or, indeed, any legal or national compensation measure.[32] Chapter 1 places section 718.2(e) into the context of reparative justice and explores important distinctions and overlaps between reparative justice, restorative justice, and reconciliation. One crucial element that this "field of related activities" requires is the necessary signpost in reparation politics – a perpetrator that acts as a historical referent. Legal discussions in Canada that have occurred in the context of reconciliation for the colonization of Aboriginal peoples have often been plagued by the question of responsibility – what was done, who is to blame, and what is the appropriate legal and political response now. As Janna Thompson similarly notes for the Australian context, "public debates that have occurred about historical responsibility and justice for Aborigines indicate that traditional ideas about reparation are difficult to apply to cases where it is not clear who (if anyone) now counts as a perpetrator or a victim or what reparation requires when a return to an ante-justice state of affairs is neither possible nor morally desirable."[33] The context of settler colonialism complicates the terrain of reparations in Canada.

Indigenous scholars insist that the recognition that Canada is a white settler regime requires an understanding of the continued political and spatial effects of internal colonialism for Aboriginal, Métis, and Inuit peoples.[34] Internal colonialism refers to "the historical process and political reality defined in the structures and techniques of government that consolidate the domination of indigenous peoples by a foreign yet sovereign settler state."[35] These scholars note that it is imperative to understand the relationship between indigenous peoples and the colonial state within a framework that recognizes the centrality of law and the impact of legal doctrines on Aboriginal communities.[36] Taiaiake Alfred argues that "'Aboriginal rights' and 'tribal sovereignty' are in fact the benefits accrued by indigenous peoples who have agreed to abandon autonomy to enter the settler state's legal and political framework."[37] The insistence on framing Aboriginal claims to the land in terms of "Aboriginal rights," for example, works to further consolidate white settler governance as it promotes a particular version of white settler history that, in turn, constructs the history of the nation through the categorical exclusion of Aboriginal history. Notably, Alfred observes: "Not throwing indigenous people in jail for fishing is certainly a mark of progress given Canada's shameful history. But to what extent does the state regulated 'right' to fish represent justice when you consider that indigenous people have been fishing on their rivers and seas since time began?"[38]

For other racialized groups, including black Canadians, nation building also included practices of spatial containment and control. For example, the practice of slavery in Canada shows that the histories of racial control of indigenous people and black people were, in some regions, intertwined. Historical records show evidence that black people often replaced indigenous people as slaves in the late seventeenth century.[39] The practice of slavery (and the disavowal of the practice of slavery in Canada), fears about interracial mixing, and practices of criminalization towards racialized groups, including Chinese and Japanese Canadians, emerge with and through the production of a settler colonial state.[40] In Canada, recovering the national story of a white settler nation has been central to recognizing the historical and political roots of projects of racialized governance and regulation. It is imperative to understand the relationship between indigenous peoples and the colonial state within a framework that recognizes the centrality of law and the impact of legal doctrines on Aboriginal communities and other racialized groups. Post-colonial scholars and legal historians identify the need to make direct connections between concrete colonial projects, the acquisition of land and territory, and the ideological and cultural formations that sustain colonial projects.[41]

The difficulty of applying traditional ideas about reparation in white settler societies stems from the fact that such societies are legally organized through a doctrine of *terra nullius* and, as a result, are anchored by the idea of white settler entitlement to the land. As Sherene Razack explains, white settler stories follow a distinct narrative:

> White people came first and it is they who principally developed the land; Aboriginal peoples are presumed to be mostly dead or assimilated. European settlers thus *become* the original inhabitants and the group most entitled to the fruits of citizenship. A quintessential feature of white settler mythologies is, therefore, the disavowal of conquest, genocide, slavery, and the exploitation of the labour of peoples of colour.[42]

As a result of the disavowal of colonial forms of expropriation and violence, a phantom perpetrator obliterated by history often haunts debates and negotiations of reconciliation and reparation in white settler societies. Consequently, responsibility for past injustice in white settler societies frequently moves away from traditional models of reparations (with clearly delineated perpetrators and victims) to a field of reconciliation politics often organized through rhetoric of national responsibility. Furthermore, in white settler societies, the acknowledgment of historical injustices and violence has taken many forms, some of which have ranged from legal, political, or monetary compensation and/or (in the case of land claims) the return of what was stolen.

In pursuing reparative justice in criminal sentencing, a particular political rationality concerning questions of historical and contemporary injustices is set in motion. The idea of taking national responsibility for disproportionate incarceration emerges through a wide array of political, legal, and ethical contexts where questions of justice and injustice, the global and local, are considered. The specifically national character of responsibility emerges out of a consideration of the idea of collective responsibility, a concept perhaps made most famous by Hannah Arendt, who suggests that two conditions must be present for collective responsibility: "I must be held responsible for something I have not done, and the reason for my responsibility must be my membership in a group [a collective]."[43] Arendt argues that "this kind of responsibility is always political ... when a whole community takes it upon itself to be responsible for whatever one of its members has done, or whether a community is to be held responsible for what has been done in its name."[44]

Questions and considerations of responsibility are also determined and shaped by forms of power that constitute political hierarchies. As Andrew Schaap explains,

> the notion of responsibility ... forms a natural part of our vocabulary of power and invests the criteria of power with a normative dimension. Consequently, to attribute power to an agent amounts to something like an accusation, while to acknowledge that one exercises power is to acknowledge responsibility, which invites moral justification.[45]

Indeed, the moral contours that contribute to articulations of national responsibility invest individuals and institutions with particular forms of power. In his book *National Responsibility and Global Justice*, David Miller advocates for an approach to the consideration of social injustices that is specifically national. He argues for an idea of national responsibility that binds the notion of "personal ethics" to institutional arrangements that "will bring about a globally fair allocation of rights, opportunities, resources and so forth."[46] National responsibility thus requires a sense of personal as well as political and institutional obligation.[47] Similarly, Farid Abdel-Nour offers an account of national responsibility that insists upon "individual national responsibility." He identifies the "individual" in discourses of national responsibility in order to move away from accounts of responsibility that posit a "meta-subject or a collective agent."[48] Abdel-Nour argues that approaches to reparations politics that aim to identify collective responsibility

> inevitably lead ... to intractable controversies over collective agency. Theorists of collective responsibility are haunted by questions pertaining to whether groups can have beliefs and intentions, and whether they can act. Without an affirmative answer to the last of these questions, they cannot ascribe responsibility to collectivities.[49]

In examining the question of national responsibility as it pertains to section 718.2(e), I follow scholars who argue that the law relies upon national narratives for meaning and that, in turn, the law constructs categories through such national narratives in order to determine certain historical "truths" and to appeal to particular forms of justice.[50] As Elazar Barkan points out, "despite the dissimilar temporality and rationality, there is an overlap between historical injustice and contemporary discrimination."[51] This book aims to contribute to the development of a historically situated legal framework that identifies the reality of past injustice experienced by racialized communities, in addition to a framework that investigates this "overlap" and recognizes the meaning of injustice and its contemporary (legal) implications both for the perpetrators and the victims.

Colonial, post-colonial, and indigenous legal scholars have long noted the many ways in which processes of criminalization have regulated and produced particular forms of racial difference in colonial and white settler legal contexts.[52] Criminalization is often recognized as one of the grounds upon which colonial and settler forms of governance produce and regulate ideas about subjectivity, violation, protection, intimacies, and civic participation. Recently, scholars have demonstrated the ways in which multicultural and emerging democratic forms of government require notions of criminalization in the regulation and governance of racialized and other marginalized groups, in different global locations. Jean and John Comaroff maintain that "criminality with violence ... has become endemic to the postcolonial condition."[53] They suggest that the twin concepts of law and lawlessness "are conditions of each other's possibility," insofar as an increasing "fetish[ization]" of the law represents a "dialectic of law and dis/order, framed by neoliberal mechanisms of deregulation and new modes of mediating human transaction at once politico-economic and cultural, moral, and mortal."[54]

The language of criminalization and law (from debates about rates of crime, types of crime, crime and poverty, and so on) evidences that the law, and practices of criminalization in particular, often functions to control and contain overlapping, but not similar, sets of people – indigenous people, people of colour, working-class and poor people, workers, immigrants, refugees, migrants, and cheap labour pools. As a result, racialized people (in Canada and elsewhere) are often invoked in the context of discussions concerning criminalization through the distinct, yet nonetheless interrelated, historical trajectories of colonialism, multiculturalism, democratization, transnational markets and economies, and racial injustice.[55] As many prison activists and scholars point out, the criminal justice system is not a place in which any kind of justice is dispensed, articulated, or imagined. Indeed, these scholars and activists suggest that the growing prison industrial complex exists as part of a nexus of government regulation, corporate and neoliberal transactional expansion, "community development," the growth of cheap and free labour for prison workers and prisoners, the military and arms development sector, corrupt economies, democratic and transitional governments, international courts and other international governing mechanisms, and the widening of the criminal justice system into aspects of everyday life.[56]

In this context, when forms of legality play a part in the recognition of historical injustice and systemic racism in the lives of Aboriginal peoples and people of colour, it is, indeed, an anti-racist legal practice. We might further consider that we are, as Gayatri Spivak suggests (in her now famous formulation), in a historical time where rights are "that which we cannot not want."[57] While we are witnessing a global wave of reconciliation, memorialization, and other commemorative and legal projects aimed at negotiating and recognizing historical forms of injustice and violence, it can also be said that such projects and their international prominence, following Spivak, are "that which we cannot not want." The ethical demands of our global order suggest that we should acknowledge historical injustices. As Wendy Brown notes, there is in "Spivak's grammar a condition of constraint in the production of our desire so radical that it perhaps even turns that desire onto itself, foreclosing our hopes in a language we can neither escape nor wield on our own behalf."[58] This book attempts to push against this bind in considerations of historical injustice and is motivated by the idea that it is necessary to investigate what appear to be anti-racist and anti-colonial legal incentives (incentives that identify a nation's own role and complicity in past injustice) and to examine how they work in implicit and/or explicit ways to consolidate a particular version of the nation that is upheld by the implementation of individual and group justice. This book is driven by the idea that social justice actors need to refract history onto their legal and political strategies as well as onto themselves in order to be better equipped to understand the shape and targets of their anti-racist platforms, the histories upon which they rely, and the colonial tricks that those invested in social justice have inadvertently reproduced in their efforts to adjust the political lens of legal practices.

The Biopolitics of Racial and Cultural Difference

In their submission to the Standing Committee on Justice and Legal Affairs, Pauktuutit argued that any new approach to sentencing could be a matter of life and death for the women in their communities. Forms of legality and criminalization bear upon questions of life and death and the powers inherent in the regulation and interaction of these spheres for particular groups of people. The work of Michel Foucault, and in particular his concepts of biopower and biopolitics, is often invoked in the context of examining the modern state and legal apparatus as well as the regulation of the life possibilities of people and entire populations. I use the concepts of biopower and biopolitics throughout the book in order to illuminate the ways in which ideas about racial difference constitute and produce particular subjects in law.

The main objective of Foucault's work was to "create a history of the different modes by which, in our culture, human beings are made subjects."[59] Law is a pivotal site for examining how citizens and subjects are produced. This process of biopolitics emerged through the Enlightenment, at a time when the idea of a respectable society became tied up with regulating the life processes of bodies. For instance, in volume 1 of *The History of Sexuality*, Foucault argues that in nineteenth-century modern Europe a bourgeois moral and social order developed through the policing of sexuality and sexual repression. This regulating mechanism took shape at the same time that scientific racism became central to the politics of the nation-state. Foucault explains:

> Beginning in the second half of the nineteenth century, the thematics of blood was sometimes called on to lend its entire historical weight toward revitalizing the type of political power that was exercised through devices of sexuality. Racism took shape at this point (racism in its modern, "biologizing" statist form): it was then that a whole politics of settlement (peuplement), family, marriage, education, social hierarchization, and property, accompanied by a long series of permanent interventions at the level of the body, conduct, health and everyday life, received their color, and their justification from the mythical concern with protecting the purity of the blood and ensuring the triumph of the race.[60]

Foucault introduced the concept of biopower in order to provide a conceptual framework to address these new configurations of power in the second half of the nineteenth century. This period saw a shift from sovereign forms of power to disciplinary forms of power that inserted themselves into the management of the life and death processes of individuals and entire populations. These new forms of power were made possible through the emergence of a range of sciences and professional discourses that rendered people and populations thinkable, translatable, and manageable to forms of government and political/economic systems. For example, life processes of birth, disease, illness, death, reproduction, and sexuality became sites of biopower and became productive forms of power. In volume 1 of *The History of Sexuality*, Foucault defines "biopower as a political technology that brought life and its mechanisms into the realm of explicit calculations and made knowledge/power an agent of transformation of human life."[61] Biopower functions through state power and is connected to state policies because certain populations can be adjusted in accordance with state processes involved in the process of nation building. Foucault suggests that manufacturing subjects in the service of state and nation requires a dual process of the operation of biopower.

The dual operation of biopower works through technologies of governance (or governmentality) that bring together both the disciplinary effects of state practices and the interpolative consequences of individual subjects. First, biopower operates directly on the body of individual subjects in order to individually classify and constitute these subjects as a population in accordance with state practice. Second, biopower operates through what Foucault describes as "technologies of the self" – the interpolative consequence of governance – which refers to the range of practices through which individuals constitute themselves within and through systems of power regulating their bodies, their thoughts, and their conduct.[62] It is these interpolative consequences for indigenous and racialized subjects that I track most closely in this book.

Foucault's concept of biopower provides a framework for understanding how specific legal practices require and constitute racial and gendered performances. In *Race and the Education of Desire: Foucault's History of Sexuality and the Colonial Order of Things,* Ann Laura Stoler reminds us that although "colonialism was clearly outside of Foucault's analytic concern," he did recognize the productive function of state racism in his formulation of biopolitics.[63] Biopolitics is the condition of emergence for biopower, insofar as biopower designates a particular mode of power, and biopolitics often refers to its manifestation in the context of political and economic regimes of power.[64] Foucault maintains that the "state can scarcely function without becoming involved with racism" and that "once the state functions in the biopower mode, racism alone can justify the murderous function of the state."[65] State racism is described as "warfare" against a particular population within a "social body."[66]

Nikolas Rose suggests that the production and constitution of political rationalities of rule occur through discourse and discursive regimes.[67] Political rationalities can be identified, differentiated, and mobilized by means of discourse analysis. In particular, as Rose points out, it is imperative to pay attention to the moral form of political rationalities ("the ideals and principles to which government should be directed – freedom, justice, equality, mutual responsibility, citizenship, common sense," and so on), the epistemological character of political rationalities (how objects of government are conceptualized), and the "distinctive idiom" of political rationalities, which is to say, the language through which historical, political, and legal reality is made comprehensible and translatable to government.[68] As will be shown through an analysis of legal and political discourse, the framework of biopower is useful because it opens up questions concerning how particular racialized and gendered bodies are organized through the political rationalities that underpin programmatic and legal governance.

Questions concerning biopower and biopolitics and their connection to state and legal practices are at the core of formulations of race that are utilized in much of socio-legal and social science literature and analysis. The biopolitical use of race in law is often highlighted through political and legal discourse.[69] The reliance upon Foucault's notion of the biopolitics of state racism can have the effect of, on the one hand, conflating race with biology and biological processes and paradigms and, on the other hand, constituting race by tracking its governmental and disciplinary effects and practices. Barnor Hesse suggests that scholarship on race falls into two analytic traditions: "race/modernity studies" and "historical modernity and the structure of racism" studies.[70] In these accounts, "racism structur[es] modernity" in particular and ongoing ways. Each of these analytic fields, Hesse argues, maintains a "biological idea of race" and, hence, reifies race in the first instance. Hesse calls for an "analytics" of "racialized modernity," where "'race invokes the historically instituted colonial relation *European/nonEuropean*' ... and racialization describes its sustained configuration in discrete markings of various assemblages of social identities (e.g. polities, corporealities, histories, knowledges, communities)."[71]

Tracing the connections between colonialism and modernity, Edward Said argues not only that the struggle for colonial dominance depends upon geographical determinations marked by armed conflict, militarized occupation, and land acquisition (though these are indeed central to the project of colonialism) but also that the colonial project is/was dependent upon persuasive and coercive representational practices.[72] Said argues that in order to solidify the "hegemony of empire" through militarized occupation, violence, and land acquisition, what was/is needed is the "imagination of empire" – the production and reproduction of a culture of empire that accompanies these material practices.[73] Rather than showing the ways in which race and gender are constituted by law or, conversely, the ways in which race and gender constitute law, the task is to break apart and uncover the very epistemologies and ontologies that are defined through colonial projects in our analysis of racial formations and racial forms of governance. The subsequent analysis of section 718.2(e) shows how the biopolitics of law are produced through distinct ontologies about race, gender, and cultural difference.

A white settler society often relies for its coherence upon the production of a particular type of racial difference, namely that of cultural difference. The idea of cultural difference has extensive colonial genealogies that are historical, sociological, scientific, anthropological, and political.[74] As Paul Gilroy reminds us, "whether biology or culture claimed ultimate precedence, an underlying logic expressed through racial ontologies ... provided important legitimation for brutality, terror, and historically mandated ethnocide of the different and the inferior."[75] Nasser Hussain maintains that racial difference has a long history, "which extends from eighteenth century conceptions of cultural difference – the primitive, the oriental despot – to nineteenth century racial conceptions based on blood."[76] What is key, however, is that these discourses consistently tie together forms of difference with forms of rule. In a reading of Frantz Fanon's work, Homi Bhabha suggests that there is a temporality to the emergence of racialized subjectivity as cultural difference embedded in Fanon's work. Bhabha notes: "Fanon writes from that temporal caesura, the time-lag of cultural difference, in a space between symbolization of the social and the 'sign' of its representation of subjects and agencies."[77] The "time-lag of cultural difference," as sign and caesura, functions as a form of biopower and simultaneously as a temporal designation of difference. These racial logics of cultural difference suggest that cultural difference, as an analytic category, should not simply be understood as social construction (that is, the social construction of race as cultural difference).[78] Instead, appeals to, and designations of, cultural difference codify and depend on the political and moral rationalities that underpin historical trajectories of colonialism and racism.

There is much literature in Canada and other white settler societies that documents the many ways in which notions of indigenousness, "Indian culture," cultural difference, and cultural distinctiveness have been produced and worked through a range of legal and political arenas, including questions of sovereignty, claims to land and resources, access to government programs, criminal justice programs and policies, and other social arenas.[79] As Paige Raibmon argues in her study of the production of indigenous identity on the Northwest Coast in the late nineteenth century and early twentieth century, "whether they used definitions of Indianness in the context of policy, religion, amusement, or science, colonizers shared an understanding of authenticity."[80] Importantly, Raibmon maintains that the production of "authentic Indians" cannot be understood as entirely a top-down process of colonial governance and administrations. Claims and performances of cultural authenticity occurred in keeping with the range of contestations and collaborations (distinctly unequal) that were constitutive of colonial projects.[81] Ann Stoler and Frederick Cooper suggest that in studies of colonial projects the colonizer and the colonized (as well as the metropole and the colony) must be understood within the same conceptual field in order to resist the tendency to "draw a stark dichotomy of colonizer and colonized" and in order to examine, among other practices and social forms, "how a grammar of difference was continuously and vigilantly crafted as people in colonies refashioned and contested European claims to superiority."[82]

Cultural difference frameworks often obscure the ongoing material violence of colonization and exploitation faced by Aboriginal communities and communities of colour in favour of designating certain bodies as being outside of the sphere of political and personal agency. Cultural diversity and cultural difference function as a particular technology of racial governance in multicultural societies. Cultural difference is one of the ways in which indigenous peoples have been managed through colonial state governance and colonial *"political rationalities."*[83] As David Scott suggests, the politics of colonial governance should be understood in relation to how it continues to structure power relations, state practices, and state projects.[84]

Sherene Razack's examination of two different legal contexts – that of sexual violence against women and gender-based asylum – reveals the perils of what she calls "culture talk" in the context of Canadian law. Echoing the sentiments of the women of Pauktuutit, cited at the outset of this introduction, who argued that "culturally sensitive" approaches to sentencing often result in further violence against Aboriginal and Inuit women, Razack argues that "culture talk is clearly a double-edged sword. It packages difference as inferiority and obscures both gender-based and racial domination, yet cultural considerations are important for contextualizing oppressed groups' claims for justice, for improving their access to services, and for requiring dominant groups to examine the invisible cultural advantages they enjoy."[85] In her examination of the perils of "cultural conversations" that occur in the legal process when the issue is violence against Aboriginal women and women of colour, Razack determines that "culture becomes the framework" deployed through the law in a white settler context in order to "pre-empt both racism and sexism in a process" that she refers to as "culturalization."[86] Using an interlocking analysis of race and gender, Razack demonstrates that "culturalized racism" works: (1) to obscure the ways in which cultural paradigms support the operation of racism in the law; (2) to elide responsibility on the part of individuals and nations; and (3) as the explanatory framework for oppression.[87] Indigenous scholars and others argue that cultural difference paradigms and cultural sensitivity frameworks are necessary to address specific processes and concerns that exist within communities. However, they also warn that cultural difference and cultural sensitivity paradigms often function as a form of racial governance that impedes indigenous practices of self-determination and can work to obscure the realities of marginalization in urban and rural communities. The challenge, as I demonstrate in the following chapters, is to examine the deployment of paradigms of culture to identify the way in which they can operate as biopolitical forms of racial governance. In short, we must examine cultural paradigms for their potential and their perils, for the partial stories they produce, and for the dominant relations they often maintain.[88]

Organization

The analysis contained in each of the chapters is based upon close readings of a range of sources, including official government documents, reports and inquiries, legal decisions, transcripts from legal hearings, public records, media reports, and reports by Aboriginal, Métis, and Inuit organizations, the African Canadian Legal Clinic, and other community groups. These texts provide for an examination of the multiple ways in which contestations concerning the production of racialized and gendered political subjectivity play out in the context of criminalization, sentencing, and reparative justice. In pursuing an analysis concerning the racial and gendered implications of this provision for indigenous people and black Canadians, the chapters are organized so as to highlight how section 718.2(e) affects different racial and gendered groups in distinct, overlapping, and contradictory ways.

In the first chapter, I set out reasons for placing section 718.2(e) in the context of restorative justice, in particular, and reparative justice, more generally. I identify definitions for restorative justice and reparative justice and explain why we must understand restorative approaches in sentencing in the context of Canadian and global trends for addressing historical injustices in the post–Second World War period. In addition, I examine three government reports that have been central to national, political, and legal debates related to Canada's new sentencing regime. I examine the report of the Royal Commission on Aboriginal Peoples entitled *Bridging the Cultural Divide* (1996), the *Report of the Aboriginal Justice Inquiry of Manitoba* (1991), and the *Report of the Commission on Systemic Racism in the Ontario Criminal Justice System* (1995) for the ways in which race and culture are understood in these significant documents concerning the overrepresentation of indigenous and racialized people.[89]

My objective in the second chapter is to address the possible meaning of reparative justice and national responsibility as it is shaped by the emergence of section 718.2(e). Following arguments made in Parliament and before the Standing Committee on Justice and Legal Affairs, I argue that section 718.2(e) shows that the impetus behind this sentencing provision obscures a focus on historical injustice and national responsibility. Instead, my analysis reveals the manner in which reparative and restorative sentencing continues to rely upon the colonial management of racialized populations, whereby Aboriginal women continue to bear the burden of this state management. I demonstrate that one of the ways in which this burden is manifest is through the obfuscation of gendered racial violence, as highlighted by the objections of Aboriginal women's advocates to this provision. I offer a brief historical account of Bill C-41 and examine the legal and political dialogue related to section 718.2(e), which includes parliamentary transcripts of Bill C-11 as well as the transcripts from the Standing Committee on Justice and Legal Affairs (which heard from forty-two witnesses, including community groups, lobby groups, legal organizations, social justice organizations, as well as individuals). Examining the arguments made by these groups, I highlight the production of gendered racial knowledge against the backdrop of concerns relating to new sentencing provisions.

Chapter 3 examines *R. v Gladue* (1999), arguably the most significant judicial interpretation of section 718.2(e) in the history of the *Criminal Code*. I examine how the production of Aboriginal identity through the idea of cultural difference obscures histories of colonialism and gendered racism that together have worked to produce contemporary over-incarceration rates. This chapter reveals that reparative justice in sentencing can work in rather pernicious ways to shore up particular forms of gendered racism while obscuring the impact of colonialism.

In Chapter 4, I examine *R. v Hamilton* (2003), a sentencing decision by the Ontario Superior Court of Justice concerning two black Caribbean women, Marsha Hamilton and Donna Mason, who were charged with the crime of cocaine importation. The decision is significant because in determining the sentence for each woman, the Ontario

Superior Court of Justice considered the impact of systemic racism on black Canadians. The fact that the court did so meant that both Hamilton and Mason received what were dubbed "reduced" sentences. *Hamilton* marked the first case in which section 718.2(e) was applied to a racialized group other than Aboriginal peoples. It was overruled by a unanimous bench of the Ontario Court of Appeal. I examine the Court of Appeal's contention that the trial judge erred in reducing the sentences for two black women charged with cocaine importation. In its attempt to curtail the use of section 718.2(e) beyond Aboriginal peoples, the court maintained that the history of colonization and slavery, which has resulted in systemic racism, is of no consequence in the sentencing hearing of two black women conscripted as drug couriers. I illustrate that the court distinguished black people from Aboriginal people by outlining competing claims to both historical disadvantage and systemic discrimination, such that Aboriginals are deemed deserving of the application of section 718.2(e) while black Canadians are understood to be outside of its possible application. This chapter examines the distinction made between systemic and cultural factors that render Aboriginal peoples deserving of the practice of restorative sentencing in contrast to other racialized communities and, importantly, the political rationalities that underpin these distinctions.

The book concludes with reflections concerning recent trends in case law and emphasizes the connections between multicultural nationalism, historical injustice, and the production of indigenous and racialized identities. What might linking considerations of historical injustice and criminal justice tell us about the justice-based aspirations of the multicultural nation? What might it tell us about the citizens and non-citizens that constitute the nation? I consider how section 718.2(e) helps us to consider our current historical moment, in which we wrestle with the past in legal considerations of the present. I conclude by suggesting how this analysis helps to advance a framework for understanding the contemporary production of indigenous and racialized identities in the context of projects concerned with reparative justice.

Culture and Reparative Justice   1

In 2012, commenting on the relationship between Aboriginal people and the criminal justice system, the Supreme Court of Canada stated: "The overwhelming message emanating from the various reports and commissions on Aboriginal peoples' involvement in the criminal justice system is that current levels of criminality are intimately tied to the legacy of colonialism."[1] In recent years, the Canadian government has sought to address the history of colonialism in the lives of indigenous people. Canada has developed an ongoing record of reconciliation and restorative justice practices in the post–Second World War period, creating a national archive of local, provincial, and national inquiries, a royal commission, and countless reports that aim to address indigenous and racialized realities in the present. With varying degrees of success, these inquiries have established a framework that inaugurates the development of a substantial political and legal architecture linking past injustices, contemporary discrimination, collective responsibility, and individual culpability. As these inquiries attest, reparation, restoration, and reconciliation profoundly shape notions of cultural and racial difference in multicultural Canada. How can we understand the kind of engagement with the past and the present that these reports and commissions undertake? How can we understand the role of race, gender, and culture as constitutive of a concern with the past in the present understanding of Canada's sentencing regime? What is the relationship between Canadian and global trends in amending historical injustice?

In responding to these questions, I suggest that section 718.2(e) must be understood in the context of the global trend of amending historical injustices. This chapter seeks to place reparative justice and restorative approaches and principles in sentencing in the broader context of global and local trends that frame political, legal, and ethical questions pertaining to historical injustices. The chapter is divided into three sections. In the first section, important similarities and differences between reparative justice and restorative justice are outlined. I address the uses of gendered and racial ideas about cultural difference in restorative justice, using the Hollow Water project by way of example. In the second section, I briefly examine three reports and commissions, similar to those noted by the Supreme Court of Canada, which have identified the root causes of disproportionate racial imprisonment and which have provided some of the institutional impetus for governmental and political support for restorative justice in sentencing and for section 718.2(e) in particular. I consider the report of the Royal Commission on Aboriginal Peoples entitled *Bridging the Cultural Divide* (1996), the *Report of the Aboriginal Justice Inquiry of Manitoba* (1991), and the *Report of the Commission on Systemic Racism in the Ontario Criminal Justice System* (1995) to be examples of reparative justice, and I briefly examine some of their findings for the ways in which they interweave issues of race, colonialism, cultural difference, and the criminal justice system in Canada.[2] In the third section, I place Canada's ongoing record of reparative, restorative, and reconciliatory justice practices in the context of the post–Second World War trend of amending historical injustices.

Reparative and Restorative Justice

The memory of historical injustice casts a long shadow in the lives of marginalized people. In recent years, Canada has engaged in a broad range of reparation, commemoration, apologies, and reconciliation practices directed at indigenous and racialized groups. The global trend of amending historical injustices has been organized in legal, political, and cultural discourse under the rubric of reparative justice. Reparative justice has taken many legal, political, and cultural forms.[3] As Janna Thompson explains, "reparative justice concerns itself with what ought to be done in reparation for injustice, and the obligation of wrongdoers, or their descendants or successors, for making this repair."[4] In addition, forms of restitution, including "material compensation; rehabilitation through legal, medical, and social services; guarantees of non-repetition through institutional reform; and 'satisfaction,' a category of diverse measures that include truth-telling, apologies, commemoration of victims, exhuming human remains from atrocities, educational activities and human rights training," can also form the basis of reparative justice projects.[5] The field of reparative justice includes literature on collective and moral responsibility,[6] apologies and forgiveness,[7] reconciliation and truth commissions,[8] memory,[9] and reparations.[10] In this sense, reparative justice includes social, cultural, political, and legal practices that orient to the past in considering the present. In Canada, for example, reparative justice is invoked in a broad range of practices that address historical forms of injustice towards indigenous peoples, including apologies, public inquiries, and a truth and reconciliation commission. Practices such as public inquiries and the Royal Commission on Aboriginal Peoples, as I show later in this chapter, fall within the rubric of reparative justice because they seek to provide an account of linking past and present forms of injustice, inequality, and marginalization.

Thompson's distinction within the category of reparative justice is useful in explaining how I use the phrase "reparative and restorative justice" throughout this book. Thompson suggests that there are two modes of reparation or reparative justice: restoration and reconciliation. Each of these aspects of reparative justice can "be understood as an account of what reparation means."[11] For example, while both modes are concerned with historical injustice, reconciliation is most often "forward-looking" and reparation is often "backward-looking," in that it seeks to restore to, or compensate for, a prior state of affairs.[12] In this sense, "restorative reparation is similar to the retributive theory of punishment, which insists that wrongdoers be punished according to the nature and severity of their crime, and reconciliatory reparation resembles the utilitarian approach to punishment, which holds that punishment should aim to produce good effects for society."[13] Restorative justice, then, is a philosophy and practice of reparative justice that temporally links past, present, and future.

Section 718.2(e) has been variously described as a remedial and restorative approach to sentencing Aboriginal offenders. Section 718.2(e) binds both aspects of Thompson's approach to reparation: restorative reparation and reconciliatory reparation. As a remedial and "forward-looking" approach to sentencing, section 718.2(e) endeavours to address the overincarceration of Aboriginal people that has resulted from histories of injustice, including the governance occasioned by the *Indian Act*, residential schools, cultural and linguistic genocide, substance abuse, and violence – the strategies and effects of settler colonialism.[14] Section 718.2(e) is therefore simultaneously "forward-looking" in its approach to the past and in its application at sentencing. Section 718.2(e) also invites a consideration of restorative reparation in that it is tethered to a retributive approach to punishment, which binds punishment with proportionality and seeks an approach that, in the words of George Pavlich, "requires the active input of victims, offenders and affected community members."[15] It is this "distinctive moral compass" that is unique to restorative justice practices, and, thus, it might be said that restorative justice in the context of the criminal justice system is categorically distinct from the restorative justice practice of a truth and reconciliation commission, though they each share a moral idea that moves away from an adversarial approach to punishment.[16]

Scholars have noted the difficulty of defining restorative justice and have offered, instead, definitional features that concern the philosophical and conceptual underpinnings of restorative justice and the idea that restorative justice is a political practice.[17] For example, Andrew Woolford has offered "basic morphological properties of restorative justice" that include the notion that restorative justice is context specific, is an active process, is negotiated and can be the subject of much contestation, and is a living, evolving model of justice.[18] There are also important considerations concerning the practices, the scope, and the goals of restorative justice projects. Restorative justice can be, and has been, used in criminal justice contexts where it must be understood with "varying meanings that [are] used to describe a diversity of events, ranging from minor offences against property and person to massive scale destruction, such as genocide."[19] While restorative justice is a form of governance that can be a transformative practice of social justice, Emma Cunliffe and Angela Cameron note that, as a political practice, "not all restorative justice practice or theory is created equal."[20] There is a vast amount of literature that points to its transformative aspirations and "much more modest statements backed by empirical research."[21] Finally, restorative justice is categorically distinct from indigenous legal orders and indigenous knowledge. Aboriginal legal orders may contain elements of restorative practice; however, these practices are distinct from projects of self-determination and self-government. As many indigenous scholars argue, Aboriginal peoples have the right to self-government as an existing Aboriginal right under section 35 of the *Constitution Act, 1982*.[22]

Culture and Restorative Justice

John Braithwaite, one of the major proponents of the Euro-Western restorative justice movement, has suggested that one of the main analyses of restorative justice follows from the simple question: What is restored?[23] There is no one theory or one practice of restorative justice, and, as a consequence, it operates and is instituted in complex and capillary ways. Restorative justice is a paradigm of justice that operates through a consideration of harm. In the context of criminal justice, restorative justice considers: who has been harmed; what historical precedents led to the harm; and how can the criminal justice system work to repair the "harm done" to the offender, victim, and community? Some have argued that "this focus helps the major stakeholders in the event – the victim, offender, and community – focus on moving forward, using the event as a sort of 'fuel' from which to re-engage and empower victims and community members towards building stronger connections."[24] However, Jennifer Llewellyn has argued that in *R. v Gladue* the use of the notion of restorative justice is misleading and limits the aims of restorative justice.[25] Llewellyn argues:

Restorative justice, as used in the Supreme Court's jurisprudence thus far is ... used loosely as a description for alternative sanctions ... The Supreme Court offers no basis from which to understand the sense in which these elements can be called restorative ... The Supreme Court's treatment of restorative justice thus promotes various mistaken impressions of restorative justice, for example, restorative justice as the imperative to "take context into account," or as community sanctions.[26]

Llewellyn further suggests that restorative justice must be understood as more than an alternative practice in sentencing and must instead be understood as a theory of justice that takes into account "the restoration of relationships as the primary goal of justice."[27] Restorative justice is thus both a theory of justice and a theory of social action instituted through legal governance.

When examining restorative justice practices in Canada and elsewhere, two trends have been noted as they concern indigenous people. On the one hand, restorative justice projects have been supported by some indigenous women's groups. On the other hand, indigenous scholars and other legal advocates have critiqued projects of restorative justice, mostly on the basis of the kinds of cultural approaches that have formed an integral part of restorative justice projects in Canada.[28] For example, echoing the concerns of Pauktuutit, the Aboriginal Women's Action Network, supported by feminist scholars, has called for a moratorium "on *new* western restorative justice or Aboriginal justice for cases of intimate violence until more research has been completed."[29] Key questions in the practice of restorative justice are whether such practices benefit and protect women and "whether or not the practice arises or is derived from an Aboriginal tradition, law or legal order."[30] Emma LaRocque argues that restorative conceptions of justice, when applied to Aboriginal communities, tend to be reductive versions of indigenous conceptions of justice. Specifically, government-produced programs of restorative justice tend to rely upon stereotypical notions of cultural difference, and, as a result, such restorative justice practices are part of "continuing colonization."[31]

The Hollow Water project, for example, which is a first-generation restorative justice project, reveals contradictions and challenges that can accompany restorative justice projects that operate through cultural frameworks that purport to be culturally sensitive. To be sure, the Hollow Water project has become "almost a mythic story" and one of the "most mature and well accepted" of any restorative justice project in Canada. In highlighting the Hollow Water project, certain caveats are necessary.[32] I do not mean to suggest that all restorative justice projects suffer from the cultural challenges confronted by the Hollow Water project. In fact, the Hollow Water project has resulted in many successes concerning violence in the Aghaming, Seymourville, and Hollow Water communities, as have many other restorative justice practices across Canada.[33] However, I use this example to outline a concern at the core of this project. Remedial, reconciliatory, or restorative justice approaches to sentencing often operate through limited paradigms when they are structured by appeals to cultural sensitivity and cultural difference.

The Hollow Water project is a community-based healing project for cases of sexual abuse and gendered violence in the northern Manitoba indigenous communities. This project encompasses neighbouring Métis communities in Manigotagan, Aghaming, and Seymourville, Manitoba: "The idea behind the CHCH [community holistic healing circle] took root first in the Ojibwa community of Hollow Water in 1984, when a group of residents and other people involved in providing social services to the community sought to grapple with the legacy of decades of alcoholism and family abuse, suicide and cultural loss."[34] The project is widely viewed as a form of self-governance for indigenous people. A resource group was formed to address these community issues, and the group determined that "many of the community's problems could be traced to sexual abuse."[35] This community-based resource group launched the community healing circle project. In 1993, the Hollow Water project received national attention when the community of 450 sentenced a couple (who had raped their two daughters numerous times) to three years of supervised probation and continued participation in the healing circle.[36]

LaRocque maintains that it is necessary to examine the Hollow Water project through the "assumptions of 'tradition' upon which Aboriginally controlled justice systems are based."[37] LaRocque argues that one of the pitfalls that plagued the Hollow Water project and other Aboriginal attempts at self-determination through restorative justice projects is that they have often relied upon stereotyped notions of "tradition" within overly simplistic cultural frameworks. LaRocque maintains that

> "typologizing" Aboriginal cultures results in gross generalizations, draws on stereotypes, reduces Aboriginal culture to a pitiable handful of "traits," and by oversimplifying, ends up infantilizing the very cultures Aboriginal peoples are trying to build in the eyes of the colonizer. Further, reducing and fitting cultural expression into chartered, boxed-in modules falls prey to simplistic, rigid, formulaic, and doctrinaire "solutions" to very complex issues and problems.[38]

She demands that an interrogation of Hollow Water and other restorative justice projects must begin with the question: "Upon whose 'tradition' is the Hollow Water decision based?"[39] LaRocque maintains that there is historical and anthropological evidence to suggest that indigenous communities in northern Manitoba have responded to crimes of sexual violence in ways other than probation and supervision. As a result, LaRocque encourages us to ask whether so-called Aboriginal models of justice that operate in a colonial context have been transformed by the racial hierarchies at the core of colonial law. She asks: "Have they [Aboriginal restorative justice programs], in fact, fallen prey to contemporary, white, leftist/liberal, Christian, and even New Age notions of 'healing,' forgiveness,' and offender rehabilitation?"[40]

The Hollow Water project also highlights the perils of so-called culturally appropriate models for indigenous women. LaRocque further explains that many "Native women expressed shock, disgust and outrage. Many said that if Hollow Water is any example of things to come with respect to 'culturally appropriate' applications of justice to women, they would fear to live under Aboriginal self-governments."[41]

LaRocque is quick to caution, however, that the dangers of such self-determination programs do not outweigh the fact that Aboriginal peoples should continue to fight for self-determination in their lives. Such programs should reject such colonizing models (if they can) and consider the totalizing effects of colonization and patriarchy in indigenous communities.

White settler regimes have long subsumed indigenous customary law into their own legal codes in order to consolidate a particular form of legal liberalism and a particular version of multicultural national life. These state responses often distort indigenous customary law and should not be confused with distinct Aboriginal legal orders. One of the functions of this legitimization is that liberal discourses invade these projects and often work to reconsolidate neoliberal aspirations of the nation. Framing restorative justice programs within a paradigm of cultural difference locks Aboriginal peoples in a colonial encounter. For the Australian context, Elizabeth Povinelli demonstrates that Aboriginal forms of justice often work to constitute the nation in white settler societies. Povinelli argues that the use of cultural paradigms in law work to interpolate Aboriginal subjects to "desire and identify with their cultural traditions in a way that just so happens, in an uncanny convergence of interests, to fit the national and legal imaginary of multiculturalism."[42]

The operation of cultural difference paradigms in the context of restorative justice projects in Canada replicates the racial hierarchies consistent with the production of white settler Canadian nationalism. Indigenous people continue to be understood through a paradigm of racial and cultural inferiority. Indeed, restorative justice programs, such as the Hollow Water project, highlight the risks that culturally appropriate sentencing models may present for the maintenance of colonial frameworks and patriarchy in Aboriginal communities, even though there is a record of restorative justice programs in Canada that are motivated by questions concerning self-determination.[43] Indigenous people are consistently drawn into legal negotiations that rely upon cultural difference and distinctly gendered frameworks that may work to obscure the very historical conditions that brought them to the legal table in the first place. Since my aim is to offer a broad framework for the consideration of restorative justice projects produced in, and directed at, Aboriginal communities, I do not examine the exhaustive literature on the range and diversity of restorative justice programs in Canada.

Race and Sentencing in Other Jurisdictions

There are currently a number of initiatives in Australia, New Zealand, and the United States that attempt to consider the negotiation of historical injustice in the context of sentencing and criminal justice. The emergence of American initiatives has included restorative justice sentencing projects and healing circles in many states and communities, including Vermont, Oregon, and Texas.[44] In Australia, so-called Aboriginal courts with regional distinctions called Nunga Courts, Murri Courts, and Koorie Courts often take place once the Aboriginal offender has pleaded guilty.[45] Much like Aboriginal restorative justice projects in Canada, the official aim of the Koorie Court, for example, is to "make court processes more culturally appropriate, to engender trust between indigenous communities and judicial officers, and to permit a more informal exchange of information about defendants and their cases."[46] In this respect, the Koorie Court is similar to Aboriginal restorative justice projects in Canada that purport to work on the basis of cultural sensitivity. Similar to the Canadian context in which restorative justice projects were borne out of national inquiries and the project of self-determination in Aboriginal communities, the Koorie Court has its "genesis in Aboriginal people's aspirations for a place in the legal system as *other* than defendants, [and these] aspirations have developed from Aboriginal people's increasing role in other legal or quasi-legal inquiries and litigation ... the stolen generations investigations, and native land title cases."[47]

Aboriginal courts in Australia similarly emerged out of a royal commission, specifically the Royal Commission into Aboriginal Deaths in Custody, which, among its many recommendations, suggested that the criminal justice system in Australia address the overincarceration rates of Aboriginal peoples by attending to the sentencing process.[48] Much like the sentencing imperative embedded within section 718.2(e), "amongst the factors that the courts have deemed to be relevant in considerations in the sentencing process are the socio-economic factors pertaining to, for example, colonization and dispossession."[49] Far from being solely dictated by Aboriginal communities, restorative approaches to justice for Aboriginal peoples continue to highlight the complex processes of racism and subjection that work within the very confines of government structures. As Annalise Acorn poignantly argues, "the seductive vision of restorative justice seems, therefore, to lie in the skilful deployment – through theory and story – of cheerful fantasies of happy endings in the victim-offender relation, emotional healing, closure, right-relation, and respectful community. Yet, as with all seductions, the fantasies that lure us tend to be very different from the realities that unfold. And the grandness of the idealism in these restorative fantasies, in and of itself, ought to give us pause."[50] The Canadian context requires that we pause to consider the gendered forms of racial governance that are constitutive of restorative justice practices.

As I show in this book, reparative forms of justice-seeking projects in the form of governmental reports and the Royal Commission on Aboriginal Peoples combine both restorative and reconciliatory approaches that are simultaneously backward-looking and forward-looking, marking colonialism as something that is past and embracing and aspiring to a reconciliatory future. These reparative (and temporal) forms of justice are tethered to questions of race and culture. When the issue of disproportionate levels of incarceration is at stake, race and culture become sites of intense contestation that give considerable content to practices of restoration and reparation in local and national contexts. Do racial categories harden in the context of contemporary projects of reparative justice? As scholars of colonial contexts note, "the otherness of the colonized person was neither inherent nor stable; his or her difference had to be defined and maintained."[51] Projects and practices of reparation are one site in which the instability of categories of otherness can be examined.

Race, Culture, and Reparative Justice in Canada
Political and national awareness of past injustices and their contemporary implications have been highlighted by a number of justice inquiries and a royal commission. There is a consistent evaluation in many of these inquiries. Overincarceration is often connected to a notion of

cultural difference in the lives of indigenous peoples. Otherness as cultural and racial difference is reified, reimagined, and codified when indigenous and racialized peoples encounter the criminal justice system. As an analysis of these documents reveals, there is often consensus in official inquiries and reports that colonialism has transformed the lives of Aboriginal peoples in ways that connect historical injustice to contemporary discrimination. For other racialized peoples, there is less agreement about the role of past injustices and racism in contemporary systemic discrimination. I examine three government reports that have been central to framing national, political, and legal debates related to the sentencing regime in Canada.

These inquiries not only identify the root causes of disproportionate racial imprisonment in Canada, but they have also provided some of the institutional impetus for governmental and political support of restorative justice practices in Canada. I review these particular documents because judges and legal practitioners use these reports extensively in the context of sentencing decisions, including those that I examine in subsequent chapters. I consider these government reports to be practices of reparative justice – they open up questions concerning the relationship between historical injustice and contemporary systemic racism and the role of perpetrators, victims, and the state. These documents have also been central to the introduction of restorative justice practices in the criminal justice system in Canada, including sentencing circles and other practices of self-determination by indigenous groups. I briefly examine the report of the Royal Commission on Aboriginal Peoples entitled *Bridging the Cultural Divide* (1996), the *Report of the Aboriginal Justice Inquiry of Manitoba* (1991), and the *Report of the Commission on Systemic Racism in the Ontario Criminal Justice System* (1995) for the ways in which they interweave issues of race, cultural difference, and the criminal justice system in Canada.[52] I highlight the manner in which cultural difference offers an official explanation for disproportionate imprisonment and disproportionate encounters with the criminal justice system. In the context of the *Report of the Commission on Systemic Racism in the Ontario Criminal Justice System*, I examine the methodological contours of the study in order to address the limitations of considering systemic racism through a prejudice/discrimination framework. Building upon this examination of official responses to the problem of incarceration for Aboriginal peoples and other people of colour, I note the ways in which these reports often employ notions of cultural difference (and cultural distinctiveness) in practice.

Bridging the Cultural Divide

It is well documented that Aboriginal peoples are disproportionately represented in Canada's criminal justice system. Patricia Monture-Okanee argues that Aboriginal peoples "are the commodities on which Canada's justice system relies."[53] She maintains that "if Aboriginal offenders were released from custody tomorrow, prisons would be empty and forced to close. Justice personnel from parole officers to correctional workers to police officers would be laid off."[54] Without question, the relationship of indigenous people to the criminal justice system is a national and international crisis. In an interview with the Canadian Broadcasting Corporation's national news program and in response to the Office of the Correctional Investigator's report that concluded that Aboriginal peoples continue to be overrepresented in Canada's criminal justice system, Monture-Okanee maintained that the "news of this [latest] report is that it is not news at all." She reiterated the fact that since 1967 there has been a flurry of official government reports that have highlighted the overrepresentation of Aboriginal peoples in Canada's criminal justice system.[55] Interestingly, in response to the Office of the Correctional Investigator's report, the then minister of public affairs, Stockwell Day, noted the following in Parliament: "I wish to emphasize that there is no empirical evidence to suggest that there is systemic discrimination against aboriginals in the corrections system. I visited personally a number of federal institutions and have spent time with aboriginals themselves, individually and in groups. I am confident in the professionalism of the people who work for Correctional Service Canada."[56] Forty years of empirical evidence chronicles the over-incarceration of Aboriginal peoples, yet official denial of the systemic forms of racism in the corrections system continues.

It has been argued that the report of the Royal Commission on Aboriginal Peoples was the first incarnation of the Canadian version of a truth commission, calling non-Aboriginal people to account for the history of dispossession and land theft that continues to affect indigenous communities.[57] *Bridging the Cultural Divide* was structured by the edict that forms the basis of many reparation projects: "*The road to the future runs through the disasters of the past.*"[58] The report was structured by the idea of "looking forward, looking back." Moving forward as a nation was framed within a temporal logic whereby the future for the nation would be populated by a rendering of the past through the commission's work. In this sense, "looking back" meant rehabilitating the colonial past so as to get closer to the injustices of history in order to ensure that they would not be duplicated or repeated. It meant drawing connections between colonial and racial policies of the past and ongoing forms of discrimination. Looking back also meant fulfilling a new moral framework that was in line with a fully enlightened idea of the nation.

Indeed, this sensibility structured the Royal Commission on Aboriginal Peoples. As it notes in the introduction,

> we turn our attention to Canadian history, presenting glimpses of the relationship between Aboriginal and non-Aboriginal people as it has unfolded at various times and places and examining ... policies that have cast a long shadow over that relationship. We argue that consideration of this history will surely persuade the thoughtful reader that the false assumptions and abuses of power that have pervaded Canada's treatment of Aboriginal people are inconsistent with the morality of an enlightened nation.[59]

Thompson argues that "past actions are connected to present [national] responsibilities by means of moral arguments ... 'We must make recompense for the dispossession of indigenous peoples because this was unjust, and injustices require reparation.'"[60] Moral arguments are at the core of the redemptive demands in the context of liberalism.[61] In *Bridging the Cultural Divide*, the colonized body remains at the centre of this redemptive drama, performing a dual role that reveals a shameful past and secures an enlightened future. Testifying before the Royal

Commission on Aboriginal Peoples, Mary Ellen Turpel argues that Aboriginal encounters with the criminal justice system cannot be separated from a history of colonial dispossession. She states:

> I would suggest that when we carefully take apart Aboriginal experiences and perspectives on the criminal justice system – or for that matter any other "issue" – a tangled and overarching web gets spun. From economic and social disempowerment to problems in the criminal justice system, Aboriginal people's issues are seemingly indivisible ... Alcoholism in Aboriginal communities is connected to unemployment. Unemployment is connected to the denial of hunting, trapping and economic practices. The loss of hunting and trapping is connected to dispossession of land and the impact of major development projects. Dispossession of land is in turn connected to loss of cultural and spiritual identity and is a manifestation of bureaucratic control over all aspects of life ... This is what I see as the experience of colonization.[62]

The invocation of colonialism works across social and political fields to structure an intact past (where explicit racial laws will remain forever) and to anchor a project of reconciliation. Courts at all levels often rely upon *Bridging the Cultural Divide* to understand the unique situation of Aboriginal peoples in Canada.[63] Further to Turpel's testimony, the Royal Commission on Aboriginal Peoples examined three possible explanations for the overrepresentation of Aboriginal peoples in prisons: (1) culture clash; (2) socio-economic disadvantage; and (3) colonialism. While the commission found merit in all three theories, it was of the view that the impact of colonialism best explained overrepresentation in prisons. The culture clash theory posits that overrepresentation arises from the clash of different approaches to justice: "Traditional Aboriginal approaches to justice often stand in direct contrast to Western traditions, and it is the conflict that Aboriginal people feel between these two diametrically different views that is responsible for over-representation."[64] The problem with the culture clash theory, according to the Royal Commission on Aboriginal Peoples, is that it does not explain why

Aboriginal people who have not been raised in traditional homes find themselves behind bars.[65]

The second explanation advanced for Aboriginal overrepresentation, the socio-economic theory, provides an explanation for this phenomenon: "As a general rule, if one wants to discover who is at the bottom of the socio-economic ladder in a country, the best place to look is in the jails, for it is there that those who are different from the majority are found."[66] The Royal Commission on Aboriginal Peoples' problem with this theory was that, while it is true that the socially and economically disadvantaged are disproportionately found in jail, the theory does not explain why Aboriginal people are found at the bottom of the socio-economic ladder: "Why are Aboriginal people, to use the Commission's words, 'poor beyond poverty'?"[67] Relating Aboriginal overrepresentation to social disadvantage misstates and oversimplifies a complex problem by ignoring the unique legacy of colonialism faced by Aboriginal people. The commission states:

> We are of the opinion that locating the root causes of Aboriginal crime in the history of colonialism, and understanding its continuing effects, points unambiguously to the critical need for a new relationship that rejects each and every assumption underlying colonial relationships between Aboriginal and non-Aboriginal society. Locating the root causes of Aboriginal crime and other forms of social disorder in the history of colonialism has other important implications related to the nature of the interventions most likely to bring about significant changes and improvement in Aboriginal peoples' lives, rather than provide merely short-term palliative relief of the underlying problems ... responding to the historical roots of Aboriginal crime and social disorder points directly to the need to heal relationships both internally within Aboriginal peoples and communities and externally between Aboriginal and non-Aboriginal people.[68]

Thinly veiled by the Royal Commission on Aboriginal Peoples' understanding is that the legacy of colonialism has resulted in a range of "social disorders" endemic to the Aboriginal community. What is produced from this understanding is that "social disorder" is a symptom of colonialism – and the task for the criminal justice system is to address these symptoms. The commission also reasoned that the special treatment of Aboriginal people is necessary because traditional sentencing ideals of deterrence, separation, and denunciation are often far removed from the understanding of justice of sentencing held by Aboriginal offenders and their community. The different conceptions of sentencing by Aboriginal people "share a common underlying principle: that is, the importance of community-based sanctions" such as healing and sentencing circles.[69] The commission does not distinguish between distinct Aboriginal legal orders and the distortion of these orders through state practice.

Even though the Royal Commission on Aboriginal Peoples highlights the impact of colonialism and colonial dispossession in Aboriginal communities, it ultimately found in its conclusion that Aboriginal encounters with the criminal justice system are framed by a clash of cultural proportions. In an often-cited quote, the 1996 Royal Commission on Aboriginal Peoples determined that

> the Canadian criminal justice system has failed the Aboriginal peoples of Canada – First Nations, Inuit and Métis people, on-reserve and off-reserve, urban and rural, in all territorial and governmental jurisdictions. The principal reason for *this crushing failure is the fundamentally different world views of Aboriginal and non-Aboriginal people* with respect to such elemental issues as the substantive content of justice and the process of achieving justice.[70]

This "crushing failure" is defined as a problem of cultural difference. From the outset, *Bridging the Cultural Divide* frames Aboriginal encounters with the criminal justice system as a cultural clash where "fundamentally different worldviews" result in disproportionate encounters with the criminal justice system. This "cultural clash" that produces a range of social disorders and that results in Aboriginal overincarceration ultimately frames the report's understanding of the overincarceration of Aboriginal peoples in Canada, notwithstanding the fact that throughout the report the commission articulates the role of colonialism in producing a range of social disorders. What results is a view of the impact of colonization on Aboriginal peoples and its legacy that is anchored in a fundamental problem of cultural difference. This anchoring obscures the very conditions of colonial violence and genocide in favour of a language of cultural difference that exists outside of the very historical and colonial conditions that produced it.

Report of the Aboriginal Justice Inquiry of Manitoba

The creation of the Aboriginal Justice Inquiry of Manitoba was a direct response to two events that occurred in the province in 1987 and 1988. The first event occurred in 1987 at the trial of two white men charged with the 1971 murder of Helen Betty Osborne, an Aboriginal woman from The Pas, Manitoba. Although the trial judge found that four men were present when Osborne was murdered, only one of the men, Dwayne Johnston, was sentenced to life imprisonment for the murder.[71] The second event occurred in 1988 when J.J. Harper, the executive director of the Island Lake Tribal Council, died following an encounter with a police officer from Winnipeg. The following day, the police department exonerated the officer involved. In both of these cases, Aboriginal community members demanded a public inquiry. Together, these two events often come to symbolize the relationship between Aboriginal peoples and the criminal justice system in Manitoba. As a result of these incidents and others, and due to tremendous community pressure, the government of Manitoba established the justice inquiry. The Aboriginal Justice Inquiry of Manitoba occurred six years before the Royal Commission on Aboriginal Peoples articulated a similar approach in relation to cultural difference explanations for the overincarceration of Aboriginal peoples. The Aboriginal Justice Implementation Commission noted, however, that a paradigm of cultural difference often relies upon notions of the inherent degeneracy and respectability of the subjects in question. The commission maintained that

> differences in crime statistics between Aboriginal and non-Aboriginal people result, at least in part, from the manner in which the behaviour of Aboriginal people becomes categorized and stigmatized. This may happen because, to a certain extent, police tend to view the world in

terms of "respectable" people and "criminal types." Criminal types are thought to exhibit certain characteristics which provide cues to the officer to initiate action. Thus, the police may tend to stop a higher proportion of people who are visibly different from the dominant society, including Aboriginal people, for minor offences, simply because they believe that such people may tend to commit more serious crimes. Members of groups that are perceived to be a danger to the public order are given much less latitude in their behaviour before the police take action. An example might be a group of Aboriginal youth who gather in a park. Because it is believed that their presence may be a precursor to more deviant action, they are subjected to controlling activities by the police.[72]

This conclusion highlights the manner in which the reality of over-policing Aboriginal encounters with the criminal justice system goes well beyond the issue of racial profiling. Although not articulated by the commission, a cultural understanding of "Aboriginal crime" is premised upon a biopolitical and racial idea – the colonial construction of the ontological degeneracy of Aboriginal people. This notion is similar to the rationale articulated in the Royal Commission on Aboriginal Peoples' policy responses to Aboriginal "social disorder" that often address the "symptom" of crime through a paradigm of cultural difference and racial degeneracy.

Understanding colonialism as the cause of contemporary over-incarceration rates (and the cause of socio-economic problems that result in increased racial profiling of Aboriginal peoples) reproduces the idea that the legacy of genocide and dispossession results in the symptom of poverty. The Aboriginal Justice Implementation Commission concludes with the following understanding of contemporary overincarceration rates:

> Historically, the justice system has discriminated against Aboriginal people by providing legal sanction for their oppression. This oppression of previous generations forced Aboriginal people into their current state of social and economic distress. Now, a seemingly neutral justice system discriminates against current generations of Aboriginal

people by applying laws which have an adverse impact on people of lower socio-economic status. This is no less racial discrimination; it is merely "laundered" racial discrimination. It is untenable to say that discrimination which builds upon the effects of racial discrimination is not racial discrimination itself. Past injustices cannot be ignored or built upon.[73]

This explanation defines past injustice as a contemporary legacy of "social and economic distress." The legal and extra-legal forms of racial governance targeting Aboriginal peoples as a feature of Canadian law are obscured.

Carol LaPrairie has identified the limitations of approaches that cast overincarceration as a problem of cultural proportions. LaPrairie argues that "what the early task force and studies failed to recognize or did not want to address, was that the disproportionate representation of Native people as offenders in the system was not tied directly to culture conflict but was grounded in socio-economic marginality and deprivation."[74] Aboriginal scholars continue to be opposed to culture-based explanations of Aboriginal encounters with the criminal justice system. In an examination of the Neil Stonechild inquiry (a case in which an Aboriginal man was taken to the outskirts of Saskatoon and left to die in the cold by two white Saskatoon police officers), Joyce Green argues that "racism in Canada is the malaise of colonialism," and she rejects the notion that racism in the criminal justice system is caused by cultural misunderstanding. Instead, Green insists that "Neil Stonechild *et al.* did not die due to a [cultural] misunderstanding."[75]

Report of the Commission on Systemic Racism in the Ontario Criminal Justice System

The Commission on Systemic Racism in the Ontario Criminal Justice System was established in 1992 by the New Democratic Party of Ontario to inquire into, and make recommendations about, the extent to which criminal justice practices, procedures, and policies in Ontario reflect systemic racism. The inquiry examined three major components of the criminal justice system: the police, the courts, and the correctional institutions.[76] The 1995 *Report of the Commission on Systemic Racism in the*

Ontario Criminal Justice System is perhaps the most influential report in Canada to document the relationship between black Canadians and the criminal justice system, including the sentencing process. In addition to this report, there are other studies that have explored systemic racism and the criminal justice system in Canada.[77]

The Commission on Systemic Racism in the Ontario Criminal Justice System acquired data for the report by mailing questionnaires to judges, lawyers, and residents of Toronto. The questionnaires contained questions related to various criminal justice processes in which the selected lawyers, judges, and Toronto residents took part. The commission also conducted a number of public consultations into perceptions related to inequality and discrimination within the criminal justice system with community members, lawyers, police officers, probation officers, and government policy makers.[78] Although the study demonstrates that black women and black men experience systemic racism and systemic discrimination in all levels of their encounters with the Ontario criminal justice system, some scholars have argued that such a methodological tool (questionnaires) is limited in scope and does not address the core systemic issues related to racism and the criminal justice system.[79] I reproduce an excerpt of some of the findings from the commission in order to demonstrate the way in which issues of racism were organized and articulated in the report. In a summary section relating to the mailed surveys to Toronto residents, the commission concluded the following:

> What should we make of these perceptions of inequality in the criminal justice system? Generally, the survey shows that a significant portion of Metro Toronto residents do not believe the justice system in practice treats everyone equally. Beliefs that judges discriminate on the basis of race are strongest among black respondents, but significant proportions of the city's white and Chinese communities share this view.
>
> Second, the survey shows that respondents of all three groups are more likely to perceive discrimination against black people than against Chinese people. This finding suggests people perceive a hierarchy of discrimination.

Third, the extent to which black Metro residents perceive bias based on age, wealth, gender and language – as well as race – indicates a widespread lack of confidence in the fairness of the criminal justice system within this community. These data clearly show that a majority of black residents perceive racial bias in the criminal justice system, and many members of Metro Toronto's black communities are also convinced that other forms of bias exist.

Since these findings deal with perceptions, they do not measure racial differences in the daily practices of the criminal justice system and their consequences. But findings of opinion are no less important than data about differential outcomes. What people think about the criminal justice system matters because the justice system, more than many other institutions, depends on the confidence of the community. This evidence, that many people lack confidence in the justice system, is a reason for grave concern and a call for action.[80]

The Commission on Systemic Racism in the Ontario Criminal Justice System organized their questionnaires and focus groups within the framework of "perception." That is to say, they considered whether people do perceive there to be systemic racism in the criminal justice system. Perception became the methodological litmus test through which to assess systemic racism in the criminal justice system in Ontario and in Canada more broadly. There are no doubt limitations to an understanding of systemic racism through the reliance on public perception as primary data. Kent Roach has suggested that

the Commission cannot be criticized for carrying out its mandate, but it does suggest something about the political definition of the problem when social and economic inequality merits less than a page and a half of analysis in a report of over 400 pages. There is a danger that many social problems particularly those involving gender, race, youth and drugs are being projected on and confined to the overly narrow canvass of the criminal process.[81]

By framing systemic racism in the criminal justice system within the context of individual perception and the interpersonal, the commission obscured the totalizing effects of racism in the criminal justice system. The historical and contemporary circumstances that contribute to systemic racism are obscured. Instead, the report produces an account of racism in the criminal justice system that is overly narrow. For example, the relationship between colonization, slavery, and the production of racial hierarchies in Canada that have led to the overincarceration of racialized peoples is decontextualized. As Frances Henry points out, the commission did not "provide a theoretical or analytic framework for the understanding of the dynamics of an increasingly heterogeneous society such as Canada."[82]

In addition, many scholars have pointed to the limitations of studies of race and racism within institutional sites that employ a framework of individual perception. Some have characterized this approach as a prejudice/discrimination framework. For example, in her excellent book *Vancouver's Chinatown: Racial Discourse in Canada, 1875-1980*, Kay Anderson exposes the limitations of any analysis of race that operates within a prejudice/discrimination framework and focuses simply on white racism. Anderson notes that a discrimination framework has established itself as "the stock in trade of liberal social science," but she insists that while "the prejudice concept has informed a long tradition of race-relations research, it is difficult to locate its explanatory value."[83] In effect, she urges scholars and researchers "to take a step beyond studying white attitudes, because it is not prejudice that has explanatory power but rather the ideology of racial difference that informs it."[84] By so doing, any systemic and historical investigation into race must take into consideration how racial categories came to be produced as a result of colonial projects in settler societies such as Canada.

By assessing "people's beliefs and experiences," the *Report of the Commission on Systemic Racism in the Ontario Criminal Justice System* obscures the very systemic and historical concerns that it aims to highlight.[85] Unless the historical and systemic argument is advanced to consider both the material practices of discrimination in the law and their connection to processes of racialization that have enabled white settler societies to prosper, legal researchers will remain caught within a framework that merely reinscribes the liberal contention that the law is somehow detached from the historical processes that both construct and sustain it. The ramifications of this approach suggest that some legal analyses will remain caught within a discrimination framework that does not take into consideration the historical and ideological links between racial thought and legal practice. Chapter 4 highlights this process at work in a case where section 718.2(e) was considered for two black women charged with the crime of cocaine importation. Similar to the context of inquiries into Aboriginal encounters with the criminal justice system, the *Report of the Commission on Systemic Racism in the Ontario Criminal Justice System* addresses the "symptoms" of racism in the criminal justice system rather than offering an analysis of the broad social and historical context in which these symptoms emerge.

The Global Politics of Reparative Justice

During the post–Second World War period, national responses to historical forms of injustice, including practices of reconciliation, memorialization, and apology, have proliferated. Scholars of multiculturalism and legal liberalism have noted a trend towards practices of reparation in the reconfiguration of multicultural states.[86] In the same period, multiculturalism has become a framework for considering issues of recognition, difference, and integration as they pertain to racialized communities in Western democracies.[87] Multiculturalism has prioritized notions of culture and difference in articulating the contours and limits of liberal nation-states. The category of "indigenous," too, has proliferated through a global matrix of international human rights law and indigenous solidarity struggles in local contexts. As Povinelli points out, there has been a "resituat[ing of the indigenous] within a complex field of national and international civil and human rights standards of acceptable and unacceptable social and cultural difference," while, simultaneously, "state, law and public struggle to piece together a new form of national cohesion in the midst of these modes of difference."[88] Nationally and internationally, the category of indigenous is organized through the politics of cultural difference and is cohered to the multicultural state form in settler nations.

Legal practices of dealing with collective, legal, and political violence, atrocity, and genocide have included trials, truth commissions, and formal reparations. One of the most recent and well documented of these practices has been the South African Truth and Reconciliation Commission.[89] The Truth and Reconciliation Commission "emphasize[d] the experience of those victimized; the development of a detailed historical record; and the priority of healing for victims and entire societies after the devastation of bodies, memories, families and friendships."[90] The commission in South Africa emerged in the context of democratic transition, where reconciliation was organized through amnesty and a victim-centred approach to recognizing racial injustice. The fact that the practice of amnesty in the context of the Truth and Reconciliation Commission was controversial is unquestionable; however, advocates of the approach suggest that the "trade-off of truth for amnesty promised not forgetting or impunity but an important picture of the past: stories and testimony that could help the nation to sharpen its moral conscience and to ensure that, never, never again will it gradually atrophy to the point where personal responsibility is abdicated."[91] There was much opposition to the amnesty process, and activists initiated lawsuits claiming that "the amnesty provisions violated the rights of families to seek judicial redress for the murders of their loved ones."[92] The Truth and Reconciliation Commission, and the amnesty process that was central to it, opened up questions concerning the distinction between collective responsibility and individual responsibility as a moral framework for addressing the racial and political violence of the apartheid regime.

Reconciliation also had important implications for the production of racial categories in the context of the South African Truth and Reconciliation Commission. As Will Kymlicka and Bashir Bashir note, "many people felt that reconciliation should aim at dissolving the racial identities that had emerged under apartheid, with its omnipresent use of racial categories ... This model implies that were it not for the artificial divisions created by earlier oppressive policies, the various groups in a divided society would and should feel that they belong in a unified political community."[93] Reconciliation often seeks to transform racial categories in either newly formed democracies or multicultural societies. An analysis of colonial histories reveals that this project of transforming racial categories is not new but, instead, has been a feature of the humanitarian idea that is central to many colonial projects. We can

follow this idea if we look to the histories of violence and discipline –
much like the residential school system – that are central to colonial
projects.[94] As scholars note, "racial categories hardened across the nineteenth century (through colonial projects), and ... this racializing shift
took place in consonance with the emergence of humanitarian concerns about the well-being of those subject to discipline."[95] Racial categories were used to justify forms of violence that were otherwise
unacceptable to an increasingly liberal social order.[96]

Since I am concerned with thinking through the ways in which a
notion of culture (which is often an amorphous and ambiguous category) gives content to these global trends in a Canadian context, we
must be attentive to these trends in the post–Second World War period
and increasingly in the post–Cold War period. In this period, we have
witnessed national and international attention being turned to questions concerning how nations should best memorialize, communicate,
adjudicate, honour, and navigate the relationship between past injustices
and their moral relevance in the present. The reparative legislation of
the kind articulated in section 718.2(e) of the *Criminal Code* has
emerged out of a global trend that has arisen since the end of the Second
World War in which responsibility for historical injustices has become
an important indicator of national unity in liberal nation-states and
transitional democracies.[97] For example, the South African Truth and
Reconciliation Commission, in particular, provided a model for truth
commissions and sought to provide an account of the atrocities of
apartheid that was at once legal, cultural, and affective. This commission
offered a global model of reconciliation whereby cultural ideas functioned as a thick transfer point between racial violence, political and
legal subjectivities, and communicative histories. In contrast to the Truth
and Reconciliation Commission, the Canadian government has used
apologies, in particular, as a way to address historical and ongoing forms
of injustice. Formal apologies, for example, have been offered to former
students of Canadian Indian Residential Schools and to Inuit peoples
affected by the Inuit High Arctic Relocation Program.[98] The Canadian
government apologized for the events of Ipperwash, which led to the
death of Dudley George; a Royal Canadian Mounted Police officer
apologized to an Aboriginal community in Sechelt, British Columbia,

after pepper spray was used against revellers during celebrations for two community youth soccer teams that won a soccer tournament in Vancouver; and Health Canada issued an apology for body bags that were sent to the Wasagamack First Nation in response to the H1N1 virus epidemic.[99] Canada also has a long history of apologizing to racial and ethnic communities for various exclusionary practices. Formal apologies have been directed towards the following communities: Chinese Canadians, Sikh Canadians, Japanese Canadians, Ukranian Canadians, Italian Canadians, and Jewish Canadians.[100] These practices suggest that reconciliation and apologies work with and through the politics of multicultural and multiracial difference in Canada.

The official apology to former students of Native residential schools was both a welcome and contested exercise. For example, the apology underscored public practices of multiculturalism and emotive reconciliation. The history of the present worked through the history of the past, and the convergences worked not only to capture public memorialization on a single day but also to reveal the links between nationalism, racism, and sentimentality. In this sense, apologies have worked, as Michel-Rolph Trouillot aptly describes, as "transformative rituals [because they] involve time ... They mark a temporal occasion: a wrong done in a time marked as past is recognized as such, and this acknowledgement itself creates or verifies a new temporal plane, a past oriented towards a future."[101] Through the transformative ritual of apology, colonialism itself is marked by "pastness" – a past that was particularly violent and radically misguided. If, in this way, colonial policies are largely viewed as being over or coming to an end, ongoing colonialism and marginalization in the lives of indigenous and other racialized people are characterized as a symptom of a different kind of problem in a liberal social order.

Apologies, such as from truth and reconciliation commissions and other reparative forms of legislation, must be understood in the context of the post–Second World War development of an international regime of human rights[102] as well as of the increasingly global "opposition to genocide, support for human rights, and the fear of being implicated in crimes against humanity."[103] The politics of reconciliation is most often associated with the context of transitional societies – those societies that have been marked by conflict, violence, and civil unrest and whose transition to democratic order has required reconciliation projects.[104] Recently, the politics of reconciliation has "migrated to the established Western democracies, and has become an influential framework for thinking about the claims of historically oppressed groups within these countries."[105] Scholars of settler contexts suggest that a notion of "collective responsibility" often becomes the filter through which the administration and demonstration of apology and remorse gains political and global traction.[106]

Although, as I have outlined earlier, justice inquiries, government reports, and restorative justice projects are distinct legal and quasi-legal practices, they follow a path that seeks to question the relationship between collective responsibility and individual responsibility in the administration of justice. Many reparative projects in Canada following the Second World War and the Cold War period arguably work on and through racial categories. Reparative legislation and reconciliation are new techniques in the management of racial and cultural difference. Scholars have noted that where colonial and settler societies were once organized through nationalisms premised upon ideas of racial superiority and so-called civilizing missions, explicit appeals to racial superiority have been more recently (and with the emergence of specific edicts of multiculturalism) replaced with an idea about "the international community" that views human rights and justice as liberal values that should frame a new global order. This shift, arguably, is no less influenced by ideas about racial governance – though cloaked in secular ideas about liberal humanitarianism. This new technique for managing historical forms of colonial and racial violence often works to reorient claims for injustice away from direct forms of legality. For example, "reconciliation is sometimes said to undermine liberal values by permitting the sacrifice of justice and the rule of law in favour of amnesty and truth, or by allowing personal moral convictions into the public institutional domain."[107]

Reparative justice works to bind the colonial past and the multicultural present through the regulation and governance of the colonized body. As Mary-Ellen Kelm succinctly notes in her excellent study *Colonizing Bodies: Aboriginal Health and Healing in British Columbia*, "'humanitarianism' became integral to the colonial project, not in some self-aggrandizing way but in a sincere fashion that saw 'doing good' as inextricably linked to racial superiority and the right to rule."[108] The locus of humanitarianism, whether in the form of "civilizing the Native" through education or in appealing to a new Canada untethered from its colonial past, continues to be filtered through conceptions of how to manage and incorporate racial difference. Section 718.2(e) proves to be a robust site for the management and incorporation of racial and gendered difference for indigenous and other racialized people.

From Incarceration to Restoration   **2**

Section 718.2(e) was enacted in 1996 as part of a comprehensive over-haul of the *Criminal Code*.[1] Even though this provision was intended to address overincarceration rates, its application has allowed for the consideration of historical and contemporary injustice and systemic discrimination in the context of sentencing. While section 718.2(e) is indeed an instance of anti-racist legal practice, "its application must be understood through its normative role in establishing the contours of legally codifiable claims to national responsibility."[2] Through an examination of official documents, this chapter examines the possible meaning of national responsibility and reparative justice that is shaped by the emergence of this legal intervention. An analysis of official documents related to section 718.2(e) reveals that this reparative legal mechanism works through the biopolitical production of "degenerate" populations, whereby Aboriginal women continue to bear the burden of state management. I demonstrate that one of the ways in which this burden is manifest is through the obfuscation of gendered and colonial violence, as is highlighted in the objections of Aboriginal women's advocates to this provision.

Canadian policy and legal interventions often follow a practice that incorporates Aboriginal, Inuit, and Métis participation in policy and law making.[3] This practice was no less evident in the move to consider the addition of the phrase "with particular attention to the circumstances of Aboriginal offenders" in the context of sentencing. At the hearings before the Standing Committee on Justice and Legal Affairs, Aboriginal groups were invited to participate in this extra-legal process. The necessary inclusion of Aboriginal spokespersons in Canadian policy making often functions to maintain both liberal multiculturalism and nationalism. This practice is consistent with the political rationalities that underpin liberal multiculturalism and integration in which Aboriginal peoples are often locked into the inevitability of inclusion. Gillian Cowlishaw describes this practice and conundrum in the following manner:

> Indigenous people have thus been placed in two mutually exclusive positions: the objects of worry and the consultants to their own problems. Aboriginal leaders are asked to become advisers to the nation ... this entails their coming inside the nation, speaking within the hegemonic discourse, and giving disturbing evidence of their otherness, whether exotic or pathetic.[4]

This chapter examines the legal and political dialogue related to section 718.2(e). This examination includes parliamentary transcripts regarding Bill C-11 and transcripts from the Standing Committee on Justice and Legal Affairs, which heard from forty-two witnesses (including community groups, lobby groups, legal organizations, social justice organizations, and individuals) on the section, after it received royal assent in 1995.[5] I follow the arguments of these debates as they proceed along three interrelated lines: the politics of incarceration rates, the restoration of Aboriginal models of justice, and the foreshadowing of "floodgates arguments" that effectively warn of the application of section 718.2(e) to groups other than Aboriginal peoples.

Reading Section 718

Section 718 of the *Criminal Code* provides:

Purpose:

718. The fundamental purpose of sentencing is to contribute, along with crime prevention initiatives, to respect for the law and the maintenance of a just, peaceful and safe society by imposing just sanctions that have one or more of the following objectives:

(a) to denounce unlawful conduct;

(b) to deter the offender and other persons from committing offences;

(c) to separate offenders from society, where necessary;

(d) to assist in rehabilitating offenders;

(e) to provide reparations for harm done to victims or to the community; and

(f) to promote a sense of responsibility in offenders, and acknowledgment of the harm done to victims and to the community.[6]

Fundamental principle:

718.1 A sentence must be proportionate to the gravity of the offence and the degree of responsibility of the offender.

Other sentencing principles:

718.2 A court that imposes a sentence shall also take into consideration the following principles:

(a) a sentence should be increased or reduced to account for any relevant aggravating or mitigating circumstances relating to the offence or the offender, and, without limiting the generality of the foregoing,

(i) evidence that the offence was motivated by bias, prejudice or hate based on race, national or ethnic origin, language, colour, religion, sex, age, mental or physical disability, sexual orientation, or any other similar factor,

(ii) evidence that the offender, in committing the offence, abused the offender's spouse or common-law partner or child,

    (iii) evidence that the offender, in committing the offence, abused a position of trust or authority in relation to the victim,

    (iv) evidence that the offence was committed for the benefit of, at the direction of or in association with a criminal organization, or

    (v) evidence that the offence was a terrorism offence shall be deemed to be aggravating circumstances;

(b) a sentence should be similar to sentences imposed on similar offenders for similar offences committed in similar circumstances;

(c) where consecutive sentences are imposed, the combined sentence should not be unduly long or harsh;

(d) an offender should not be deprived of liberty, if less restrictive sanctions may be appropriate in the circumstances; and

(e) all available sanctions other than imprisonment that are reasonable in the circumstances should be considered for all offenders, with particular attention to the circumstances of aboriginal offenders.[7]

I will not engage in a close reading of the text of section 718 in this book. Rather, my focus in this chapter will be on the dialogue that it prompted in Parliament and through the public hearings regarding its addition to the *Criminal Code*. Nevertheless, to place this political discourse in context, it is worth noting a number of points about the language and structure of section 718. The Bill C-41 proposals were meant to reduce the reliance on incarceration in Canada for all offenders.[8] Section 718 outlines the traditional aims of sentencing, which include denunciation ("denounce unlawful conduct"), deterrence ("deter the offender and other persons from committing offences"), separation or incapacitation ("to separate offenders from society"), and rehabilitation ("to assist in rehabilitating offenders"). In section 718.1, under the heading "fundamental principle," the concept of retribution in the sentencing process is outlined. As scholars point out, although the specific term "retribution" is not used in the statute, the connection between the gravity of the crime and the degree of responsibility on the part of the offender is a retributive concept.[9] Retribution in this formulation is congruent with a "just desserts" model of sentencing, where "the severity of any punishment should be directly proportional to the seriousness of the crime committed."[10] Moreover, as Tim Quigley asserts, "by inserting [retribution] in a separate section entitled 'Fundamental principle,' Parliament may well have elevated retribution to a higher position among the aims of sentencing."[11]

The most significant addition to section 718 was the introduction of restorative justice principles in the context of sentencing. Section 718(e) ("to provide reparations for harm done to victims or to the community") and (f) ("to promote a sense of responsibility in offenders and acknowledgement of the harm done to victims and community") articulate the restorative justice vision in the context of sentencing. Section 718(e) and (f) together include the first restorative justice principles to be included in the *Criminal Code*. One of the motivating factors behind this proposal was to narrow the disparity between Euro-Western conceptions of justice and what was deemed by the framers of the legislation to be "Aboriginal justice models." As will be evidenced later in this chapter, Aboriginal women's groups have exposed the violent and colonial fault lines in this approach.

The Talk of Bill C-41

On 13 June 1994, the Honourable Allan Rock, then minister of justice, presented Bill C-41 for its second reading in the House of Commons within the Parliament of Canada. In his presentation to Parliament, Rock assured his colleagues that the bill was not the "product of the so-called elites, the professionals, the government administrators of the system." Instead, he maintained that the bill reflected the "values that Canadians have told us are important to them in the treatment of offenders."[12] Bill C-41 was introduced to Parliament at a time when there was "a widely felt need in Canada for uniform and effective statements in the code for what sentencing is to achieve."[13] Rock's comments highlight an appeal to the nation where the values of Canadians represent the penal and moral ideas that underpin this change in the regime of criminal law and sentencing procedure. At the outset of the debate, the opposition leaders cast criminal sentencing in a national arena, questioning whether criminal sentencing is central to the constitution of a just nation, a nation that views justice as its fundamental goal. The Honourable Pierrette Venne of the Parti Québécois stated:

> It is deplorable that the bill tries to sneak through the back door the concept of a parallel system of justice for Aboriginals. It is so well hidden that it is almost necessary to read Clause 718.2(e) twice to discover this enormity hidden under nine sneaky words ... What kind of just society do we have in mind now in terms of sentencing? ... Does the Minister of Justice leave it up to his predecessors, the illustrious instigators of Canadian liberalism, these great humanists who in 1970 had no other means to create their just society but [through] mass imprisonment under the War Measures Act?[14]

Adjudication for crime may well be the task of the nation; however, there is a concern that the introduction of section 718.2(e) would ultimately set up a parallel system of justice for Aboriginal and Inuit peoples. Venne suggests that this proposal would produce a particular kind of exception embedded within criminal law, one that can be compared to other moments in history where such legal mechanisms produced forms of mass imprisonment. We might also consider that Venne's derision of Bill C-41 is less a response to the reality of overincarceration than it is an attack on the Liberal government's record of providing justice, based on the 1970 invocation of the *War Measures Act*.[15] The logic of her statement works to designate what she describes as the Liberal Party's approach to justice as misguided – one that has seen ordinary Canadians criminalized yet would give lighter sanctions to "real criminals."[16] Another opposition leader, the Honourable Paul E. Forseth of the then Reform Party, reinforces an appeal concerning the links between nationalism and criminal law in his party's formal response to Bill C-41 in the House of Commons. He states:

> In many respects, the Canadian Criminal Code is a national document, it is a particularly Canadian creation and has been one of the things that has bound us together as a nation. How we as a society write down the limits of personal conduct and define our sense of

national morals reflects the basic character of what it means to be a Canadian. The written code gives substance to the national sense of community.[17]

By this logic, the *Criminal Code* belongs to the realm of the national whereby the national and moral underpinnings of "personal conduct" reveal "the basic character of what it means to be a Canadian." Of interest here is the way in which the code signifies the everyday practices of law and order as well as the moral economies of personal conduct as expressed through the language of nationalism. This proposition effectively conjoins criminal law to national aspirations and works to delineate and determine who falls within the nation and outside the nation.

The Politics of Overincarceration

In his introduction of Bill C-41 to the House of Commons Standing Committee on Justice and Legal Affairs, Rock referred to the inclusion of the phrase "with particular attention to the circumstances of Aboriginal offenders" as being a direct result of the need to remedy and take national responsibility for overincarceration rates. Rock stated:

> Nationally aboriginal persons represent 2% of Canada's population, but they represent 10.6% of persons in prison. Obviously, there is a problem here. What we're trying to do, particularly having regard to the initiatives in the aboriginal communities to achieve community justice, is to encourage courts to look at alternative measures where it's consistent with the protection of the public – alternatives to jail – and not simply resort to that easy answer in every case.[18]

As Philip Stenning and Julian V. Roberts have pointed out, Rock's assertions concerning section 718.2(e) seem to be anchored in two interrelated postulations. These assumptions include: (1) that the problem of overrepresentation of Aboriginal people in Canadian correctional institutions is at least partly a product of inappropriate sentencing of Aboriginal offenders and (2) that modifying the sentencing methodology for Aboriginal offenders would contribute in a significant way to alleviating this problem.[19] There are a number of historical and political erasures that constitute this moment in which the motivation for reparative legislation is transformed into a national crisis of overrepresentation in prison populations. Historical violence against Aboriginal peoples is divested of meaning through a national appeal for reparative legislation. What is the utility of anchoring appeals to justice through reparative legislation in ahistorical narratives that depict the present through a quantifiable/statistical frame of reference? Rock's postulation uses the field of statistical representation as a conduit to his policy concern. What role does statistical representation play in Rock's support of a reparative approach to sentencing? As Talal Asad explains, statistical representation often "refers to the process by which experience is transformed from one form (raw data) into another (finished text). Here, experience is thought of as itself capable of modification and directly open to public inspection."[20] Aboriginal peoples have been utilized as Canada's "raw data" for national incentives (such as policy and law) for some time. This kind of quantification continues the colonial project.

As noted in Chapter 1, justice inquiries that link Aboriginal overrepresentation to social disadvantage (through various social indices) oversimplify a complex problem by ignoring the unique legacy of colonialism faced by Aboriginal people. This culture clash paradigm views the impact of colonization on Aboriginal peoples, and its legacy, as being anchored in a fundamental problem of cultural difference. The discussions concerning overincarceration rates reflect this cultural approach to understanding Aboriginal encounters with the law. In Rock's address to the Standing Committee on Justice and Legal Affairs, he employs an appeal to "community justice" as one of the ways in which Canada can take national responsibility for the overincarceration of Aboriginal peoples. As George Pavlich illustrates, it is imperative to unsettle this notion of "community justice" since it is most often posited as a realm of "freedom" for Aboriginal peoples as well as being praised as a legal and national response to an overextended penal system.[21] What does this appeal to community justice obfuscate in the context of a debate concerning the overincarceration of Aboriginal peoples?

Since a discussion of the numbers (the rates of overincarceration) emerges as the need to address the possibility of alternative and/or community sanctions, this discursive paradigm conceals the material consequences of penal sanctions as well as the histories of violence and systemic racism that result in overincarceration rates. A focus on the "numbers" enables the marking of Aboriginal populations as having a "social problem" (that of overrepresentation in prisons) that needs to be solved. Promoting community justice models to address over-incarceration rates obscures the onus incumbent upon the state to address the relationship between historical injustice and contemporary incarceration. This obscurity highlights the realization that even as the state attempts to address national responsibility in law through this sentencing provision, the state remains committed to an understanding of overincarceration rates in which it officially severs the relationship between colonial injustice and contemporary incarceration rates. This result reveals the limitations in the ability of the criminal justice process to attend to forms of marginalization and structural violence.

Restoring Aboriginal Models of Justice

Aboriginal women's groups were vehemently opposed to Bill C-41's proposal for alternatives to incarceration for Aboriginal people. Testifying before the Standing Committee on Justice and Legal Affairs, Aboriginal women's groups working on issues related to violence against women exposed fault lines in many of the arguments that suggest that the particular reference to Aboriginal offenders would result in more culturally appropriate mechanisms through which to sentence Aboriginal offenders. Women's groups maintained that "restoring Aboriginal models" of justice was not only a historical impossibility and a fallacy but also, more critically, legal and government shorthand for the continued management of indigenous peoples. This idea is congruent with arguments about the ways in which appeals to "tradition" and/or culturally appropriate sanctions may result in nothing more than creating and/or "inventing" certain practices in order to follow government dictates.[22] Scholars suggest that the inscription of "tradition" on women's bodies results in both patriarchy and colonialism working together to determine group identities and the symbolic and material conditions of belonging.[23] Justin B. Richland suggests that missing from "analyses of 'invented' tradition and the 'politics of native culture' is the fact that the notions of tradition and cultural difference have come to have their own lives within the indigenous communities that they were once used to diagnose."[24]

Notably, Aboriginal women's groups did not address the promise of reparative justice. Instead, their submissions to the Standing Committee on Justice and Legal Affairs emphasized the need to address the violence in Aboriginal communities and, particularly, the ongoing, systematic violence that Aboriginal women face at the hands of male perpetrators – violence that is reinforced when the state ignores it. Pauktuutit (the Inuit women's association of Canada) explained that the model of governments shirking their responsibility in Inuit communities has had particularly devastating effects on women and children. I have outlined Pauktuutit's submission to the committee because they offered more extensive submissions than any other women's group.[25] One reason for their extensive submissions is because sentencing circles, as a form of restorative justice, have been used extensively in remote Aboriginal and Inuit communities.[26] In addition, while the cases invoked by Pauktuutit appear to be few and dated, more recent empirical assessments of the use of sentencing circles in cases of intimate violence show similar and equally concerning trends. For example, Emma Cunliffe and Angela Cameron find that where trial court judges have used sentencing circles in cases of intimate violence in northern Canadian Aboriginal communities "Aboriginal women's experiences of violence are largely excluded from the realm of institutional concern" and that "judicially convened sentencing circles present a deceptively simple solution to the complex and longstanding problem of Aboriginal people's experiences with the Canadian criminal justice system."[27] The concerns of Pauktuutit and other Aboriginal women's groups have come to fruition since the introduction of restorative justice principles in the sentencing process and the use of sentencing circles in particular "to satisfy the requirements of section 718.2(e), which calls on courts to consider alternatives to incarceration for Aboriginal offenders in reasonable circumstances."[28]

Martha Flaherty, speaking for Pauktuutit, points out that "the underlying intent is to empower a community to deal with its own problem in a way that meets broader social goals, not just narrow legal ones. In many Inuit communities we are now being asked to take over responsibility for implementing these alternative models."[29] The transfer of responsibility for incarceration rates to Aboriginal and Inuit communities, with the intent of having a community "deal with its own problems," highlights the manner in which government responses to overincarceration continue to rely upon the notion that "social problems" are somehow both the ontological property of indigenous people and the collective responsibility of these communities. Remarkably, this approach obscures both the official stated intent of the provision (to take national responsibility for overincarceration rates) and a more general political concern in reparations politics that motivates an ethical stance on the part of states. As the women of Pauktuutit point out later in this chapter, being forced into this culture- and community-bound paradigm does little or nothing to address the broader historical, social, and political context of their lives. In particular, Aboriginal and Inuit women's groups speaking before the Standing Committee on Justice and Legal Affairs rejected being forced into this culture paradigm on three interrelated bases: (1) community justice models are often not relevant to the histories of particular indigenous communities; (2) culture-based community justice models do nothing to address the multifaceted issue of violence against women; and (3) fundamentally, culture-based justice models do not address overincarceration rates.

In their submissions, Aboriginal women's groups warned that so-called "culturally appropriate" (or community-based) legal mechanisms did not have any "cultural relevance" to certain communities and, furthermore, that cultural approaches to sentencing have, and would continue to have, serious and violent implications for the women in their communities. Pauktuutit began by noting that the practices deemed culturally appropriate for Inuit communities by justice officials and the Canadian government have no relevance to Inuit culture or history. Ruby Arngna'naaq states:

> The only alternative we are aware of being used in [our communities] has been focused on sentencing processes. Specifically, a sentencing

circle was requested for one case involving an Innu – by the way, it wasn't an Inuk, but an Innu – sexual assault offender. The sentencing circle has not been used in Inuit communities ... although we have heard that judges serving the Inuit community say they would like to use these types of circles in our communities, even though they are not part of our tradition.[30]

Pauktuutit frames its submission to the committee by emphasizing that legal projects that function through a paradigm of culture further enable both cultural erosion and the colonial management of indigenous populations. On the one hand, such projects work to further erode Aboriginal and Inuit cultures (by instituting sentencing circles in communities where circles bear no historical or contemporary relevance). On the other hand, Pauktuutit's submission before the Standing Committee on Justice and Legal Affairs highlights that Aboriginal and Inuit encounters with the law (and government) may further entrench perilous ideas about indigenous cultures.

Stating that the sentencing circle is "not a part of our tradition" works not only to lock Aboriginal and Inuit groups into a discourse of "tradition" but also to cohere Aboriginal identity and practices to a paradigm of culture. The attempt to disrupt government intervention in communities (through the imposition of sentencing circles) by pointing out that the government got it wrong (both in terms of naming and in terms of particular histories that are indigenous to Inuit communities) paradoxically reinscribes the narrow cultural terrain of Aboriginal and Inuit encounters with government and legal officials. This encounter keeps Inuit communities within the very discursive frameworks they aim to contest. This symbolic and material bind carries consequences for women in their communities as they attempt to confront and live with experiences of violence. Pauktuutit points out that "cultural misunderstandings," and other legal forms of violence against women, permeate Aboriginal encounters with the sentencing process. Government appeals to the governing possibilities of restorative justice expose the material consequences of these proposals for Aboriginal women. In order to think through some of these concerns, I reproduce excerpts from narratives related to violence against Inuit women presented by Pauktuutit at the public hearings into Bill C-41:

> In one case a man pleaded guilty to having committed sexual assault on a young woman. In this case, we are told by the judge that the woman told the young man that she did not want to have sexual intercourse, and yet he went ahead, despite her crying, telling him no and pushing him away. The accused told her he had also sold his soul to the devil and that she would die if he did not complete intercourse. The judge also informs us that he accepts this as a death threat and [that] the accused was drunk at the time of the attack. In this case the accused was given a suspended sentence for two years. In coming to his decision, the judge stated:
>
> > "We can understand why this kind of offence is a serious crime under our law, the Parliament of Canada speaking for all of us has made a law under which the Court may send a person to jail for up to 10 years for this offence. When a person goes to jail for more than two years, they can be sent to a penitentiary in Southern Canada which is a place murderers and sexual perverts go. It is not a good place for an Inuit or a young man but if necessary to teach people that sexual assault is a serious crime, the Court will send even young men to the penitentiary."
>
> In another case, a father was convicted of indecently assaulting his daughter, with violence, over a period of years. While condemning the act of incest, the judge noted the accused had no previous criminal record and stated: "I have nothing before me to indicate that he is anything but a good hunter and a competent provider for his family." The accused received a six-month sentence.[31]

In both of these cases the imposition of "culturally appropriate" models has little to do with addressing the issue before the court. Emma LaRocque demonstrates that the appeal to "cultural appropriateness" in the context of sentencing is manifestly about the impact of colonization in indigenous communities:

> The issue of cultural appropriateness is now accepted as central to creating effective services for Aboriginal individuals, families and communities ... The result has been a growing complex of reinvented "traditions" ... which have become extremely popular even while lacking historical or anthropological contextualization ... much of what is unquestionably thought to be tradition is actually syncretized fragments of Native and Western traditions which have become highly politicized because they have been created from the context of colonization.[32]

LaRocque highlights that community justice models amount to the continued management of indigenous populations through the deployment of signifiers that appeal to "tradition" or "values" that emerged from the colonial context. In presenting these cases to the Standing Committee on Justice and Legal Affairs, it is clear that Pauktuutit did not consider the penal sanctions offered to the men in these contexts (and the narrative tropes upon which these penal sanctions relied) to be appropriate. The sentences were mitigated through a paradigm of culture, and, in their view, these sanctions do not incorporate a "multi-faceted" understanding of violence against women – one that would address the material context of violence in indigenous women's lives as well as the continued colonial, political, and legal system that supports indigenous women's subjugation.[33]

In addition, Pauktuutit is also forced into another paradigm that is central to Western criminal law – the "punishment as retribution" paradigm. This paradigm is yet another example of the limits of the criminal justice system's potential to address the social and historical context of indigenous people's lives. By having to focus on crime's formal manifestation (the core of criminal law) through state response and having to navigate this punishment-retribution paradigm in law, Pauktuutit is forced into an approach that does not expose the violent moral economies through which violence against women is rendered comprehensible in law. It is forced to enumerate, explicate, and identify event by event (empirical evidence) the inadequacies of the system. That is to say, by negotiating retribution in criminal sentencing, Pauktuutit finds itself contesting the punishment-remediation nexus related to criminal sentencing as well as the inadequacies of a cultural-based approach to sentencing. Underlying this punishment-retribution paradigm in Western law is the assumption that incarceration is a logical response to crime. As a consequence, two narrative and political traps borne out of colonialism continue to be manifest: (1) violence against women is expressed as an individualized experience that requires a (crime/retribution) response by the criminal justice system and (2) culture becomes the only viable platform through which to make claims about violence against women comprehensible on this conceptual terrain, which obscures the complex relationships between patriarchy, heterosexism, and colonialism that condone and produce violence against women.

In other examples offered before the Standing Committee on Justice and Legal Affairs, this culture-retribution bind becomes fully evident. At the public hearings, a member of Pauktuutit stated:

> In another case, the judge said:
>
>> For the people of [this specific Inuit region] there is no prima facie age restriction when it comes to sexual intercourse. The acculturation process does not include the terms "statutory rape," "jail bait" and other terms suggesting prohibition. Rather, the morality or values of the people here are that when a girl begins to menstruate she is considered ready to engage in sexual relations. That is the way life was and continues in small settlements ... It is clear on the material before me that each of the accused was raised with this attitude and value. I note each one did not consider their actions "wrong" until confronted with the police and the Code.

This case involved three men who sexually assaulted a 13-year-old girl. In the eyes of the judge, these men were simply doing what their culture permitted. Each accused was sentenced to one week's imprisonment based on the cultural defence discussed above. While culture was not accepted by the judge as a defence, it was used to mitigate the sentence. The case was appealed and each accused was sentenced to four months. The appeal court did not correct or comment on the trial judge court's misinterpretation of Inuit values. In effect, both levels of Court condoned this misinterpretation.[34]

The culture-retribution language in this passage takes us through a number of narrative detours that expose the legal logic at work in the sentencing practices described. First, the judge in question secures his articulation of repugnant cultural practices present in Aboriginal communities within both a racial and spatial rhetoric that maintains that "certain ways of life" continue in "small settlements."[35] The utility of sealing certain "cultural practices" (violence against women) within a demarcated zone of aboriginality presents violence against women as naturalized phenomena that require little legal intervention. Indeed, as Pauktuutit points out, the sentences given by both the trial judge and the appellate judge reflect this presumption. The recounting of indigenous practices (supposed or actual) that are deemed repugnant – sexual, violent, or otherwise – has always served larger aims for both national and liberal aspirations.

For the Australian settler context, Elizabeth Povinelli points out that sexual practices have always haunted the liberal nation and have been subsumed into a civilizational discourse mediated through law and the "national archive." Povinelli emphasizes that the legal and anthropological categorizing of Aboriginal practices serves a double purpose that is mutually constitutive: to bolster liberal legal multiculturalism through a frame of toleration and, second, to demarcate a legal zone of repugnant aboriginality.[36] In the case outlined earlier, cultural and moral abhorrence (in the form of an age of sexual consent) exposes the malleability of the limits of multicultural tolerance. In this case, age of consent was culturally specific. Given the extensive case law drawn upon by Pauktuutit, multicultural tolerance appears to be more malleable in the face of violence against women. In the cases recounted in the public hearings, Pauktuutit's submission highlights the ways in which the court legitimized violence against women through a paradigm of culture. Moreover, we witness the ways in which the sex–culture–violence nexus, as told through the judge's evaluation of the evidence, determines a liberal and multicultural language of toleration ("that is the way life was and continues").

Furthermore, the impact of framing violence against women through a paradigm of culture takes on a particular materiality on the bodies of Aboriginal women:

> In another series of cases the judges established a special category of sexual assault when determining the sentence. These involved cases where the Inuit women victims were unconscious due to sleep or intoxication. In these cases, the judge accepted the unconsciousness of the victim as a mitigating factor. If no physical injuries were sustained, the judge concluded no harm or injury was done to the victims, as they were not conscious at the time of the assaults.[37]
>
> In a case where a 36 year-old man attacked a sleeping 22 year-old woman, the judge denounced the offence but in a way that was degrading to Inuit women. "You might think that the next time you've had a few drinks and you've seen a woman lying around, asleep [sic]. First of all, you have no right to force yourself on any woman, asleep or any other way ... They're not there just to keep you happy ... no man can simply go along helping himself to whatever he thinks is available." This unfortunate use of "whatever" to describe Inuit women is, in our view, offensive and degrading.[38]

Together, these narratives expose the implications of appealing to culturally appropriate and/or Aboriginal models of justice in the context of sentencing. Beyond the fact that many Aboriginal activists and scholars have pointed to the futility of "restoring Aboriginal models of justice" through Western legal frameworks, framing rationales for sentencing through modalities of culture supports liberal legal multiculturalism while obfuscating the material violence against Aboriginal women. Culture is utilized as an epistemological frame of reference (for both Aboriginal groups and government officials) and winds its way through "restorative governmentalities" that structure appeals to race-based sentencing.[39] National responsibility for overincarceration rates not only comes to be played out on the bodies of Aboriginal women but is also notably absent in political discourse purporting to institute a legal provision aimed at taking national responsibility for overincarceration rates. This mode of racial governance has material consequences for women, where the attempt to restore "Aboriginal models of justice" through a legal paradigm of culture reinstalls the maintenance of legal and coercive control exercised by the (colonial) state on Aboriginal women.[40]

Legal scholars have since noted that the apprehensions of Aboriginal women's groups have been realized in practice. In an analysis of available decisions in which a "judicially convened sentencing circle" was used as a restorative justice practice in sentencing Aboriginal men for intimate violence, Angela Cameron and Emma Cunliffe found that "women's voices and experiences [were] inadequately represented in the judgments written by trial court and appellate judges about the conduct of sentencing circles and the sentences they recommend." They conclude that the absence of women's experiences "presents real challenges to the institutional construction of sentencing circles as a restorative practice that provides a more just means of sentencing Aboriginal offenders."[41] The concerns identified by Pauktuutit further echo the extensive body of literature pertaining to the gendered implications of restorative justice. This literature has called attention to the following aspects of restorative justice in the context of violence against women in general and violence against indigenous women in particular: (1) restorative justice requires a more comprehensive understanding of the racial and gendered implications of violence against women;[42] (2) many restorative justice practices concerning violence against women have been "poorly executed";[43] and (3) the possible eradication of violence against indigenous women must be understood through a framework that recognizes the realities of ongoing colonialism.[44]

Between the public hearings and the debates that Bill C-41 prompted in Parliament, there has been much talk related to the specific addition of the phrase "with particular attention to the circumstances of Aboriginal offenders." In parliamentary debates, these "nine sneaky words" were interrogated for the door they might open for a consideration of the way in which race, ethnicity, and culture (seemingly conflated) can or will mitigate a sentence. In Parliament, the debate proceeded in a manner that highlighted both the racial and moral logic of "floodgate arguments." For example, Venne stated:

> When you talk about alternatives, you seem to be saying that we should add other categories of delinquents to the list in paragraph 718.2(e) ... Are you proposing that we should have a more exhaustive list or do you want us to add minorities according to their sexual orientation? In that case, wouldn't we be introducing one system of justice for Aboriginals, one for Blacks, one for Jews, one for gays, and so on? That's what I am wondering.[45]

Here we see the racial lines that are central to the production of "floodgate arguments." These are arguments that effectively warn of the possible extension of race-based sentencing to groups other than Aboriginal. The concern articulated is that the addition of the phrase "with particular attention to the circumstances of Aboriginal offenders" would lead to a range of parallel justice systems. This position suggests that aboriginality and/or racial and sexual minority status would mitigate crimes that are deemed "serious" and, consequently, would not result in sentences that are, in the view of the opposition parties, properly retributive.

This position, which was debated in Parliament and which links race to the notion of retribution in criminal sentencing, was outlined by a then Reform Party member through the use of a narrative about sentencing practices. The Honourable Dick Harris, who represented the Bulkley Valley riding in Prince George, British Columbia, stated:

> A section in the bill deals with the treatment of offenders of aboriginal descent. About two weeks ago a native Indian was convicted of sexual assault. At the same time he issued a death threat against his victim. The fellow went to court and was found guilty. That is a very serious crime in my book and would be considered so by most Canadians ... The person was found guilty. The evidence in court showed that the person had a prior arrest and convictions for armed robbery. However, the judge with his creative thinking or because of political

pressure or the influencing forces to make politically correct decisions, decided that instead of dealing with the crime as one that has a specified punishment in the Criminal Code, to have a sentencing circle ... The sentencing circle of elders determined that this man who was convicted of sexual assault and while assaulting his victim said: "If you do not co-operate with me, I'll kill you," who had previous sentences for armed robberies which is a serious crime, whether your gun is registered or not, was given a sentence of one year banishment ... He was to go out into a remote area for a year and be counselled by some elders.[46]

There is obvious disdain in this narrative regarding the extent to which sentencing circles and/or sentences that are deemed by the sentencing judge to be culturally appropriate can be considered properly retributive. However, also apparent in this narrative are the links between race and retribution. At stake, according to Harris, is the way in which laws outlining the limits of multicultural tolerance may be perversely bent as a result of the judge's good intentions (which have been produced apparently by political pressure). We see the way in which race and aboriginality collide to produce what the member of parliament is suggesting is a "very serious crime in [his] book and would be considered so by most Canadians."

There are a number of questions that emerge from this connection between race and retribution. In what ways can an amendment such as 718.2(e) mitigate a sentencing process based upon the punishment principle of retribution? Moreover, can race mitigate the determined "seriousness" of an offence? Studies conducted in the United States report that where crime is associated with particular racialized communities, such as the crimes of drug possession and trafficking, penal sanctions tend to rely heavily on incarceration. The inverse is also true. For example, data collected by the Sentencing Project shows that the criminal justice response to the crime of drunk driving (a crime that is disproportionately committed by white males) tends to result in fewer penal sanctions.[47] The relationship between race and the use of retributive penal sanctions cannot be overstated. The moral fears related to the development of "parallel systems of justice" and/or "cultural justice," which arguably result in no less severe sanctions, are of little consequence when cast alongside the material reality of overincarceration for Aboriginal and other racialized communities.

It is also important to point out that in the context of public hearings before the Standing Committee on Justice and Legal Affairs, the political concerns relating to the possible extension of this provision to groups other than Aboriginal people was notably more nuanced than the overtly racist fears encapsulated by the excerpt from the Parti Québécois and Reform Party in Parliament noted earlier. For example, Julian V. Roberts, a professor of criminology, testified before the committee, suggesting that the particular reference to Aboriginal peoples in the provision is misguided given the fact that in some provinces other racialized populations, such as black Canadians in Ontario, are disproportionately incarcerated. Roberts stated:

> Remember what this statement is supposed to do. It's supposed to give judges some guidance as to the direction sentencing should be taking ... If you look at the data in Ontario prisons, you will find that black residents of the provinces of Ontario are over-represented significantly relative to their numbers in the general populations ... All sorts of other offenders, particularly visible minorities, are affected. It's not just aboriginal offenders ... I would question the wisdom [of] focusing exclusively on aboriginal offenders, and I would suggest wording that would be a little more forceful in terms of use of incarceration.[48]

Roberts argues that the problem of overincarceration is a problem affecting a number of racialized communities in Canada. As a consequence, he suggests that amendments should consider overincarceration generally, the use of penal sanctions specifically, and the disproportionate jailing of Canada's racialized communities. Roberts demands that the committee "question the wisdom" of this particular legislative reference to Aboriginal peoples.

In this context, the law has apprehended the social problem of differential incarceration and, in so doing, as Roberts's statements suggest, emptied the social problem of incarceration of any historical resonance related to the connections between colonization and contemporary overincarceration rates among racialized communities. There are a number of tensions that this proposal gives rise to. First, what is at stake in considering the disproportionate incarceration of racialized people more broadly? Second, would the consideration of racialized incarceration address the specific realities in and of specific communities? As I show in subsequent chapters, case law concerning the application of section 718.2(e) to groups other than Aboriginal peoples suggests that the terrain of racial/cultural comparison and its gendered implications raises questions about the efficacy of anti-racist platforms rooted in social identity claims. In a case that is examined in Chapter 4, for example, the Ontario Court of Appeal distinguished black peoples from Aboriginal peoples, finding that Aboriginals were deemed deserving of the application of section 718.2(e) while black Canadians were understood as being outside of its possible application.[49]

Finally, Aboriginal groups that were not (wholly) representing Aboriginal women's interests, such as the Assembly of First Nations and the Federation of Saskatchewan Indian Nations, were supportive of the reference to the "circumstances of Aboriginal offenders" in the purposes and principles of the sentencing section of the *Criminal Code*. Not only were these Aboriginal groups supportive of the reference to Aboriginal offenders in the provision, but they also argued that the amendment does not go far enough in addressing the gravity of the situation concerning the relationship between Aboriginal people and the criminal justice system.[50] The support for the provision on the part of certain Aboriginal groups is based upon the notion that since certain communities currently administer ("successful") practices related to sentencing, this provision should be promoted.[51] Indeed, Aboriginal communities have determined that community initiatives is a domain where alternative discursive spaces for political and legal practices can emerge and maintain themselves, both parallel to and within, legal discourses. It is perhaps in this context that the social crisis of overincarceration can be leveraged to the benefit and production of alternative political ends. Despite the claims that such practices of "self-determination" should continue in the context of particular Aboriginal communities and where such claims may carry practical utility and strategic and/or political aims, the impact of such penal sanctions on the lives of Aboriginal women is difficult to ignore.[52]

Conclusion

This chapter grows out of an attempt to understand how we might think of the historical, political, national, and social narratives and consequences that have motivated Canada to take national responsibility for the disproportionate levels of overincarceration for Aboriginal peoples. I have outlined the numerous and contradictory ways in which the "problem of incarceration" is articulated as a matter of politics and policy that ultimately obfuscates the very histories that constitute this contemporary national and international crisis. The debates surrounding this provision collectively emerged along the following lines: the politics of overincarceration rates; the "restoration" of Aboriginal models of justice; and "floodgate arguments," which warned of the possible extension of this sentencing provision to groups other than Aboriginal people. While the debates generally proceeded along these distinct lines, the discursive frameworks that gave rise to these debates had one thing in common – the history of colonization and its continuing economic, political, and social consequences on the lives of Aboriginal peoples, and on the structuring of Aboriginal/Canadian relations, were remarkably absent.

What can we make of this paradoxical absence in the context of the government move to consider reparative legislation? Racial governance in sentencing works in three constitutive ways. First, by insisting that certain cultural practices (violent, sexual, and otherwise) are particular to Aboriginal communities, culture becomes the ontological property and ordering mechanism for Aboriginal encounters with reparative legislation. Second, by utilizing culture as a political and national strategy, reparative justice can work to strengthen the aspirations of a multicultural nation by insisting upon, and mediating, "justice" through cultural toleration. Finally, third, cultural toleration, national benevolence, and civility underwrite each other in ways that divest "national responsibility" of any reconciliatory or reparative meaning. The frame of culture and cultural difference emerges concomitantly with this compensatory sentencing mechanism, which means that cultural and racial superiority claims become the legal pivot upon which this form of racial governance proceeds. This shift has had a material impact on certain groups, particularly Aboriginal women.

To legislate (and imagine) reparative justice outside of this political frame would require recognition of the ways in which histories of colonial violence, genocide, and systemic racism, along with global and economic relations of labour and production, interweave with government policies in criminal justice at the local and national level. These practices may include increased social and economic rights, practices of self-determination, and reclamation of land. Finally, since these connections were not expressly made in the historical and political precedents that resulted in a change in legislation, is this new sentencing methodology merely a form of goodwill national politics that supports Canada's status as a multicultural nation? Can these discursive politics in sentencing be harnessed to impact the material reality of overincarceration rates?

Her Aboriginal Connections 3

On the night of 16 September 1995, Jamie Tanis Gladue, in the midst of a quarrel, ran towards her common law husband, Reuben Beaver, and stabbed him, causing his death. At the time, Gladue was celebrating her nineteenth birthday with friends and family as well as with Reuben Beaver. According to court documents, Gladue suspected that Beaver was having an affair with her older sister, and this suspicion peaked when Gladue's sister, Tara Chalifoux, left the party with Reuben Beaver. During the course of the evening on 16 September, Gladue raised this suspicion to friends at the party, explaining that "the next time he fools around on me, I'll kill him."[1] Later that evening, Gladue found Chalifoux and Beaver emerging from Chalifoux's unit in the townhouse complex where they all lived. Gladue suspected that they "had been engaged in sexual activity and confronted her sister, saying, 'You're going to get it. How could you do this to me?'"[2] Beaver and Gladue returned to the townhouse unit that they shared, and a quarrel ensued outside of their townhouse unit. The quarrel was witnessed by a neighbour who ultimately saw Gladue run towards Beaver with a large knife in her hand and "heard Beaver shriek in pain and saw him collapse in a pool of blood."[3]

Gladue was born in McLennan, Alberta, in 1976 and was one of nine children. Her mother was Cree and her father was Métis. In 1994, when Gladue was pregnant with her first child, Beaver was convicted of assaulting her and was given a fifteen-day intermittent sentence with one year's probation.[4] In September 1995, when the event in question took place, Gladue was five months pregnant with their second child. After the night of the attack, there were bruises on Gladue's arm and on her collarbone that "were consistent with her having been in a physical altercation on the night of the stabbing." However, the trial judge found that "the facts as presented before him did not warrant a finding that the appellant was a 'battered or fearful wife,'" because stabbing Beaver twice highlighted the aggravating factors that ultimately rendered her the aggressor.[5] It has been noted by legal practitioners that the transcripts of the preliminary inquiry in *R. v Gladue* reveal that Gladue did not kill in a jealous rage as depicted in the Supreme Court of Canada but that she was responding to having just been a victim of abuse and to the fact that her sister actually had been raped by her common law partner.[6] Furthermore, following the stabbing, Gladue was diagnosed as suffering from a hyperthyroid condition, "which was said to produce an exaggerated reaction to any emotional situation. [Gladue] underwent radiation therapy to destroy some of her thyroid glands, and at the time of sentencing she was taking thyroid supplements which regulated her condition."[7]

On 3 June 1996, Gladue was charged with second degree murder and on 11 February 1997, following "a preliminary hearing and after a jury had been selected, [she] entered a plea of guilty to manslaughter."[8] At trial, she was sentenced to three years' imprisonment and given a ten-year weapons prohibition. Gladue appealed the decision to the British Columbia Court of Appeal on the grounds that the trial judge erred in not following the directives set out in section 718.2(e) of the *Criminal Code*.[9] Section 718.2(e) signals a particular focus on Aboriginal peoples in the sentencing process and states: "A court that imposes a sentence shall take into consideration the following principles: ... (e) all available sanctions other than imprisonment that are reasonable in the circumstances should be considered for all offenders, with particular attention to the circumstances of aboriginal offenders."[10] Gladue appealed to the Supreme Court of Canada on four interrelated grounds: (1) that the judge did not consider her Aboriginal status when imposing her sentence; (2) that the judge erred in not considering her "rehabilitative efforts" during the seventeen months she spent awaiting trial;[11] (3) that the judge failed to consider the impact of Beaver's abuse and violence towards her during their relationship; and (4) that the judge "considered Ms. Gladue's apparent intent to harm Mr. Beaver as an aggravating factor when evidence of provocation was used as a basis for reducing the murder charge to manslaughter."[12] The Supreme Court of Canada allowed the appeal on one ground. Although the trial judge erred in not considering Gladue's Aboriginal background, the sentence was appropriate given the seriousness of the offence. The Court's decision dealt exclusively with the judicial interpretation and application of section 718.2(e) of the *Criminal Code*.

Gladue is arguably the most significant precedent-setting case for the judicial interpretation of section 718.2(e) of the *Criminal Code*.[13] It was not until 1999, when the Supreme Court of Canada released *Gladue*, that the meaning of this particular subsection of the *Criminal Code* was interpreted judicially and thus acquired the status of legal precedent. As Jonathan Rudin, the program director of the Aboriginal Legal Services of Toronto, explains, "in the context of aboriginal offenders, *Gladue* provided an opportunity for judges, with the assistance of defence counsel, Crown attorneys and community agencies, to work together to fashion sentences that would not simply perpetuate the revolving door from the street to the jail and back again."[14] In *Gladue*, the Court reasoned that the historical overrepresentation of Aboriginal peoples in Canada's penal system warranted the practice of creative sentencing in order to remedy incarceration rates for Aboriginals. As Rudin notes, the purpose of the amendments of Bill C-41 and the "*Gladue* decision was not necessarily to reduce rates of offending in Canada, but rather to lessen the country's reliance on incarceration as a response to such behaviour."[15]

Much has been written about *Gladue*. In this chapter, I will focus on the proceedings of the Supreme Court of Canada, which is an overlooked procedural aspect of *Gladue* in the academic literature but, nevertheless, an important feature of the case. It provides, I argue, the blueprint for the racialized and gendered structure of the *Gladue* process. *Gladue* is a rich site through which to consider notions of cultural and racial difference in the context of reparative jurisprudence. My analysis is motivated by the following questions. What did the event of Gladue's murder of her common law husband become in law and through law? How were claims to "aboriginality" and therefore "worthiness" (worthy of the application of remedial or reparative sentencing) organized and legally managed in this case by the defence counsel, the Crown attorneys, and the panel of judges at the Court? What does this legal management tell us about the racialized and gendered structure of particular identity-making practices and requirements that constitute restorative and reparative approaches to sentencing?

To give substance to these questions, my analysis is divided into two parts. In the first section, I use court documents, including facta, the decision from the trial proceedings, the British Columbia Court of Appeal decision, a video recording of the Supreme Court of Canada proceedings, as well as the Court's decision in order to examine the deployment of cultural difference in this case. My analysis of this case reveals that knowledge about the cultural difference of Aboriginal peoples is central to how the Court articulates notions of "aboriginality" in relation to section 718.2(e). I examine the position of the defence counsel; the Crown attorney; the Aboriginal Legal Services of Toronto (ALST), which served as the community intervenor in this case; and the panel of judges from the Supreme Court of Canada. In the second section, I identify some of the debates that have circulated following the Court's decision in *Gladue.* One of the objectives of the chapter is to suggest that *Gladue* signals and signifies something more than the "judicial and political reception of a promising decision"[16] and something more than a "call to action"[17] for the judiciary to consider the overincarceration of Aboriginal peoples.

Gladue: The Legal Terrain

The Supreme Court of Canada Proceedings
While Gladue appealed on the four bases outlined earlier, only the issue of whether the trial judge erred in not considering her Aboriginal status was considered during the proceedings of the Supreme Court of Canada. In order to consider the significance of her Aboriginal status, and whether in fact Gladue was sufficiently Aboriginal, the parties followed

a similar methodology in making their submissions. First, it was argued that what was required to determine whether Gladue was (what I describe as) *adequately Aboriginal* was the legal interpretation of the legislative intent behind section 718.2(e) and whether, in fact, it was intended by Parliament to remedy overincarceration rates. Second, it was determined that what was required was the need to elucidate legal interpretations of "aboriginality" and, concomitantly, the legal recognition of Aboriginal identity.

I examine three interrelated encounters from the Court's proceedings between defence counsel and then Chief Justice Antonio Lamer that are derived from a video recording of the proceedings. I consider these particular moments for what they reveal about the production of Aboriginal identity and ideas concerning cultural difference in the application of remedial sentencing. First, I attempt to demonstrate how the actors in this legal exchange (the chief justice and the defence counsel) devise questions around a national story of origins in which Canadian law often comes to be legally comprehensible through a national story of white racial innocence.[18]

Gil McKinnon, acting for the defence, began with the following statement: "The mischief this section 718.2(e) was meant to overcome was the disproportionate numbers of Aboriginal incarceration. Aboriginal over-incarceration was the clear target of Parliament's concern."[19] Following this statement, Chief Justice Lamer and the defence counsel had the following exchange:

> CHIEF JUSTICE LAMER: I have some difficulty with that. Surely the section says alright you must take into account *the particular nature of Aboriginal people and take into account their customs* and what might be [considered] serious conduct by other groups would not be perceived as serious conduct for other groups ... To then go to the disproportionate number of people who are in jail ... If after taking into account the fact that they are Aboriginal people you are still left with a disproportionate number of Aboriginals in a given jail, like in Yellowknife I think it's 92% or 90% of Yellowknife, am I to understand that your argument is that we should not send ... that in order to correct these disproportionate [numbers] and I am postulating

that these sentences are appropriate, that we should go to an improper sentence.

DEFENCE COUNSEL: No, no.

CHIEF JUSTICE LAMER: Just because there are too many Aboriginals in a given jail then that opens the door to many other considerations like certain groups might consider incest less serious than other groups. And I'm not necessarily referring to a particular group, whether Aboriginal or other ... but it might be considered. Are we then to say [that] the sentence for incest for that special group would be less because of certain attitudes? I don't know. I have difficulty with that.

DEFENCE COUNSEL: I think if I may, My Lord Chief Justice, respond in this way. I think the distinction here is with the Aboriginal offenders, the Aboriginal people, the First Nations of this country that Parliament has clearly focussed on in this principle of restraint in imprisonment in subsection e. Parliament has spoken. And, I submit the reason they have spoken is because of their concern with the disproportionate numbers of Aboriginals in the jails. But that doesn't mean, My Lord, and I'm not going to submit to this Court in the next phase of my argument that Aboriginals should not be going to jails in the appropriate case. I'm not submitting that. I'm submitting that I wish to persuade this Court that there should be a different emphasis of sentencing objectives when dealing with Aboriginal offenders who do not pose a real risk to reoffending. Because I submit that unless this Court is prepared to put some teeth into the nine words in subsection e then Counsel will be coming before this Court in twenty years making similar arguments about disproportionate numbers.[20]

What is the relationship between this exchange and the argument I make about the centrality of cultural difference paradigms in Canada's new sentencing regime? Chief Justice Lamer begins by operating within a cultural difference framework ("take into account their customs"), and, from within this cultural framework, he questions a narrative shift to claims of injustice in the context of overincarceration rates ("but to then go to the disproportionate number of people in jail"). Chief Justice Lamer's response proceeds within a cultural difference framework, and it becomes difficult to reconcile links between historical injustice and contemporary overincarceration rates. We also witness, through the operation of the politics of acknowledgment (acknowledging the numbers of Aboriginal people in Canadian prisons), a pedagogy of national moral reprehension. Chief Justice Lamer is effectively concerned with a kind of "floodgate argument" as it relates to the "crime permissibility" that he views as being potentially read into section 718.2(e). Where are "we" going to draw the line between remedial forms of sentencing and seemingly abhorrent cultural practices or a practice of cultural relativism that may operate in the courts? This "floodgate argument" operates through a moral fear (not unlike floodgate arguments concerning national borders where there is a fear of being overrun by those deemed outside the nation) that is signalled by the fear of cultural practices ("certain attitudes"), which may or may not consist of practices signifying sexual and/or cultural degeneracy. The collapsing of the sexual and the cultural is significant here, as it signifies what Michel Foucault describes as a "dense transfer point for relations of power" where evidence of sexual alterity works to reconfigure the contours of lawful sexual practice.[21]

There is a critical incongruence in Chief Justice Lamer's inquiries into incarceration rates in Canada. He questions a move from the politics of cultural difference ("the section says alright you must take into account the particular nature of Aboriginal people and take into account their customs") to a sentencing methodology that demands that cultural paradigms must come into play precisely because of overincarceration rates. Chief Justice Lamer's questions seem to dislodge the historical connections between the impact of colonialism, dislocation, violence, and poverty on contemporary overincarceration rates. Emerging from this approach is the productive story of degeneracy and respectability whereby the social and political construction of Aboriginal people and Aboriginal cultures as vectors of degeneracy and a threat to national livelihood works to promote the idea of (European) whites as *de facto*

Canadian (moral) citizens and as belonging to the nation. Chief Justice Lamer's statements successfully function to maintain the idea that liberalism favours pluralism (a paramount feature of Canadian nationalism). Moreover, embedded within Chief Justice Lamer's questions is the idea that cultural difference may require a punishment-based sentencing regime intent on retribution rather than on remediation.

While attention is paid in this exchange to the material fact of the overrepresentation of Aboriginal peoples in Canadian prisons, this social fact emerges concomitantly with national fears about sexual and cultural difference. Powerful constructions of respectability function as a symbol and pedagogical tool for entitled citizenry as a way of ensuring that those bodies deemed degenerate are contained through the representation of moral reprehension. Whether or not there are disproportionate numbers of Aboriginal people in Canadian prisons, there is a moral compass to crime that is drawn through cultural formations of respectability and degeneracy. In the end, it is this moral compass that produces Gladue's deemed "worthiness." The consideration of the legislative intent behind section 718.2(e) in the Supreme Court of Canada proceedings delineates these racial lines.

In another critical exchange from the proceedings, "impossible authenticity" emerges through a paradigm of difference concerning the location of Aboriginal identity – in practice, in the body, or in spirit.[22] The defence counsel began this exchange maintaining that section 718.2(e) is meant to be a principle of restraint in the context of criminal sentencing as it relates to the "plain meaning of the words" contained in the phrase "with particular attention to the circumstances of Aboriginal offenders."

> DEFENCE COUNSEL: If you look at the plain meaning of the words, I submit that you might agree that there is a principle of restraint.
>
> CHIEF JUSTICE LAMER: Given the very expansive definition, it is under Section 11 of the Indian Act, there is a great variety of lifestyles amongst Aboriginals and there are a great many Aboriginals who come within that definition who are no different from the mainstream of Canadian society. There are some Aboriginal people, I think ...

that well recently we had some data that had to do with paying taxes or not ... no it was voting, electing the Chief and we had some data before us with regards to the proportion of people who are very remote from Indianness. It was an Indian band, that they were very remote culturally from Indianness that there was no more an Indianness in them than a Caucasian or the neighbour ... then I guess in those circumstances, what is there particular about?

DEFENCE COUNSEL: Well, well, well.

CHIEF JUSTICE LAMER: See, because there was this question about being off the reserve or not being on the reserve. Ok, just being off the reserve may not be enough. But, some people have been more or less assimilated into our society. Fortunately or unfortunately, I'm not getting into that. Maybe later on but, I'm not getting into that. The fact is they have been assimilated so much that there is not Indianness or Aboriginalness, if that is a word, left in them. I guess in a case like that it would have no bearing on the sentence.

DEFENCE COUNSEL: It may. Two things. The sentencing judge has the option of dealing with every individual as he comes before the Court. I think it would be a very dangerous perspective of a sentencing judge to impose his interpretation or his view [regarding] the extent to which the individual offender is still a part of his culture.

CHIEF JUSTICE LAMER: There could be evidence of that. He is the president of Chrysler Canada and has never been to a reserve or anything like that. It is a question of evidence.

DEFENCE COUNSEL: But innately, My Lord.

CHIEF JUSTICE LAMER: Pardon?

DEFENCE COUNSEL: Innately. Innate. The innermost being. In the innermost part of his soul he is Aboriginal.[23]

What is at stake and what is produced in this exchange? A sense of bewilderment is induced in Chief Justice Lamer when defence counsel's claims to aboriginality turn on the idea that aboriginality is elusive and is a manifestation of the "innermost being of one's soul." The incommensurability that emerges in the proceedings is not simply because of different approaches to recognizing the meaning of Aboriginal identity in law. The body and the spirit are evidently marked by difference, collapsing a distinction between body and soul for indigenous people. How can the reparative aspirations of the Canadian nation be realized if their target (both literal and figurative) keeps slipping on either an evidentiary terrain or a metaphysical terrain? Or does this slippage reveal that legal reparation, in the end, has little to do with the claims of Aboriginal peoples and much to do with the redemptive aspirations of the nation?

At work in this passage are the contestations surrounding competing claims to "aboriginality" and the (impossible) search for the truth conditions of such claims. The defence counsel and the judge each promote a different index for assessing and determining cultural claims to aboriginality. I will attend to each in the operation of their specificity. Chief Justice Lamer promotes a distinctly evidentiary claim, what I will call a request for a "biography of aboriginality." In his assertion that aboriginality is "a question of evidence," Chief Justice Lamer maintains that, since some Aboriginal people may be "very remote culturally from Indianness, that there was no more an Indianness in them than a Caucasian or the neighbour," the onus would be incumbent upon the Aboriginal defendant to produce themselves as (what I call) adequately Aboriginal through a range of cultural difference signifiers. Chief Justice Lamer is suggesting that there ought to be a way that the law can identify "degrees" of Aboriginality. In this instance, the identification of aboriginality is bound and associated with a range of specific practices – geographies that together form a kind of temporality that attaches identity (and economies) to cultural difference. Defence counsel promotes a kind of metaphysical/essentialist claim, one that effectively promotes a "s/he just is or isn't Aboriginal" claim. It is important to point out that it was after a series of exchanges with the chief justice in relation to how the Court might assess degrees of aboriginality that the defence counsel moved to this metaphysical space of aboriginality as a litigation strategy. Notably, both positions are anchored by the production of a form of difference that is at once metaphysical and concrete, material, and evidentiary.

In this exchange, we come to know that some Aboriginal people are perceived to bear greater claims to authenticity than other Aboriginal people and, moreover, that Aboriginal identity is not necessarily a cultural signifier but, rather, a question of metaphysics. As a result, Aboriginal identity in law can be overwritten by a range of significations that have little to do with indigenous cultures, practices, identities, and commitments. The defence counsel and the chief justice are not only applying circumscribed understandings of Aboriginal identity in order to legally assess ideas about aboriginality, but they are also claiming the authoritative space of identity. As Emma LaRocque argues,

> one of the most severe problems the Native person is faced with today is that he is defined outside himself. That is, other cultures and other people have defined who he is supposed to be as well as what he was supposed to have been. He has been defined, categorized, and mythologized by books, movies, missionaries, educators, anthropologists – and every other "ologist." He has been set apart by legality and even by economic status.[24]

There is a systemic erasure of Aboriginal peoples from the very terms through which aboriginality is represented across social and political domains. Similarly, Elizabeth Furniss argues in her ethnography of cultural and political contestations in Williams Lake, British Columbia, during a land claims dispute:

> These cultural forms – the ideas of history, identity, society, and indigenous "difference" that permeate Canadian literature, film, art, and popular culture – are not secondary derivatives of political/economic practices. Instead, these cultural representations and practices are central to the very process of establishing and perpetuating colonial relationships. The cultures of modern Western societies, and settler cultures in particular, continue to be profoundly influenced by the ideological legacy and the ongoing practices of colonialism. In Canada, there has been no radical break with the past: Canadian culture remains resolutely colonial in shape, content, meaning, and practice.[25]

The production of culture and aboriginality emerges out of diverse legal, political, social, and cultural sites ranging from the *Indian Act* to land claims, popular culture, and the everyday workings of the criminal justice system.[26]

In yet another exchange, Chief Justice Lamer, continuing to probe the connection between overincarceration and culture, encourages defence counsel to articulate who is at "fault" for Aboriginal encounters with the criminal justice system, and he questions whether an idea of responsibility was what Parliament intended with the addition of the provision. In this exchange, Chief Justice Lamer identifies an incongruence at work in the Supreme Court of Canada proceedings. How can this provision be about cultural difference when national responsibility is at stake?

> CHIEF JUSTICE LAMER: It appears to me when Parliament says "have a look at everything" [that is, all circumstances of Aboriginal offenders] and that they had not mentioned that we particularly look at Aboriginal people [in their individuality] because many of them *are* different from the mainstream. Ok, but there has to be something that is different [in the approach to sentencing Aboriginal offenders]. It seems to me that what Parliament is saying is that we have a look at the fact that she is Aboriginal because there might be some additional consideration ... that will justify non-imprisonment.
>
> DEFENCE COUNSEL: But, My Lord Chief Justice, I go back to the same point ... She [Gladue] squarely falls into this circle of disadvantage that this Court, no, not this Court, but that people have recognized for 100 years as the legacy of our system or our approach towards Aboriginals ...
>
> CHIEF JUSTICE LAMER: What you are saying in essence ... is that the difference between a non-Aboriginal woman in this circumstance and an Aboriginal woman in these circumstances is that we're at fault, that we're partly faulty [sic] for her being or becoming what she became.
>
> DEFENCE COUNSEL: Well maybe we are.

CHIEF JUSTICE LAMER: Well, I think *that* has to be your argument ... I gave you examples if I were a sentencing judge ... say well, I have evidence that imprisonment will be harsher (because of the circumstance of Aboriginals in Canadian prisons) and I'm not going to imprison or I will imprison very shortly because the hunting season is coming up and that man must get out in time to go to the hunt to gather food. I would [offer a mitigated sentence] if I had that kind of evidence.

DEFENCE COUNSEL: My Lord, Chief Justice, the reason I have framed my submission the way I have rather than on a fault-based approach [is that] I prefer to invite the Court on a positive level into taking the approach that I advance to you ... and to look at the restorative values of justice that are inherent to the Aboriginal people ... that's why I've approached it the way I have rather than getting into pointing of fingers about who's to blame for this.

CHIEF JUSTICE LAMER: Well, I agree with you but a sentencing judge has to find a difference other than the general proposition that the person is an Aboriginal. Unless one is saying, well, because the person is an Aboriginal we will treat that person more leniently because we are partly responsible for that person becoming what he or she became.[27]

The chief justice insists that the argument the defence counsel should be making is that the distinction between non-Aboriginal peoples and Aboriginal peoples in the sentencing process should be related to the fact that "we" are at "fault" for what the Aboriginal offender has "become." Presumably, the "fault" that the chief justice points to is the impact of colonization. However, far from following this line of reasoning, the chief justice suggests that a consideration of "fault" is bound up with the presence of cultural practices in indigenous communities (whether the "hunting season is coming up"). Notably, at various points throughout the proceedings, a number of the Supreme Court of Canada justices (Chief Justice Lamer, Justice André Bastarache, and Justice Frank Iacobucci) use the "hunter/gatherer" colonial construct to anchor what they mean by cultural practices.

Section 718.2(e) requires that a sentencing judge consider "alternatives to incarceration for all offenders, while paying particular attention to the circumstances of Aboriginal offenders." The nine words associated with aboriginality in this provision were understood through a lens that might read: "while paying particular attention to the *characteristics* of Aboriginal offenders." What is it in this provision that demands a focus on the "characteristics" of cultural difference (the degree of cultural difference) rather than a focus on the "circumstances" that could lead to a focus on the systems that sustain Aboriginal subjugation in Canada? Why do legal forms of reparative justice require a focus on cultural difference rather than on a historical/systemic view of "circumstance," even when the actual legal language is thinly veiled through a paradigm of historical injustice?

ALST

As community intervenor, the ALST argued that the phrase "circumstances of Aboriginal offenders" signals a demand for judges "to respond to the systemic problems faced by Aboriginal people in the criminal justice system in general, and in the sentencing process in particular" in order to fully recognize "their exposure to systemic discrimination in the criminal justice system and the social, economic and cultural dislocation that they face as a legacy of colonialism."[28] In effect, the ALST situated the provision within the context of colonial histories. Drawing upon years of litigation, the ALST attempted to (1) address the cultural bind that plagues Aboriginal encounters with the law and the criminal justice system in particular and (2) insist upon a historical grounding of section 718.2(e). Indeed, the ALST was the only group to make submissions to the court that addressed the issue of colonization. In pursuing this historical analysis, Justice Bastarache raised the question as to whether a sentencing proceeding was the legal place in which to address these historical considerations (as will be shown in subsequent chapters, this concern would become a central feature of the ensuing case law):

> JUSTICE BASTARACHE: In reading all your material on that [systemic factors facing Aboriginal peoples] I couldn't see how it could be resolved through sentencing.

KENT ROACH FOR THE ALST: My Lord, it is true that not one sentence will cure all of these problems but all of this combined [systemic and historical factors], we submit, requires judges to think hard and twice about the circumstances all Aboriginals face before sentencing yet another Aboriginal offender to prison. In our submission, both Courts failed to engage in this important exercise [in the *Gladue* case] by only examining the particular circumstances of the case they ignored the broader context in which Aboriginal people come before the Court.[29]

The ALST maintains that the recognition of the historical and systemic relationship between Aboriginal peoples and the criminal justice system is a distinct move away from considerations of the Aboriginal offender's "individual identity as an Aboriginal person" that was the sentencing methodology prior to the enactment of section 718.2(e) in 1996.[30] The ALST argues that section 718.2(e) demands a focus on systems that produce subjugation rather than solely on the individual experience of subjugation. The ALST endeavoured to debunk "myths and stereotypes" about Aboriginal peoples "that the trial judge and other courts both before and after the enactment of section 718.2(e) have applied."[31] Recognizing that Canadian colonial law continues to identify Aboriginal peoples through overly simplistic and racist constructs, the ALST must begin where the current Canadian law currently sits with respect to Aboriginal peoples – in the realm of myth and stereotype.

The ALST outlines five myths that have affected Aboriginal people in the context of the sentencing process. In addressing these myths and stereotypes about Aboriginal offenders, the ALST has followed earlier attempts by the Supreme Court of Canada to "respond to rape myths about women and sexual violence [where it] recognized the existence of stereotypes of Aboriginal accused."[32] The following myths have been identified: (1) "the connection to community myth," which operates in law through a paradigm of worthiness whereby "Aboriginal persons who are somehow connected to their community are more deserving of consideration";[33] (2) the "urban Aboriginal myth," which is structured through the idea that a "person living in an urban area is somehow not an Aboriginal person for the purpose of sentencing" (as in the trial judge's assessment of Gladue);[34] (3) the "Aboriginal offence myth," which "relates to the types of charges that are somehow seen to be 'Aboriginal offences'";[35] (4) the "noble savage" myth, which is "represented by cases which stress the fact that the offender does not speak English or French and does not have experience with urban settings or prisons as a reason to develop a different sentence";[36] and (5) the "restorative justice myth," which dictates that section 718.2(e) "only applies when the offender can be placed into what one court of appeal has described as 'truly aboriginal programs or healing processes.'"[37]

The ALST argues that this approach would exclude many Aboriginal peoples from the remedial nature of the provision that demands a consideration of "alternatives to incarceration."[38] The idea of cultural difference constitutes these myths and stereotypes. For example, the "urban Aboriginal" myth is often affixed to the idea that those indigenous peoples living on reservations or in rural areas are somehow more culturally attached to Aboriginal history and identity. Indeed, as I show later in this chapter, this myth and stereotype was at work in the trial judge's analysis of Gladue's claims to Aboriginal identity. In another example, the "connection to community" myth establishes the idea that to "qualify for a sentencing circle, an accused must have deep roots in the community in which the circle is held and from which the participants are drawn. Those without such roots are not entitled to sentencing circles and thus are presumably less Aboriginal."[39] This myth operates through the idea that those who are deemed "less Aboriginal" are somehow not anchored in both the community and certain cultural practices. As Chris Anderson highlights, borrowing a quote from Marilyn Dumont, the cultural signifier of the circle often comes to epitomize the idea that Aboriginal people are locked within a paradigm of culture and are subject to continued colonial management. Dumont affirms:

> There it is again, the circle, that god dammed circle, as if we thought in circles, judged things on the merit of their circularity ... yet I feel compelled to incorporate something circular into the text, plot, or narrative structure because if it's linear then that proves that I'm a

ghost and that native culture really has vanished and what is all this fuss about appropriation anyway ... There are times when I feel that if I don't have a circle or the number four or legend in my poetry, I am lost, just a fading urban Indian caught in all the trappings of Doc Martens, cappuccinos and foreign films.[40]

Dumont highlights that colonial stereotypes that have come to define Aboriginal cultures are challenged by Aboriginal peoples living in urban areas. Dumont also points to the manner in which Aboriginal peoples are themselves interpolated into these constructs that come to define their very existence when navigating the colonial world in which they are forced to live.

What does it mean to fashion social justice responses in the context of a sentencing proceeding around the aim of targeting stereotypes and the dislodging of myth that operates in litigation strategies and judicial reasoning? The approach outlined by the ALST works to expose the frameworks within which Canadian law continues to operate with respect to Aboriginal people. In the proceedings, a number of the judges consistently employed the "urban Aboriginal myth," the "connection to community myth," the "restorative justice myth," and the "noble savage myth." The ALST highlighted the manner in which stereotypes and myths about Aboriginal people and Aboriginal communities have worked in tandem with the law to sustain systems of subordination in order to produce a focus on individuals rather than a focus on systems of governance, which would result in a broader approach to the judicial interpretation of the circumstances of Aboriginal offenders. The ALST attempted to historicize these myths, to move them out of the realm of the individual, and to show them as part of a sustained, ordered, disciplinary mechanism of racial value. Moreover, the ALST also historicized these myths by showing that they are a consequence of the colonial context of which they are part. It stated:

The experience of colonialism by Aboriginal people in Canada is not simply a historical fact, it is a contemporary reality. The reserve system created under the *Indian Act*, RSC 1985 c.1-5, was established not to respond to the needs of Aboriginal people, but to implement the federal government's policy to isolate Aboriginal people from the general population. Various federal policies, including those of enfranchisement, encouraged or forced Aboriginal people who left reserves to assimilate and leave behind their cultural identities. Residential schools were another instrument of assimilation and colonialism. The traumas caused by forced dislocation from community and the often brutal conditions of these schools are still felt by those who attended the schools, their children and grandchildren ... Although the ultimate remedy for colonialism may be self-government, the existing system must make accommodations if it is not to perpetuate the legacy of colonialism, including social and economic dislocation. A refusal to recognize how the conditions of colonialism and forced attempts at assimilation have estranged many Aboriginal people, particularly in cities, from their cultures and communities leads to myths and stereotypes that suggest that only a subset of all Aboriginal offenders are truly Aboriginal and eligible for consideration under s. 718.2(e).[41]

The ALST proposed that understanding the connection between the production of myth and stereotype and the reality of colonization would mean that the history of colonization and the genocide and constitutive function of colonial violence would enter the arena of law. Given how firmly rooted myth and stereotype are for Aboriginal peoples, how can we measure the success of such a litigation strategy?

The Supreme Court of Canada's Decision

The decision of the Supreme Court of Canada dealt exclusively with the judicial interpretation of section 718.2(e) and with the degree to which Gladue's aboriginality would affect the sentence of three years' imprisonment with a ten-year weapons prohibition. The decision found, first, that the directive from Parliament was that section 718.2(e) was meant to address overincarceration rates and, second, that, although the trial judge erred in not considering Gladue's Aboriginal status, it had correctly decided that she would not benefit from the remedial intent of section 718.2(e), because her crime was considered to be "too serious."

The Judicial Interpretation of Section 718.2(e)

The Supreme Court of Canada reasoned that section 718.2(e) "cries out for recognition."[42] The Court ruled: "It is reasonable to assume that Parliament, in singling out aboriginal offenders for distinct sentencing treatment in s. 718.2(e), intended to attempt to redress this social problem to some degree. The provision may properly be seen as Parliament's direction to members of the judiciary to inquire into the causes of the problem and to endeavour to remedy it, to the extent that a remedy is possible through the sentencing process."[43] Drawing extensively from both social science research and following conclusions that were made by the Aboriginal Justice Implementation Commission and the Royal Commission on Aboriginal Peoples, the Court ultimately accepted one of the main conclusions of the Royal Commission on Aboriginal Peoples and quotes directly from its report entitled *Bridging the Cultural Divide*:

> The Canadian criminal justice system has failed the Aboriginal peoples of Canada – First Nations, Inuit and Métis people, on-reserve and off-reserve, urban and rural – in all territorial and governmental jurisdictions. The principal reason for this crushing failure is the fundamentally different world views of Aboriginal and non-Aboriginal people with respect to such elemental issues as the substantive content of justice and the process of achieving justice.[44]

Gladue is another episode in this cultural clash story. What is apparent in this instance are the ways in which the impact of gendered racial violence, and the often-violent personal histories that follow from this violence, become used as evidence of a colonial cultural clash story.

The Politics of Aboriginality

The Supreme Court of Canada found that the trial judge erred in not considering Gladue's Aboriginal status at the time of sentencing. The Court outlined the trial judge's explanation there was "ambiguity as to the applicability of the provision to aboriginal people who do not live in rural areas or on a reserve."[45] The Court's decision quotes directly from the trial court's decision:

> The factor that is mentioned in the *Criminal Code* is that particular attention to the circumstances of aboriginal offenders should be considered. In this case both the deceased and the accused were aboriginals, but they are not living within the aboriginal community as such. They are living off a reserve and the offence occurred in an urban setting. They [*sic*] do not appear to have been any special circumstances because of their aboriginal status and so I am not giving any special consideration to their background in passing this sentence.[46]

Noting that "this understanding of the provision was unanimously rejected by the members of the Court of Appeal," the Court found that the trial judge had erred in not considering Gladue's Aboriginal status at the time of sentencing.[47] The Court quotes directly from the report of the Royal Commission of Aboriginal Peoples:

> The class of aboriginal people who come within the purview of the specific reference to the circumstances of aboriginal offenders in s. 718.2(e) must be, at least, all who come within the scope of s. 25 of the Charter and s. 35 of the Constitution Act, 1982. The numbers involved are significant. National census figures from 1996 show that an estimated 799,010 people were identified as aboriginal in 1996. Of this number, 529,040 were Indians (registered or non-registered), 204,115 Métis and 40,220 Inuit.
>
> Section 718.2(e) applies to all aboriginal offenders wherever they reside, whether on- or off-reserve, in a large city or a rural area. Indeed it has been observed that many aboriginals living in urban areas are closely attached to their culture. See the Royal Commission on Aboriginal Peoples, Report of the Royal Commission on Aboriginal Peoples, vol. 4, Perspectives and Realities (1996), at p. 521:
>
> > Throughout the Commission's hearings, Aboriginal people stressed the fundamental importance of retaining and enhancing

their cultural identity while living in urban areas. Aboriginal identity lies at the heart of Aboriginal peoples' existence; maintaining that identity is an essential and self-validating pursuit for Aboriginal people in cities.

And at p. 525:

> Cultural identity for urban Aboriginal people is also tied to a land base or ancestral territory. For many, the two concepts are inseparable ... Identification with an ancestral place is important to urban people because of the associated ritual, ceremony and traditions, as well as the people who remain there, the sense of belonging, the bond to an ancestral community, and the accessibility of family, community and elders.

Section 718.2(e) requires the sentencing judge to explore reasonable alternatives to incarceration in the case of all aboriginal offenders. Obviously, if an aboriginal community has a program or tradition of alternative sanctions, and support and supervision are available to the offender, it may be easier to find and impose an alternative sentence. However, even if community support is not available, every effort should be made in appropriate circumstances to find a sensitive and helpful alternative. For all purposes, the term "community" must be defined broadly so as to include any network of support and interaction that might be available in an urban centre. At the same time, the residence of the aboriginal offender in an urban centre that lacks any network of support does not relieve the sentencing judge of the obligation to try to find an alternative to imprisonment.[48]

The Supreme Court of Canada clarifies that all Aboriginal peoples as defined by the *Canadian Charter of Rights and Freedoms* and the *Constitution Act*, whether they are status Indians, non-status Indians, Inuit, or Métis, fall within the purview of section 718.2(e).[49] Furthermore, the Court proposes that the recognition of aboriginality is associated with a range of specific practices and geographies that together attaches identity to time and space. According to this formulation, cultural identity for Aboriginal peoples, whether living on or off reserve, is produced and propelled by "the sense of belonging" to a kinship "network," where "ceremony and tradition" enshrine a sense of attachment to an "ancestral community." The challenge with this formulation is the evidentiary threshold that it demands. In what way can Aboriginal people articulate (and present evidence of) a sense of belonging, of kinship and ceremony, and of ancestral community that will not simply reduce culture to identity? This challenge has been examined in cases concerning land title. Examining *Delgamuukw v British Columbia* (a significant land title case launched by the Gitksan and Wet'suwet'en peoples), Val Napoleon demonstrates the ways in which the oral histories presented by the Gitksan peoples were treated by the Supreme Court of British Columbia as "cultural artefacts" rather than as "evidence about their societies including land ownership, resource management, social structures, governance systems, histories, economies and spirituality."[50]

Gladue: The Interpretive Terrain

Since much has been written about the Supreme Court of Canada's decision in *Gladue*, I will examine some features of the interpretive trends that have followed it. I illustrate that embedded within each of these aspects of *Gladue*'s influence is a racial and gendered logic through the management and disciplining of particular bodies. I organize the analysis of the legal interpretations of the *Gladue* decision along four thematic lines: *Gladue* and/as restorative justice; *Gladue* and the definition of "serious crime"; *Gladue*, overincarceration, and the use of conditional sentences; and *Gladue*, "aboriginality," and gendered racial violence.

Gladue and/as Restorative Justice

The introduction of section 718.2(e) to the *Criminal Code* was the result of a two-fold national and legal incentive. The first imperative was to address overincarceration rates of Aboriginal peoples and the second motivation was to address the disparity between the Euro-Western conception of retributive justice in the context of punishment (whose goals in the context of sentencing include deterrence, denunciation, and the separation of the offender from society) to include sentencing alternatives that would recognize that "most traditional Aboriginal conceptions of justice place a primary emphasis on the ideals of restorative justice."[51] The 1996 report by the Royal Commission on Aboriginal Peoples identified these principles in the context of sentencing and criminal justice.[52] Restorative and community approaches to justice have long been a feature of indigenous legal systems in many Aboriginal and Inuit communities; however, it is important to note the distinctions between restorative justice and indigenous legal orders.[53] Restorative justice should not be conflated with indigenous legal orders.

It has been argued that restorative justice is a more culturally sensitive sentencing mechanism for Aboriginal offenders. However, Aboriginal and non-Aboriginal commentators suggest that *Gladue* "reflected a limited and misguided understanding of restorative justice."[54] This case was unique to the extent that the Court found that section 718.2(e) of the *Criminal Code* was a remedial sentencing aim. Furthermore, "the Court found that the principle of restraint outlined at section 718.2(e) (i.e., the idea that 'imprisonment should be resorted to only where no other sentencing option is reasonable in the circumstances') would necessarily be informed by this re-orientation" to restorative justice principles.[55] *Gladue* effectively changed the terrain of sentencing methodology and procedure in Canada.

There has been much criticism directed at the Supreme Court of Canada's insertion of restorative justice principles in the context of sentencing, particularly, as noted in Chapter 1, its use as shorthand of the application of alternative approaches to imprisonment with little emphasis on how these approaches can be considered restorative.[56] Restorative justice must be understood as more than an alternative practice in sentencing. As a category of governance, it has been argued that restorative justice "does little or nothing to enable subjects to engage politically with, and to substantially alter, the broader social conditions that have generated their suffering to begin with."[57] For example, Annalise Acorn argues that restorative approaches to justice can also be characterized as "compulsory compassion" approaches to justice whereby compassion, and narratives of compassion, "forms both the procedural and conceptual structure of restorative justice."[58] Acorn argues that compassion invites all of the parties in the legal encounter (judges, defendants, and lawyers) to right (actual and perceived) wrongs and injustices. In the context of sentencing, how does a focus on compassion in criminal sentencing mask a historical and/or more fundamental violence?

Significantly, some scholars point out that the problem with the introduction of restorative justice in sentencing proceedings is that it too often slides into a cultural language that not only obscures the legal conditions that Aboriginal people must endure as a result of colonization but also reinforces ideas about the presence of customary law in indigenous communities. For example, Emma LaRocque argues that in the context of restorative justice "much of what is unquestionably thought to be tradition is actually syncretized fragments of Native and Western traditions which have become highly politicized because they have been created from the context of colonization."[59] In addition, there are a number of ethnographies that demonstrate the ways in which forms of indigenous customary law must be understood as distinct from restorative justice and through colonial contestations and interactions with relations of power, historicization, land claims, and issues concerning self-determination.[60]

The decision of the Supreme Court of Canada in *Gladue* has had far-reaching implications for judicial practice. Several years after the decision in *Gladue*, members of the Aboriginal and judicial community noted how little had changed in the sentencing process and outcome for Aboriginal offenders. In response to the complacency in jurisprudence, a special court called the Gladue Court was established in Toronto.[61] The purpose of the court was to provide judges with the information they required to carry out the directives from the Supreme Court of Canada's decision in *Gladue*. The objective of the court was "to establish this criminal trial court's response to *Gladue* and s. 718.2(e) of the *Criminal Code* and the consideration of the unique circumstances of Aboriginal accused and Aboriginal offenders."[62] The court's most distinguishing characteristic was the role played by the Gladue Court worker (who was Aboriginal) in providing critical information to the judge through an extensive sentencing report designed to give the judge an understanding of the particular needs and circumstances of the Aboriginal defendant.

The report, known as a Gladue report, was the result of detailed interviews with the offender and family members, exploring issues as wide-ranging as the offender's childhood, his/her relationship with family members and the police, past experiences of racism or sexism, any abuse suffered, any community support mechanisms utilized in the past, whether they were effective and why, employment background, whether other family members had been convicted of a crime, any health or addiction issues, and educational opportunities.[63] The interviews were compiled with a view to relaying critical information about the offender to which a judge would typically not have access. These interviews were viewed as an essential part of examining the underlying causes of the criminal behaviour, and they were part of the efforts made to implement sanctions that were appropriate given the broader systemic context in which Aboriginal peoples have come into contact with the criminal justice system. The idea behind a Gladue report was that a judge will be more likely to address "unique circumstances of Aboriginal offenders" in the life of an individual offender if she or he understands the particularities of what this might mean. Gladue reports have typically required significant participation from the offender and his or her family and friends. The report writer is also deemed better equipped to assist the judge if she or he is aware of relevant and "culturally sensitive" community resources to which an offender can be referred.[64] Many Gladue reports have, for example, highlighted the experience of non-Native adoptions, alcoholism on reserves, and the impact of being exposed to violence at an early age to explain the unique circumstances of the offender. Many of these sentencing reports show the ways in which colonialism has resulted in a range of "social disorders" with no consideration of the broader context in which subjugation occurs.[65]

Gladue and the Definition of "Serious Crime"

Gladue was sentenced to three years of imprisonment and given a ten-year firearms prohibition. According to the Supreme Court of Canada, this sentence is generally considered appropriate for manslaughter.[66] Some have argued that the "most ambiguous part of *Gladue* is the applicability to serious offences."[67] Although the Court found that the trial judge, as well as the British Columbia Court of Appeal, erred in not adequately applying section 718.2(e), "it dismissed the appeal of the sentence on the basis that, given the seriousness of the offence and the aggravating factor of spousal violence, three years of imprisonment was not unreasonable."[68] The judicial ambiguity derives from the Court stating that section 718.2(e) would not likely affect the sentence when a "serious crime" was committed, noting that "the more violent and serious the offence the more likely it is as a practical reality that the terms of imprisonment for aboriginals and non-aboriginals will be close to each other or the same, even taking into account their different concepts of sentencing."[69] This determination has not only led to an array of judicial ambiguity but has also obscured the fact that people of colour endure harsher legal sanctions whether or not the crime is deemed to be a "serious offence."[70] A number of questions are relevant when *Gladue* is considered in relation to serious offences. Does the application of section 718.2(e) affect the sentence when a crime is deemed a "serious offence"? Does identity or "aboriginality" mitigate the determined "seriousness" of an offence? Do the traditional sentencing principles of deterrence and denunciation override appeals to reparative or restorative sentencing based upon histories of colonization, violence, and systemic incarceration?

These questions have raised a concern about the relationship between the interpretations of section 718.1 of the *Criminal Code*, which reads: "A sentence must be proportionate to the gravity of the offence and the degree of responsibility of the offender," together with the remedial nature of section 718.2(e). What emerges from an interpretation of these two subsections of the *Criminal Code* is a three-part mediated approach to the governance of criminal sentencing whereby proportionality, responsibility, and the remedial nature of section 718.2(e) together come to reconcile the determination of "serious offence."[71] There are a number of factors that are taken into consideration in the context of the legal test for proportionality in sentencing. For example, Chris Anderson argues that what is required for Aboriginal offenders in the sentencing process is both a "responsible subject" (which can be operationalized as a remorseful subject or a subject that is willing to participate in a process of rehabilitation, as in the case of *Gladue*, for example) and a subject that is recognized as adequately Aboriginal and is found to have a relationship to tradition and/or community. Anderson argues that what materializes from this formulation, consistent with the applicability of restorative justice or Aboriginal justice approaches to remedial sentencing, is "the production of peaceful subjects through an acceptance of individual and community responsibility, predicated and wrapped in discourse of 'tradition.'"[72]

Kent Roach argues that *Gladue* currently "represents two disappointing steps back: the failure to reduce Aboriginal overrepresentation and the focus on the seriousness of the offence."[73] In *Gladue*, the Supreme Court of Canada suggested that "the more serious the offence and perhaps the more serious the characteristics of the offenders, the more likely the sentence will be the same for non-Aboriginal offenders."[74] Reviewing case law that concerns, in part, the seriousness of an offence, Roach demonstrates the considerable regional variations with such determinations. For example, the "Ontario Court of Appeal has no cases in which *Gladue* does not apply" and "British Columbia and Saskatchewan Courts of Appeal appear to have operated on the assumption that *Gladue* does not really apply in cases that are particularly serious."[75] In Quebec, it appears that "a number of Quebec cases make reference to *Gladue* only to find that it has no impact on sentencing given the seriousness of an offence."[76] In order to evaluate such regional distinctions, it is necessary to understand the historical context of Aboriginal encounters with the criminal justice system in each location. Recently, the Supreme Court of Canada has ruled that the application of *Gladue* principles must be applied in every case, even those cases where the offender is a serious offender who breaches a long-term supervision order.[77] In *R. v Ipeelee*, the Court reasoned that judges must consider an Aboriginal defendant's past "in each and every case regardless of the seriousness of the offence."[78] I address this significant decision in the conclusion.

Gladue, Overincarceration Rates, and the Use of Conditional Sentences
Canadian sentencing legislation contains a conditional sentence option (section 742.1) that diverts cases from the criminal justice system when, in the opinion of the investigating officers and other authorities, it is

appropriate.[79] Although "*Gladue* was not a conditional sentence case ... it has frequently been interpreted as a justification for the use of conditional sentences even though the judgement clearly indicates that it applies to all alternatives to imprisonment, as well as reductions in terms of imprisonment."[80] This justification for the use of conditional sentences has emerged out of the Supreme Court of Canada's integration of the Canadian Parliament's aspiration to reduce the population of Aboriginal peoples in Canadian prisons.[81] However, the reality of conditional sentencing for Aboriginal people is that it is a particularly coercive penal mechanism, and, furthermore, conditional sentences do not necessarily result in a person not being subject to imprisonment. As Roach notes,

> the process of net widening affects aboriginal offenders who make up a significant percentage of those offenders subject to conditional sentences in the western provinces and who may be disproportionately subject to having their conditional sentences breached. For aboriginal offenders who breach conditions, a conditional sentence may very well mean jail. If the breach is established early in the sentence, it may even result in imprisonment for a longer period than if they went directly to jail.[82]

Roach contends that conditional sentences, and the possible breach of conditional sentences, may effectively result in longer prison terms for Aboriginal people in particular.

Conditional sentences widen the carceral network for marginalized people whereby house arrest and other community sanctions function as a mode of racial governance where the community effectively works as part of the "regulatory terrain" for Aboriginal peoples.[83] Conditional sentences for Aboriginal people often mean being sent back to the "community," where there are few programs and services available for reintegration. Furthermore, conditional sanctions may also function as code for "community sanctions" for Aboriginal offenders. Community sanctions can function through paradigms of culture whereby Aboriginal women who are enduring violence are often disproportionately affected by sanctions that do not address the conditions of both patriarchy and colonization in their lives. For example, in *R. v Morris*, a band chief assaulted his wife over a period of a number of hours, and a talking circle had been recommended to the judge, "but the Aboriginal Women's Society had expressed reservations about the use of the sentencing circle because of the violence of the offence and the political power of the accused."[84] The concerns of the Aboriginal Women's Society were noted, and the accused received one year of imprisonment.[85]

Conditional sentences have not affected the incarceration rates for Aboriginal people since the *Gladue* decision in 1999. In fact, in October 2006, the Office of the Correctional Investigator of Canada released a report that demonstrated that the incarceration of Aboriginal peoples had continued to rise at dramatic rates regardless of provisions such as sections 718.2(e), restorative justice initiatives, and/or conditional sentencing.[86] Indeed, many outside the government have argued that *Gladue* would not help the disproportionate representation of Aboriginal peoples in Canadian prisons, and, since the implementation of section 718.2(e) in 1996, prison rates for Aboriginal peoples have in fact increased. As noted in the introduction, Aboriginal peoples continue to be disproportionately represented in Canada's criminal justice system, and incarceration rates for Aboriginal women have increased since the decision in *Gladue*.[87] In 2007-08, "Aboriginal adults accounted for 22% of sentenced custody, while representing 3% of the Canadian population."[88] Toni Williams has found that in cases where the *Gladue* methodology is applied to Aboriginal women,

> there is a danger of social context analysis portraying lawbreaking by Aboriginal women as over-determined by ancestry, identity and circumstances, thereby feeding stereotypes that render the criminalized group more vulnerable to criminalization. This focus on the Aboriginal woman's personal history, family, and community shifts attention away from questions about societal discrimination and exclusion and about the role of criminal and penal practice in exacerbating the problems of Aboriginal societies and individuals.[89]

Williams's analysis suggests that we must think critically about the ways in which social context in sentencing continues to be filtered through ideas of cultural difference and cultural distinctiveness. In cases where *Gladue* is applied, social context is often identified as social disorder and dysfunction, and these issues effectively become the (ontological) property of Aboriginal peoples.

Importantly, scholarly responses to section 718.2(e) have addressed the relationship between the application of section 718.2(e) and the incarceration rates for Aboriginal peoples. Philip Stenning and Julian Roberts note that while the overincarceration rates of Aboriginal peoples are a national problem, there is no evidence to suggest that "the problem has arisen as a result of discriminatory sentencing *per se*," thereby suggesting that changes to sentencing methodology legislated by section 718.2(e) would have little effect on decreasing incarceration rates.[90] The second response has maintained that "sentencing practices can address problems not caused exclusively by the sentencing process itself."[91] This position attempts to understand the direct relationship between colonialism, ongoing colonialism, and incarceration rates for Aboriginal people. While both approaches insist that the overrepresentation of Aboriginal people in Canadian prisons is a national crisis, they have a differing view of the impact of the sentencing process. Rudin and Roach predicted ten years ago that *Gladue* would be ineffectual in addressing issues of overincarceration rates.[92] Roach suggests that the failure of *Gladue* is not simply a result of the "way courts have applied the precedent" but of the way that "court(s) also noted that sentencing decisions made by judges do play a role" in incarceration rates.[93]

Gladue, "Aboriginality," and Gendered Racial Violence

The case of *Gladue* raised legal and political questions about what kinds of practices, commitments, and performances come together to constitute a legally discernable "Aboriginal person" and/or a legally comprehensible notion of "aboriginality." The trial judge rejected the idea that Gladue was adequately Aboriginal because of the fact that she was living off of a reserve in the urban centre of Nanaimo, British Columbia, and noted that, when asked about the racial makeup of McLennan, Alberta (Gladue's birthplace), her defence counsel described McLennan as a "regular community." The judge maintained that she was not "within an Aboriginal community as such," and, consequently, he did not think that any consideration should be given to her Aboriginal status in the context of sentencing.[94] The Supreme Court of Canada rejected this view and reasoned that status Indians, non-status Indians, Inuit, and Métis peoples come within the scope of section 718.2(e) "wherever they reside, whether on- or off-reserve, in a large city or rural area."[95]

Gladue, however, was not the first case to highlight legal contestations surrounding constructions of Aboriginal identity. This case invites us to think through the impact of ongoing colonial violence in the lives of Aboriginal peoples. In a white settler context such as Canada, these debates are profoundly embedded within colonialism and colonial legal processes and are affected by the differential impact these processes have on Aboriginal women.[96] Identifying Gladue as an "Aboriginal subject" functioned through a legal manoeuvre that turned the history of colonialism, ongoing colonialism, and colonial violence into culture in the language of law. She became comprehensible in the law through cultural paradigms. Even when the chief justice initiated a discourse of "fault" and "blame" on the part of the nation in considering Aboriginal peoples' particularity in the sentencing process, "blame" was reconceptualized through a consideration of what it might have to do with the "hunting season."

Very little has been written about the impact of the *Gladue* decision on Aboriginal women's experience of violence and the ways in which the law effectively denied Gladue's experience of violence by transforming her into the aggressor.[97] Moreover, the Supreme Court of Canada's decision did not make any reference to the violence in Gladue's life other than to note that her partner had been charged with assaulting her in the past.[98] Nor is it considered, as noted at the outset of this chapter, that the transcripts of the preliminary inquiry into the *Gladue* case reveal that Gladue did not kill in a murderous rage as depicted but, rather, may have been responding to having just been a victim of abuse and to the fact that her sister was a victim of sexual assault.[99] The Court determined that Gladue's crime was a "serious offence" and did not consider her participation in a serious offence to have been mitigated by any other aspect of her history or her own experience of violence.

There is much evidence to support the position that women's violent acts are disproportionately a result of systemic disempowerment and violence. Furthermore, Aboriginal and other marginalized women charged with the homicide of abusive partners often plead guilty in higher number and forego the use of possible defences, such as self-defence, out of a concern that the defence may be ineffective and, thus, they may receive a more severe sentence in higher numbers.[100]

The Supreme Court of Canada's disavowal of Gladue's experience of violence implies that if Gladue experienced domestic violence it was inconsequential – a theme that emerges in other cases where Aboriginal women encounter the law.[101] For example, even though there were bruises on Gladue's body; there was a neighbour who had witnessed the altercation ("it sounded like someone got hit and furniture was sliding, like someone pushed around" and "the fight lasted five to ten minutes, it was like a wrestling match");[102] and Gladue's partner had previously been charged with assaulting her, the Court did not find that the evidence relating to Gladue's experience of violence was relevant in this case. Even in the face of an "evidentiary record" of physical attacks, the Court found that the violence perpetrated against Gladue was insignificant. This is a familiar legal story and one that Sherene Razack has discussed in the context of the legal response to the murder of Pamela George, an Aboriginal woman working as a prostitute who was murdered by two white men. Razack argues that the gendered racial violence that George endured "was characterized as a natural by-product of the space and thus of the social context in which it occurred, an event that is routine when the bodies in question are Aboriginal."[103] Similarly, there was nothing exceptional about Gladue's experience of domestic violence (and, therefore, her experience of violence was neither legally credible nor comprehensible, even in the face of evidence). In fact, violence against Aboriginal women was naturalized in this case. Moreover, in a twist of her experience of violence, it was her participation as the "aggressor" that compounded the aggravating factors that ultimately led to the conviction.[104] This is not new legal terrain for Aboriginal women, who are "familiar with the denial and reverse onus claims of the dominant group, [and who] have wondered ... if Aboriginal women's stories of oppression are even 'translatable' for the court's benefit."[105]

Conclusion

Gladue did not benefit from the remedial incentive mandated by section 718.2(e), because although it was determined that section 718.2(e) was relevant in her case, the crime of stabbing her common law husband was considered legally to be "too serious" to warrant a consideration of the remedial incentives of section 718.2(e). However, the legal story of Gladue has formed the bedrock of Canada's sentencing regime as it relates to considerations of aboriginality and race. What does the Supreme Court of Canada recognize and accomplish in the case of *Gladue*? What are the features of the sentencing methodology outlined by the Court that bear upon the remedial intent behind section 718.2(e) of the *Criminal Code*?

The aim of section 718.2(e) of the *Criminal Code* is to address the overincarceration of Aboriginal peoples that has resulted from a history of colonialism, dislocation, and systemic poverty. Leading very quickly into an analysis of the *Gladue* decision, remedial sentencing is addressed through a focus on the "cultural characteristics" of Aboriginal identity. Apart from the fact that the Supreme Court of Canada has reasoned that all Aboriginal persons in Canada fall within the legal purview of section 718.2(e), aboriginality is defined as culture that is calculated through degrees of cultural difference, whether evidentiary or metaphysical. Not dissimilar to other claims to accommodation in law, the legal methodology for assessing the "characteristics of aboriginality" or the "degree of aboriginality" functions through a paradigm of culture that is legally operationalized as cultural difference.

The official recognition of colonialism outlined in *Gladue* functions through what can be described as a meta-narrative or a kind of meta-discourse that operates to promote a nation's place in the international moral arena. *Gladue* functions as a judicial precedent in the context of sentencing whereby this meta-narrative of a "history of colonialism," evidenced by the extensive use the Court makes of both social science research and national public inquiries, takes the legal form of "judicial notice" in legal reasoning. This approach does little to disrupt how the law actually functions in complicit ways with ongoing colonialism, violence, and gendered racism. The relationship between criminality and a politics of reparative justice in the context of criminal sentencing is particularly pernicious. The dilemma that *Gladue* sets up is that while the intent of addressing the systematic incarceration of Aboriginal peoples (which includes the interweaving of carceral networks into every aspect of their lives) is appealing as a national project, and appealing to social justice advocates, the functionality of remedial sentencing as a program of government in the context of sentencing highlights how ineffective this project is as a tool to address the material reality of overincarceration. Since the determination in *Gladue* was that the ameliorative intent behind section 718.2(e) applies to all offenders, the Court's decision in *Gladue* effectively left the door open for other considerations of systemic disadvantage in relation to the criminal justice system. As is highlighted in the following chapter, the analysis in *Gladue* specifically opened the door to the possibility of the consideration of systemic racism, and specifically anti-black racism, in the prison system and sentencing process.

This chapter demonstrates that the consideration of remedial sentencing raises questions relating to the concern that such practices in criminal sentencing may "inadvertently redraw the very configurations and effects of power that they seek to vanquish," while further intensifying "the power of the state and its various regulatory discourses."[106] At the start of this examination, I posed the following question: What did the murder of Gladue's common law husband become in law and by law? *Gladue* raises questions about the efficacy of reparative justice in sentencing procedures and serves as a legal template for the consideration of these strategies. *Gladue* also sets the stage for the consideration of systemic racism in the sentencing process. In their decision, the Court stated:

> Not surprisingly, the excessive imprisonment of aboriginal people is only the tip of the iceberg insofar as the estrangement of the aboriginal peoples from the Canadian criminal justice system is concerned. Aboriginal people are overrepresented in virtually all aspects of the system. As this Court recently noted in *R. v. Williams*, [1998] 1 S.C.R. 1128, at para. 58, there is widespread bias against aboriginal people within Canada, and "[t]here is evidence that this widespread racism

has translated into systemic discrimination in the criminal justice system."[107]

The recognition of "widespread racism" and "systemic discrimination in the criminal justice system" left the legal door open to the consideration of systemic racism and the overincarceration of other racialized communities in Canada's criminal justice system. I will consider this context in the following chapter. Finally, this case also highlights the fact that Aboriginal women's bodies and Aboriginal women's experiences of violence often function as the terrain upon which claims to national responsibility are legally organized and legitimized.

Racial Injustice and Righting Historical Wrongs

4

On 20 February 2003, the Ontario (Canada) Superior Court of Justice released *R. v Hamilton*, a decision that judicially considered the issue of systemic racism in the sentencing hearing of two black women, Marsha Alisjie Hamilton and Donna Rosemarie Mason, both of whom had pleaded guilty to illegally smuggling cocaine into Canada from Jamaica.[1] Justice Casey Hill reduced the sentences for Hamilton and Mason based on his view of how systemic racism had affected their lives and their crimes. Justice Marc Rosenberg followed the legal precedent set by *R. v Gladue* (1999), where the Supreme Court of Canada reasoned that the demand of section 718.2(e) of the *Criminal Code* required that Canadian judges address the overincarceration of Aboriginal peoples and consider remedial or restorative justice principles in the application of alternative sentencing.[2] In this chapter, using *Hamilton* and the Ontario Court of Appeal's decision in *Hamilton*, I examine the different ways in which a biopolitics of cultural difference is contingent upon invoking and enacting historical racial and cultural narratives, both for the particular subject before the court, as a consequence of the racial community to which they belong, and for the court, as the (moral) arbiter of the nation.

I argue that these racial narratives invite the subject before the court into a discourse of reparative justice by circumscribing their claims to personhood along racial and cultural lines. I also consider the racial and gendered implications of reparative justice in the marking of racialized women as particularly culturally and racially degenerate. This chapter is divided into two sections. The first section of the chapter is divided into three parts and is substantiated by the following data: the transcripts from the sentencing hearing, the pre-sentence reports for Hamilton and Mason, the sentencing decision, and the media reports surrounding the decision in *Hamilton*. I examine the sentencing proceedings and suggest that *Hamilton* must be understood within an analytic framework that links legal-juridical discourses at the local/national level to complex histories of migration. I also demonstrate the connections between *Gladue* and *Hamilton* and, specifically, the factors in *Gladue* that may permit considerations of systemic racism and reparative justice in the sentencing process.

In the second section, I examine the decision of the Ontario Court of Appeal to overrule *Hamilton* and focus on its contention that the trial judge erred in reducing Hamilton and Mason's sentences on the basis that there was no evidence "to suggest that poor black women share a cultural perspective with respect to punishment that is akin to the aboriginal perspective."[3] Furthermore, I examine the claim by the Ontario Court of Appeal that sentencing is not the place to right historical wrongs. I also examine the various litigation strategies by the intervenors in this case. The intervenors in this case included the Native Women's Association of Canada (NWAC), Aboriginal Legal Services of Toronto (ALST), and the African Canadian Legal Clinic (ACLC). These intervenors highlight the various ways in which this provision has created a number of (new) tensions and contradictions in the implementation of restorative approaches in sentencing.

Hamilton: Cross-Examination and Evidence

The sentencing hearing of Hamilton and Mason was uncharacteristically long, owing to the number of witnesses and the large amount of evidence related to systemic racism and the criminal justice system that was entered into the proceedings by Justice Hill. The following section examines the cross-examination of security personnel posted at a "satellite border" in Jamaica, the racialization of the concept of deterrence, and the introduction of evidence by the judge related to systemic racism and the criminal justice system.

Marsha Hamilton

On 9 November 2000, Marsha Hamilton arrived in Toronto from Montego Bay, Jamaica, with her one-year-old son. A Canada customs officer, believing that Hamilton looked "suspicious," detained her for further investigation. As a consequence of her being detained, Hamilton acknowledged to having swallowed ninety-three pellets containing cocaine before leaving Jamaica. She was then admitted to hospital, where traces of cocaine were found in her urine. At this point, a physician concluded that her medical condition was critical. As part of his rationale for sentencing, Justice Hill noted that Hamilton, a Canadian citizen, was twenty-six years of age at the time of her arrest and was twenty-eight at the time of sentencing. Admitted in the context of the trial as evidence, it was noted that Hamilton was also a single mother of three children, with no prior criminal record. She attained a Grade 9 education and had supported her family on social assistance. At the hearing, Hamilton addressed the court and displayed remorse for her actions. Hamilton explained: "All I have to say is I'm sorry, I'm truly sorry, but I made some mistakes in the past, and I look forward to getting a job and taking care of my kids now." Many scholars point to the ways in which remorse operates as a disciplinary function in sentencing hearings. Some argue that subjects must appear adequately remorseful in order to benefit from the remedial incentives in provisions such as section 718.2(e).[4] Justice Hill sentenced Hamilton to twenty months of house arrest, noting that a two-to-three-year sentence was the customary sentence given for the offence that she had committed.[5]

Donna Mason

Donna Mason arrived at Pearson International Airport in Toronto from Kingston, Jamaica, on 14 May 2001. A customs officer felt that Mason was a "suspicious" traveller, because her plane ticket was paid for in cash by a third party. The customs officer detained her for further investigation. After a personal search in which she expelled nine capsules of cocaine, Mason was arrested and transported to a hospital where she excreted a total of seventy-four capsules. Mason was thirty-one years of age at the time of her arrest and was thirty-three at the time of sentencing. Mason, a single mother with three children, had attained a Grade 12 education and supported her family through full-time employment supplemented by welfare assistance. Mason was a Jamaican citizen with "permanent resident" status under the *Immigration and Refugee Protection Act*.[6] Her children were Canadian citizens. Mason addressed the court and displayed remorse for her actions. Mason explained: "I just wanted to say I'm very sorry ... I'm just asking that you just give me a second chance to better my life with my children and that I can show the Court that I can do better in life."[7] Justice Hill sentenced Mason to twenty-four months less a day of house arrest, noting that he granted this sentence (instead of the two-or-three-year sentence normally given for such an offence) because Mason would have faced deportation as a "permanent resident" under Canadian law if her sentence exceeded two years.[8]

Drug "Mules" and Cheap Labour: Canadian-Style Border Policing
After opening arguments, the hearing began with the calling of a witness, Neil Armstrong, a security investigator for Air Canada. Armstrong testified to working undercover and accompanying flights from Toronto to Jamaica in order to police the possible "drug lines" between Kingston, Jamaica, and Toronto's Pearson International Airport.[9] Armstrong testified on behalf of three Air Canada security investigators about the range of activities that he and his colleagues were involved with in Jamaica. He stated:

All three of us are former police officers ... We are predominantly concentrating on Jamaica. Two of our flights we attend to Jamaica, them being 982 and 984, it's predominantly known. They're seasonal flights. 984 – just to give you a little overview, 984 is a Kingston bound flight ... Montego Bay is our 982 flight ... Over the past years, from my previous experience, those are one of the major flights for drug importations. Jamaica is a drug source country. *Marijuana is not indigenous to Canada, neither is hash oil.*[10]

Armstrong further described his working trips to Jamaica:

> In the Kingston airport, as I said originally, it is predominantly a business crowd. It's a business link more than it is a vacationer's link. We do offer *our services* to, believe it or not, the farming community up here in Canada. We bring in – transport farmers for – what's it called – pickers, I guess for the vegetables and stuff up here in the Holland Marsh and down in the Windsor area. So, we developed that conduit for them.[11]

This excerpt from the sentencing hearing is reproduced in order to make some preliminary links between the policing of racialized people (in particular, Jamaicans and other black Caribbean people) at Canadian satellite border crossings and the legal importation of cheap labour pools from the global south in support of the Canadian agricultural industry. In this sentencing hearing of two black women charged with the crime of cocaine importation, it is possible to observe the inter-dependency of racial profiling and the economic ends to which this policing is a part. Canada has a long history of drug importation and prohibition laws that differentially affect racialized peoples.[12] For example, "the Opium Act 1908, targeted the Chinese immigrant community by outlawing the importing and distribution of opium for recreational smoking at a time when both the trade and the mode of ingestion were firmly identified with Chinese men ... Race also featured in the development of the legislation and gave direction to enforcement practices."[13] *Hamilton* is but one episode in a long history of drug enforcement policies that disproportionately affect racialized peoples.[14]

Armstrong's testimony highlights the connections between racial governance (in the form of satellite security patrol and the "war on drugs") and transnational labour practices. These transnational policing mechanisms were also highlighted by signage that is displayed at the Jamaican airports in Kingston and Montego Bay. The Crown entered this signage as evidence. It was installed by the government of Jamaica and contains a visual image of a black woman behind bars. The sign states:

DRUG MULES BEWARE!
You will be caught!

New detection measures at both international airports will clearly
identify drug mules and other couriers.

Cocaine swallowers risk:

- Intensive drug testing
- Arrest by the police
- Long prison terms
- Separation from loved ones
- Death!!!

If you manage to make it to Britain or the United States,
you'll most likely be caught there too.

It's a plane ticket to Hell!!

A Message from the Ministry of National Security.[15]

The inscription of the black female body as a site that requires surveillance, policing, and inspection in the context of such a visual/ symbolic display reproduced in a Canadian legal decision reveals the image of the black woman as symbolic of both criminalization and external threat. In light of the increased surveillance and policing in Jamaica by the British government, Julia Sudbury has examined the way in which the very category "drug mule" has largely emerged through "the confluence of events, media coverage, and official responses that created a racialized moral panic" around "Jamaican drug mules 'flooding' the UK."[16] Importantly, as noted in the decision, Canada has used "British techniques," including ion scanning, in its own "crackdown" at satellite borders in Jamaica.[17] Sonia Lawrence and Toni Williams note that "[a]t ports of entry they [Canadian officials] struggled to keep 'the tidal wave of drugs flooding over our borders out of the country;' in neighbourhoods that housed large populations of impoverished Black people, they sought to subdue the 'murderous' Jamaican gangs or 'posses' that dominated the crack-cocaine trade."[18] The legal inscription of the black female as cocaine importer signifies how the very practice of criminalization is most fully realized on the racialized and gendered body.

Edward Royle, acting for Mason, used racialized and gendered frameworks as a legal strategy. He stated:

> Why are black people over represented in drug offences in the Greater Toronto area, and specifically for the context of this case, over represented in drug importation schemes ... We all perhaps have views on it, and certainly we've heard evidence in the course of these proceedings, that Jamaica or other parts of the West Indies are a transshipment point for cocaine that originates in Columbia, therefore it seems not surprising, given the geographical location of the West Indies, and the fact that the West Indian population is primarily black, or at least the English speaking West Indian population is primarily black, that persons from that geographical region would of necessity perhaps, well, perhaps not of necessity, but logically be over represented in the commission of the offences that geographically originate in that area of the world ... So that the submission of the defence is that her gender and her race are factors that must have an impact on the court's consideration of what is appropriate here. We're dealing with a first offender, a woman who has two young children, who it would appear, has been gainfully employed since she was about 17 years of age, in fast food restaurants or in the nursing home environment, whose life consists of looking after her children, going to work. There's no indication of criminal behaviour at all in her background or predisposition towards any behaviour that would have her come into contact with the criminal community. I make the observation that she lives in an area of the city which is rather notorious for its criminal activity. She lives at Driftwood Court, which is sort of in the heart of the Jane/Finch area, which is certainly recognized as a high crime area.[19]

The connections between racialized policing, security, and transnational labour practices reveal that practices of legal and racial governance, as Avtar Brah notes, "[have] a particular set of economic, political and cultural circumstances" and are "produced and reproduced through specific mechanisms."[20] Mason and Hamilton are produced as context-ualized racialized and gendered subjects by their lawyers. Whether this ploy is strategic matters little. These carceral networks of transnational border policing invite us to map the contours that promote a particular kind of nationalism that works through legal discursive strategies (both linguistic and visual/symbolic) in the courts. David Tanovich, borrowing from the *Report of the Commission on Systemic Racism in the Ontario Criminal Justice System*, has also highlighted the range and capacities of the carceral networks that the "war on drugs" has pursued in Ontario specifically:

> No evidence shows that black people are more likely to use drugs than others or that they are over-represented among those who profit most from drug use. Events of the last few years do show, however, that intensive policing of low-income areas in which black people live produces arrests of a large and disproportionate number of black male street dealers. Similarly, intensive policing of airline travellers produces arrests of a smaller, but still disproportionate, number of black female couriers. Once the police have done this work, the practices and decisions of crown prosecutors, justices of the peace and judges operate as a conveyor belt to prison.[21]

The real consequences of these strategies become clearer as more evidence is revealed in the proceedings.

"Not the Most Sophisticated Woman in the World:" Racializing Deterrence

Anthony Doob, a criminologist, was called as an expert witness on the issue of deterrence in sentencing and drug-related crime. Doob's testimony, as well as a large body of social science research related to the "deterrence effect" in sentencing, became the grounds upon which deterrence was debated in the proceedings.[22] In effect, deterrence refers to the range of ways in which sentencing can (or may) serve the purpose of crime reduction or the increased "perception of risk" on the part of the potential "offenders."[23] Doob was called to testify to the merits of the principle of deterrence in the context of drug crime and sentencing. As noted in the decision, "Dr. Doob's opinion questioning the efficacy of the general deterrence objective in sentencing, frequently referred to as a 'somewhat speculative' purpose, is more or less widely shared by jurists, academics and law reforms alike."[24] Doob's speculation about the limited effects of the principle of deterrence, supported by Counsel for Hamilton and Mason, was met with some resistance by both the Crown and Justice Hill – so much so that in his final decision Justice Hill included a section entitled "The Attack on General Deterrence."[25]

General deterrence theory operates through the legal supposition of the rational or reasonable actor. In the course of Counsel for Mason's opposition to the theory of deterrence, a narrative about a sentencing theory was transformed into a racialized and gendered pronouncement about the ways in which Mason and Hamilton were ejected from the very category of the "reasonable person" because of both their racial and cultural affiliations. Defence counsel for Mason, Edward Royle, stated:

> How many people really do comment or consider the cost benefit analysis in committing these kinds of offences, and, in particular, does a person in Ms. Mason's situation make that kind of cost benefit analysis? In my respectful submission, Your Honour, they don't. *This particular offender you have before you, while certainly she's not stupid, Your Honour, and not mentally challenged in any way, is not the most sophisticated woman in the world.* If I could just be anecdotal for a moment here, to illustrate why I say that, yesterday after court concluded, I turned around to notice that Ms. Mason was in tears, and I asked her why, took her outside and asked her what the problem was, and she commented to me, Your Honour, that, "Oh, because he said I'm going to get three years." And as you recall, that was Mr. North's [Crown prosecutor] comment in summarizing what his position on sentence was going to be. Ms. Mason had no concept, Your Honour, that Mr. North in making a submission to your Court was any different than a ruling of this court with respect to the sentence she was going to receive. *That's how little she understands the intricacies of what's happening in this Courtroom.*[26]
>
> *And it's unfortunate, Your Honour, one would like to think that since she's been here every day, she would understand a little bit better exactly*

what's going on, but she doesn't. I'm sure much of what we're saying here is absolute gibberish to her. I mean, she understands what the purpose of the exercise is, namely to determine what punishment she is going to receive for the offence to which she's pleaded guilty, but beyond that, she has very little understanding of the issues here, and not even an understanding of the respective role of counsel, the judge and exactly what's happening in the courtroom.[27]

And, yet, this is the person who is expected to undertake this cost benefit analysis before committing an offence and be deterred by potential consequences of what she does. Your Honour, the bottom line is, most accused people just don't think that way, and especially someone like Ms. Mason. And the impact of that line of reasoning in here is just so out of whack with the reality of the situation, that it just – it's just absurd.[28]

I mean, if I were sitting down contemplating a criminal act, Your Honour, I would sure think of the consequences very carefully. I think any rational person would. But the average accused just isn't like that, and that may well be a reason why there can be no justification or no empirical data in support of the proposition that general deterrence is applicable in diverting the potential offender from a course of conduct that is illegal.[29]

In promoting the view that general deterrence does not have an impact on crime prevention, the defence counsel depicted Mason as an irrational, unsophisticated, and unintelligent woman. The political rationalities that underpin such a racialized and gendered characterization not only render Mason outside of the category of "the rational actor" but also work to cast her as being plagued by the impossibility of her racially marked and gendered social location. The dehumanizing effects are palpable. Counsel for Mason promoted a view of a pitiable character. Representations of people of colour work to promote the idea that "black inferiority is attributed to cultural deficiency, social inadequacy, and technological underdevelopment [which] thrives in a climate that is officially pluralist."[30] Counsel for Mason used the particular strategy of distinguishing himself, in contrast to his client, as a rational person who would engage in a "cost benefit analysis" (an analogy for the theory of general deterrence) if he considered engaging in a crime.

What is at stake in this powerful exchange in the context of the sentencing hearing? Played out in this situation (ostensibly in Mason's interest since it is her lawyer acting on her behalf) are the moral underpinnings to the universal grounds upon which traditional theories of sentencing (in the form of general deterrence) rely. Furthermore, the litigation strategies that accompany these theories of sentencing expose the moral logics that necessarily require the delineation of both respectable and degenerate subjects through a discourse of liberal legal rationality. Consequently, Royle is produced as the rational lawyer and Hamilton and Mason are sealed within a biopolitics of race that emerges out of the production of cultural and racial difference. This ontological and legal position maintains persistent (historical) connections between racism at the national and local level and the global economy.

The Heroism of the Judge

Justice Hill requested that the parties make submissions on what he thought to be "sub-issues" related to general deterrence.[31] Justice Hill interrupted the proceedings and introduced a large body of social science research, government reports, reports from public inquiries, newspaper articles, and law association articles.[32] He instructed the parties to make submissions in relation to this new body of evidence. In outlining his rationale for introducing this body of evidence, Justice Hill stated: "As a trial judge at this port of entry, Brampton, responsible for the Pearson International Airport, I think it's fair to say that having done this for almost nine years, that I have been struck by the number of single-mother, black women who have appeared before me over that time period. And it leads me to wonder whether this is a group that is targeted for courier conscription by the overseers ... Where that takes us, I'm not sure."[33] The fact that Justice Hill suspended the proceedings in order to enter new evidence was variously described as "heroic"[34] – that he "brought his own agenda and pre-conceived conclusions,"[35] that he was endorsing "judicial activism," that he "assumed the role of research director and independent investigator,"[36] and that he effectively "took on the combined role of advocate, witness, and judge, thereby losing the appearance of a neutral arbiter."[37] It is imperative to point out, as David Tanovich has, that "section 723.3 of the *Criminal Code* gives a trial judge jurisdiction to order the production of evidence that would assist in determining the appropriate sentence."[38]

Justice Hill's insertion of new evidence in the sentencing hearing raises a number of questions in light of the way in which cultural and racial difference work in the sentencing process. Informed by Richard Rorty's work, Kirstie McClure maintains that pluralism and toleration are played out through the moral underpinnings of the aspirations of multiculturalism as well as through the individual subjects who embody this aspiration.[39] McClure explains that toleration "not only locates the 'moral worth' of 'bourgeois liberal culture' in its 'tolerance of diversity,' but goes on to identify the 'heroes' of that culture as those who have 'enlarged its capacity for sympathy and tolerance.'"[40] The sentencing hearing of Hamilton and Mason exposes these moral undercurrents of multiculturalism that produce particular subjects through national aspirations – the heroes, the villains, the mediators, and the imagined citizenry. Effectively, Justice Hill's "activism" and "heroism" widen the legal consideration of systemic racism in the law at the same time that it works to consolidate a national discourse about multicultural tolerance and humanitarianism in Canadian law.

This consolidation, however, requires the marking of racial and gendered subjects as degenerate while absolving the white subject to the space of a tolerant liberal judge. How does it come to be that such a humanitarian gesture conceals the systemic racism at work in the sentencing process? In the context of Canadian peacekeeping in Somalia, Sherene Razack has demonstrated that "what the Somalia Affair has to teach us is that the dehumanization of others is more easily accomplished and condoned when we understand those others to be different and when we understand ourselves to be standing outside of the world's crises as impartial and compassionate observers."[41] I suggest that a similar project of dehumanization is at work in the sentencing hearing of Hamilton and Mason. Playing the "compassionate observer," the judge's insertion of evidence relating to system racism does little to disrupt the "dehumanization" of black women at work in the proceedings.

During closing arguments, and after being repeatedly confronted by Crown prosecutor J. North about these evidentiary submissions to the hearing, Justice Hill explained why he entered this evidence. "I sit in this courthouse," he elucidated, "and do most of the assignment courts for the Superior Court [of Ontario] ... the face of importing that I see are black women charged with the crime of cocaine importing, beyond the percentage of black women that I see in a shopping centre or other public forum." Speaking directly to the Crown prosecutor, Justice Hill further explained:

> Yesterday morning I had a pretrial at 9:30, Mr. North [Crown prosecutor], to put a case in point. I came in here at ten o'clock ... I remanded the case of Brooks and Erhirhie, two black women. Five minutes later, I started *this* case again, two black women. So in the space of about seven or eight minutes, I had four women on the right side of the courtroom who had the following in common: they were black women charged with importing cocaine. Given the percentage of the black population to the general population of 2.2 percent, in a group of 100 people, we would expect to find one black man and one black woman. So if I found 400 Canadians, I would expect to find four black women or I could walk into my own courtroom and find four black women, who all coincidentally are charged with importing cocaine. All of which is to say that this is the face of importing at this port of entry in terms of who's being charged. What does it mean? I have already said it has nothing to do with the propensity of black people to commit criminal offences. I have already said it has nothing to do with racial profiling, in terms of enforcement techniques. So what does the reality mean? Does it mean this is a particularly vulnerable group ... Black women find themselves doubly disadvantaged frequently because of the effects of racial inequality ... And so, the women I see in the years that I have been here, are often single, black women and single mothers carrying a huge burden, very few employable skills, little prospect for the future with respect to attracting stable employment at much more than a subsistence level, with the burden of child care of young children. And I suppose that's why I interjected this issue into the case ... I'm

trying to figure out when I see black women before me, day in, day out, assignment court after assignment court, what it means in terms of the crime of cocaine importing, and what it should mean to me, if anything, as a sentencing judge obliged to apply equality principles, constitutional principles in the exercise of a discretion, which sentencing is.[42]

The Crown prosecutor's closing arguments stated that "there is no social science evidence that black people are, black women, are over represented with respect to importing the crime – the crime of importing cocaine."[43] In response, Justice Hill replied:

Well, I'm not sure I agree. The RCMP and Canada Customs have produced no data to you. They are the people who could uniquely have answered that question. So that leaves us with the issue of, we know that with respect to schedule two offences, the number of black women who are incarcerated. And we know with respect to drug offences generally that a higher percentage of black women – I'm sorry – a higher percentage of women appear to be charged proportionately to their male counterparts with respect to cocaine importing, that with respect to other importation crimes or trafficking or possession. I sit in this courthouse and do most of the assignment courts for the Superior Court. So – apart from doing federal trials – that the face of importing that I see are black women charged with the crime of cocaine importing, beyond the percentage of black women that I see in a shopping center or other public forum.[44]

In repeatedly challenging the Crown's position that there is no evidence to indicate that black women are disproportionately incarcerated for drug-related crimes, Justice Hill's insistence upon considering the systemic nature of Hamilton and Mason's drug offences is significant.

Hamilton: Sentencing

Hamilton and Mason pleaded guilty to cocaine importation. As a consequence of both women's pleas, their case deals solely with the issue of the "appropriate" sentencing for them. In the course of the hearing and in the decision, the admission of details about their personal lives reveals the process through which the "face" of cocaine importation is racially marked and gendered. In *Hamilton*, Justice Hill applied this reasoning to the context of the black Canadian experience of systemic racism.[45] He maintained that the applicability of the impact of systemic racism in the criminal justice system and "historical disadvantage" on the Aboriginal community in Canada, in the context of the sentencing outlined in *Gladue*, demanded a similar approach to "other definable groups" who "shared these attributes or history." Justice Hill noted that this "restorative justice" approach should include a consideration of both the particular use of incarceration and its duration. As he explained in *Hamilton*,

> I understood the Crown to take the position that the statutory refer-
> ence to aboriginal offenders was included in part on the basis of
> aboriginal Canadians' estrangement from the Canadian criminal
> justice system and their special and long-standing views respecting
> traditional sentencing objectives. In turn, it was submitted by the
> Crown that other definable groups were not meant to be included
> in a similar analysis unless they too shared these attributes or history.
> Whether or not for other groups s. 718.2(e) permits, or compels, a
> similar approach to that articulated in Gladue ... respecting aborig-
> inal offenders, the purposes and principles of sentencing and the
> exercise of sentencing discretion in accordance with Charter values
> commands consideration of systemic factors in this case insofar as
> they are related to the commission of the offences for which the ac-
> cused have been convicted. This is the essence of equity and individ-
> ualized sentencing.[46]

He categorically suggested not only that section 718.2(e) of the *Criminal Code* requires that systemic racism be taken into account in sentencing but also that the *Canadian Charter of Rights and Freedoms* demands a consideration of systemic factors in *Hamilton*.[47] Beyond the fact that the judge maintained that these communities share "attributes and histories" that render them commensurate with the remedial aspirations of this provision, he does little to untangle the intricacies of these histories.

In a section entitled "Social Context and Sentencing," Justice Hill maintained that "in [his] view, systemic and background factors, identified in this case ... should logically be relevant to mitigate the penal consequences for cocaine importers conscripted as couriers."[48] He granted sentences that were otherwise an exception to the historic sentencing patterns for such offences. Borrowing from *Gladue*, he specified his rationale for weighing the systemic factors and other background factors present in the lives of Hamilton and Mason by framing his rationale around the following questions. What combination of systemic background factors contributed to this particular offender coming before the courts for this particular offence? How has the offender who is being sentenced been affected by, for example, substance abuse in the community, poverty, overt racism, or family or community breakdown?[49] Furthermore, borrowing from an Irish Law Reform Commission's report, Justice Hill reasoned that a "just" sanction for Hamilton and Mason requires a consideration of how society bears a responsibility for the social and past historical conditions that play a role in the commission of an offence. Quoting from the commission's report, Justice Hill concurred:

> Society bears a responsibility for such conditions and as a corollary, has obligations towards offenders whose personal history or whose offence suggests a link between the offending conduct and the presence of such conditions ... We are not suggesting that society's ills can be cured by the adoption of a socially-concerned sentencing policy ... All we are saying is that retribution on its own can rarely afford sufficient justification for the imposition of a particular sentence. Society must bear a degree of responsibility for the incidence of crime, and this responsibility does not end upon a finding of guilt at the close of a criminal trial.[50]

The framework that Justice Hill proposed in assessing a just sentence operates through a legal framework that links history (past injustice produces society's contemporary ills) and systemic discrimination directly to the subject before the court. Assessing the application of "socially concerned sentencing," where "retribution can rarely afford sufficient justification," suggests that national responsibility for injustice comes into the purview of legal accountability relative only to the historical and social conditions that have brought the subject before the courts. As a consequence, the negotiation of reparation through criminal sentencing necessarily requires that "contending narratives shape the identity of both perpetrators and victims, as each side is invested in a particular interpretation of historical events."[51]

In *Hamilton*, the interlocking systems of race and gender frame the material conditions that mitigate the application of a just sentence. Justice Hill maintained that

> it would be unfortunate if combining the discussion of race and gender in this case obscured the importance of either issue ... It is apparent that women, and especially African Canadian women, like the offenders here and so many others, are virtue tested by drug operation overseers deliberately preying on their social and economic disadvantage ... Each of the offenders in this case has three young children. Each is a single mother with no financial assistance from their children's fathers. Each requires welfare to survive. In Canada, the feminization of poverty is an entrenched social phenomenon with a multiplicity of economic barriers faced by women.[52]

Justice Hill attempted to point to the interlocking nature of race and gender in the lives of women of colour. He did so in order to suggest that both race and gender structure the lives of Hamilton and Mason. Justice Hill made the necessary link between the system and the individual by contextualizing their lives within the larger framework of the reality of both gender and racial bias in society and in the criminal justice system. This quote reveals the manner in which the lives of women of colour are used as a productive legal platform through which discourses linking racial bodies to crime and poverty frame the legal assessment for the applicability of reparative justice. The particular marking of "African Canadian women," to be sure, inscribes citizenship/immigrant status as a primary marker through which such claims are made. The effect is that Hamilton and Mason come to be legally comprehensible as subjects within the terms that link their blackness to poverty and crime – indeed, to abhorrence – that requires national consideration.[53]

In an effort to summarize the cumulative effects of the systemic and background factors that led to the commission of their crimes, Justice Hill produced a succinct narrative, linking race, gender, motherhood, poverty, and crime – the narrative basis through which Hamilton and Mason emerge as recognizable legal subjects. He explained that

> offenders like those before the court are subject to both the systemic economic inequality of women caring on their own for young children and the compounding disadvantage of systemic racism securing their poverty status. These individuals, almost inevitably without a prior criminal record, are in turn conscripted by the drug distribution hierarchy targeting their vulnerability. Poor, then exploited in their poverty, these women when captured and convicted have been subjected to severe sentences perpetuating their position of disadvantage while effectively orphaning their young children for a period of time.[54]

The racialization at work through this excerpt reveals that the black female body effectively becomes the pivot point through which criminalization and victimization are legally linked. Furthermore, Justice Hill itemized a five-point legal calculation that justifies his application of section 718.2(e) to the sentencing of Hamilton and Mason. His five-point legal calculation includes the facts that they both pleaded guilty, were first-time offenders, were single mothers of three children, demonstrated real remorse, and spent four days in custody.

Justice Hill further reasoned that the consideration of individual autonomy (and criminality) comes into the legal purview relative to the social/historical context, which together operate to produce an idea of social/national responsibility:

> We believe in individual autonomy and that individuals must bear responsibility for the exercise of their choice, including a choice to break the law. We do however believe that the exercise of choice is often influenced by social factors, and in its treatment of offenders,

including its sentencing policy, society should recognize some responsibility for the social environment in which much crime is committed.

The application of section 718.2(e) thus operates through a legal calculus whereby the legal notion of responsibility emerges through the combination of individual autonomy (circumscribed through race and culture in *Hamilton*) and a legal notion of past or systemic injustice (the need to account for "some responsibility for the social environment"). These biopolitical forms of racial knowledge implicate the very meaning of reparative justice. The consideration of systemic racism through the operation of such biopolitical forms of racial knowledge does not take full account of the connections between the material practices in the law that work to ensure the subjugation of people of colour and Aboriginal peoples, the narratives that circumscribe the claims to personhood in the court, and the national story of innocence that underscores the ideological impetus behind the legal redress of racial injustice.

I am not the first to point out the limitations of the *Hamilton* decision in addressing systemic racism in the criminal justice system. Lawrence and Williams also question the "progressive potential of social-contextual analysis in the sentencing process."[55] They argue that

> social contextualization of a courier's circumstances does not contest but, rather, tends to reinforce three critical elements that sustain harshly punitive measures: the demonization of drugs, the culturally embedded identification of such substances with members of racialized communities, and the rationality of interdiction and penal practices.[56]

Furthermore, Lawrence and Williams suggest that Justice Hill's approach "does not question how crimes are constructed, sentences determined, or policing methods decided upon," but, instead, his use of

> social-context analysis and intersectionality theory is problematic because these theories are employed first to explain why black women

are likely to commit a certain crime and only then to argue that the punishment being meted out is overly severe. A more critical use of these theories would explain the severity of the punishment by reference to how law-enforcement and penal processes operate on offenders' social contexts and respond to intersectionality.[57]

While Lawrence and Williams suggest that it is a "social-context analysis" that limits the progressive potential of the *Hamilton* decision, I would echo that it is the reliance upon the legal construction of the cultural degeneracy of black communities that fundamentally restricts the potential of *Hamilton* to be an adequate legal precedent for addressing systemic racism in the criminal justice system. Past injustices in Canada were perpetrated in the name of a state that was founded upon, and organized on and through, ideas about cultural and racial difference. The race-based sentencing initiative at work in section 718.2(e), as applied in *Hamilton*, is rooted in a jurisprudence that, on its face, attempts to address the relationship between race and (in)justice in Canada. Inclusion and compensation for past injustices along racial lines may serve to assuage national responsibility. However, the culturalization and gendered racialization at work in *Hamilton* also serve to confine or circumscribe the historical narrative of past injustice that frames contemporary understanding of racial injustice in Canada.

The racialization at work in *Hamilton* is signalled by the discourses of race, gender, citizenship, community, crime, and poverty that together construct Hamilton and Mason as abhorrent, disenfranchised, and categorically suspect. Naming and codifying past injustice and systemic racism in the law does not address the production of gendered, cultural, and racial degeneracy that plagues the sentencing hearing. Unless the legal and historical record is advanced to consider both the material practices of discrimination in the law and their connection to identity-making processes of gendered racialization that enable the nation to position itself legally as the moral arbiter of "just sanctions," projects of reparative justice will continue to reinscribe the liberal contention that the law is somehow detached from the historical processes that both construct and sustain it. In setting out his reasoning in *Hamilton*, Justice Hill proclaimed that "judging in a multicultural society necessarily recognizes the importance of perspective and social context in judicial decision-making."[58] Significantly, national responsibility in a multi-cultural society materializes only relative to categorical racialized, gendered, and culturalized inscriptions on subject populations in sentencing decisions. The discursive transformation of the story of cocaine importation, for example, into one that is organized around (and against) the consideration of systemic racism in the law, through the invocation of certain populations such as "criminal," "offender," "substance abuser," and "racial minority," thus encodes the discourse of citizenship (or "worthy" citizenship) into the discourse of law and order.

Following the *Hamilton* decision, the media was characteristically divided among those who saw the decision as "special treatment" for black Canadians and others who applauded Justice Hill's efforts to account for systemic racism in sentencing. Members of the African Canadian community and the ACLC viewed the decision in *Hamilton* as a legal victory. In the *Toronto Star*, Margaret Parsons and Marie Chen, lawyers from the ACLC, state that

> the decisions by ... Justice Casey Hill of the Superior Court of Justice in *R v Hamilton* not only recognize the systemic disparities faced by African Canadians but also affirm the role of the sentencing judge, albeit limited, in remedying injustices and the effects of such systemic racism ... Hill also placed weight on the systemic and background factors relevant to the women such as the overrepresentation of women (including black women) in federal prisons, the feminization of poverty and the compounding disadvantage of systemic racism.[59]

While recognizing the limited role of the sentencing judge in remedying systemic racism, the members of the ACLC suggest that *Hamilton* is a welcome addition to the jurisprudence in Canada concerning race.

Conservative reaction to the decision argued (not surprisingly) that *Hamilton* "invites the question of which ethnic group will be next in line claiming systemic racism in order to gain preferential treatment in the courts."[60] Other right-wing reaction holds that *Hamilton* amounts to nothing less than special treatment for black Canadians: "Shaving off a sentence simply because of skin colour serves no purpose. It's special treatment. It ignores individual responsibility and insults law-abiding members of the community."[61] I maintain that the narrative about the application of a fair and just sentence in *Hamilton* is specifically a story about race and the nation. Following the contributions made by other scholars, I argue that regulating bodies of colour in the context of the application of section 718.2(e) is part of the historical manufacturing of Canada as a white settler society, with a social hierarchy that is ultimately maintained through a methodical, ordered, structured, and controlled disciplinary system of racial value.[62]

Competing Claims of Cultural Difference and Racial Injustice

On 3 August 2004, the decision in *Hamilton* was overruled by a unanimous bench of the Ontario Court of Appeal. The decision was critical of several aspects of the trial judge's decision. The appeal court was most disapproving of the fact that Justice Hill of the Superior Court of Ontario had introduced several hundred pages of materials on which the parties were expected to make submissions, thus substantially broadening the scope of the sentencing hearing. It suggested that the "trial judge effectively took over the sentencing proceedings and in doing so went beyond the role assigned to a trial judge."[63] Reports from the pages of national newspapers were no less critical of the trial judge's decision. On 5 August 2005, the *National Post* supported the Ontario Court of Appeal's decision in its editorial. In particular, the newspaper is critical of what it refers to as "race-specific sentencing guidelines." The editorial states:

> In a bout of social activism, an Ontario Superior Court Justice, Casey Hill, converted [a] joint sentencing hearing into a public forum on the challenges facing black single mothers. After sending lawyers roughly 700 pages of his own research on the subject, Justice Hill effectively concluded that the offenders were the real victims. On the basis that their race, gender and financial circumstances placed them in an untenable situation in which they were easy targets for higher-ups in the drug trade, he decided to spare them jail in favour of house

arrest ... Thankfully, saner heads have prevailed. On Tuesday, the Ontario Court of Appeal unanimously rejected the Superior Court's findings.[64]

The Ontario Court of Appeal began by stating:

Sentencing is not based on group characteristics, but on the facts relating to the specific offence and specific offender as revealed by the evidence adduced in the proceedings. *A sentencing proceeding is also not the forum in which to right perceived societal wrongs, allocate responsibility for criminal conduct as between the offender and society, or "make up" for perceived social injustices* by the imposition of sentences that do not reflect the seriousness of the crime.[65]

Its decision effectively reduced the possibility of section 718.2(e) being applied to groups other than Aboriginal peoples. The court distinguished black people from Aboriginal people by organizing possible and competing claims to both historical disadvantage and systemic discrimination, such that Aboriginals are deemed deserving of the application of section 718.2(e), while black Canadians are understood as being outside of its possible application. The court's distinction between Aboriginal peoples and black Canadians was grounded in the reasoning that Aboriginal peoples have experienced colonization, have endured systemic discrimination, and have culturally specific justice models that together warrant the consideration of alternative sentencing. Black Canadians, the court reasoned, experience systemic racism (unconnected to the history of slavery), but they do not, as a cultural group, have culturally specific justice models, analogous to those in Aboriginal communities. These tensions form the basis of the legal arguments presented to the court.

Appellant's Factum

The Crown organized their facta into four sections that included the particulars of the case, a summary of the facts, the multiple grounds of their appeal, and the sentence that they requested. The Crown requested that Hamilton and Mason be sentenced to a term of two to three years of imprisonment.[66] The grounds for appeal included: (1) that Justice Hill erred in the type of sentencing hearing that he conducted; (2) that Hill erred in his treatment of the "social context" issue; (3) that Hill erred in "reducing the sentence ordinarily imposed for this type of offence and offender due to the delay occasioned by the extended sentencing hearing"; (4) that Hill "erred in distinguishing [this case] from cases in which [the Ontario Court of Appeal] provided clear sentencing guidelines on the basis of 'purity adjusted weight'";[67] (5) that Hill "erred in over emphasizing the sympathetic personal circumstances of the offenders and under emphasizing the need to generally deter the commission of the offence"; (6) that Hill "erred in affording mitigation of [the] sentence based in the potential for deportation; and (7) that the Crown outlined their position in terms of what was a "fit sentence in this case."[68]

Justice Hill: The "Research Director"

The Crown maintained that Justice Hill "erred in engaging in the broad inquiry that he did, basing the inquiry on his own evidence and observations, and reaching conclusions not urged on him or in some cases not supported by counsel for the Respondents or by any admissible evidence."[69] While noting that section 723 of the *Criminal Code* permits judges to introduce "direct evidence" and "make reference to social context even where it may be based on personal knowledge," the Crown argued that Justice Hill nonetheless "exceeded the boundaries of this broad jurisdiction."[70] The Crown maintained that Justice Hill "improperly assume[d] the role of research director and did improperly become an independent investigator when he raised issues not supported by the parties."[71] In delivering the evidence, Justice Hill noted that he was well within jurisdiction and accordingly labelled the materials that he presented to the parties as "Section 723 Criminal Code Sentencing Materials," signalling that section 723 of the *Criminal Code* indeed permitted a sentencing judge to enter evidentiary materials into the proceedings.[72]

Individualized sentencing is the backbone of Canada's sentencing regime. For example, Lawrence and Williams maintain that a "contextual analysis [in sentencing] does not depend on the existence of a special provision such as s. 718.2(e) but may occur as a routine part of an individualized sentencing process."[73] Individualized sentencing promoted by the Crown assumes that offenders exist outside of the social and historical context that brings them into direct contact with the criminal justice system. Moreover, individualized sentencing assumes that the judge and judicial practices exist outside of the context of a racist criminal justice system, which has been well documented by Canadian courts at all levels,[74] justice inquiries,[75] a royal commission,[76] government-supported studies,[77] independent research,[78] and community groups.

The Social Context Issue
The Crown construed that in order to extend the application of section 718.2(e) to groups other than Aboriginal people, the burden would be incumbent upon the defendant to argue that their individual situation was adequately similar to those of Aboriginal offenders in order to justify a similar remedial sentencing approach. Therefore, the Crown argued that the first error that Justice Hill made in the treatment of the "social context" issue was the "failure to determine if the individual circumstances of ... Hamilton and Mason were sufficiently similar to those of Aboriginal offenders to justify a similar sentencing approach."[79] The Crown used the Supreme Court of Canada's decision in *Gladue* in order to justify their argument. The Crown argued that the Supreme Court of Canada had followed the directive of Parliament in maintaining that the purpose of enacting section 718.2(e) was threefold: (1) "to respond to the problem of over-incarceration in Canada in general"; (2) "to respond to the more acute problem of disproportionate incarceration of Aboriginal people"; and (3) "to encourage the principles of restorative justice to be applied when sentencing Aboriginal offenders."[80]

Furthermore, the Crown argued that in prior decisions the Ontario Court of Appeal had indicated that what was required for the application of remedial sentencing to groups other than Aboriginal peoples was evidence of a causal relationship between the "circumstances of the offender" and the commission of an offence. To this end, the Crown quoted *R. v Borde* and argued that *Borde* set a precedent that dictated that "background factors" must be sufficiently similar and be determined to have played a role in the commission of the offence in order to warrant the application of remedial sentencing.[81] *Borde* is a decision of the Ontario Court of Appeal where Justice Rosenberg maintained that there was a need to take into consideration "systemic racism and background factors" in the sentencing of black youths. (However, such systemic factors did not operate to reduce the sentence of Quinn Borde, an eighteen-year-old black male charged with the "possession of a loaded restricted weapon, aggravated assault and using a firearm in the commission of an indictable offence," because Justice Rosenberg noted that his crimes were "too violent" for such considerations to affect the sentence.)[82] As an excerpt from *Borde* demonstrates,

> the appellant's fundamental submission is that because of the similarity between the plight of Aboriginal Canadians and African Canadians, the court should adopt a similar form of analysis for the purposes of sentencing. Further, he submits that the background of the appellant exhibits many of the same factors often found in the background of Aboriginal offenders including poverty, family dislocation, chaotic child rearing and alcoholism. I accept that there are *some similarities* and that the background and systemic factors facing African Canadians, *where they are shown to have played a part in the offence, might be taken into account in imposing sentences.*[83]

The Crown took the position that there must be a distinct relationship between the notion of "individual circumstance" and the commission of an offence. Furthermore, this relationship must be considered to be "sufficiently similar" to the histories and contemporary circumstances of Aboriginal peoples. Moreover, the Crown submitted that in order for individual circumstances to be determined to be sufficiently similar, the individual in question must be part of a larger community where the presence of alternative conceptions of rehabilitation and/or justice is culturally specific (in this case, the community of Jamaican Canadians and/or African Canadians, which are communities that are seemingly collapsed in the Crown's facta). To this end, the Crown further quoted the Ontario Court of Appeal's decision in *Borde* in order to justify this argument regarding the need for culturally specific justice models for the application of remedial sentencing to be warranted. In *Borde*, the court stated:

> Further, an important part of the *Gladue* analysis hinged on the fact that the traditional sentencing ideals of deterrence, separation, and denunciation are often far removed from the understanding of sentencing held by aboriginal offenders, and their community. At para[graph] 70 the *Gladue* court noted, "most traditional aboriginal conceptions of sentencing place a primary emphasis upon the ideals of restorative justice. This tradition is extremely important to the analysis under s. 718.2(e)." *This link for the African Canadian community is missing from the fresh evidence.* The importance that the Supreme Court attached to the sentencing conceptions of aboriginal communities results from the specific reference to aboriginal offenders in s. 718.2(e). In this regard, aboriginal communities are unique.[84]

This statement demonstrates the manner in which the Crown's position continues to make an argument that is consistent with the culturalization of people of colour. By invoking a discourse of tradition ("most traditional aboriginal conceptions of sentencing place a primary emphasis upon the ideals of restorative justice"), the Crown insisted that it is this type of cultural tradition that is the missing link for the African Canadian community when considering the applicability of section 718.2(e). The black Canadian community is posited as not having a viable "distinctive culture," since there is no "tradition" of restorative justice present in this community. (The singular monolithic construction of the "African Canadian community" will be addressed later in this chapter.) The Crown argued that the *Gladue* decision has placed an overarching emphasis on the concept of cultural specificity of restorative justice and that, most importantly, there is no evidence in *Hamilton* to suggest that the diasporic black community in Toronto has "cultural values" consistent with a restorative approach to sentencing and/or rehabilitation. The Crown stated that Justice Hill

> erred in superimposing upon the Black community an approach to sentencing that does not necessarily fit. In adopting this approach,

they failed to consider whether the sentences would restore relationships between the offenders, their victims and their communities.
Moreover, they failed to consider whether these principles are even
relevant to the Jamaican-Canadian community.[85]

What does this argument accomplish? In addition to narrowing the
application of section 718.2(e) to groups other than Aboriginal peoples,
this argument serves the productive function of ensuring that the application of section 718.2(e), in general and in particular, is sealed within
a framework of culture and cultural difference, even though the notion
of cultural approaches to justice is neither present in the direct reading
of the statute nor in Parliament's intent when the statute was amended.
Moreover, Aboriginal communities and black Canadian communities
are effectively cast against one another through a framework that as-
sesses both the presence and the "value" of cultural practices.

The second error that the Crown outlines concerning Justice Hill's
treatment of the "social context" issue is that since the defence counsel
did not provide adequate evidence suggesting that systemic factors
played a role in the commission of the offence, Justice Hill erred in
suggesting that drug importation was at all systemic among black
women in Toronto. The Crown argued that Justice Hill made the link
to systemic racism and systemic disadvantage merely because "the
Respondents were members of disadvantaged groups and shared some
of the external characteristics of members of that group."[86] Furthermore,
the Crown argued that Justice Hill

> commented at length, and with obvious sympathy, about the barriers
> faced by many Black women and the opportunities denied to them.
> The clear implication was that such women commit crimes almost
> unwillingly, out of desperation. The corollary is that they are less
> morally blameworthy and therefore entitled to less severe sentences.
> There was simply no evidence to support this assumption.[87]

Justice Hill used a range of government reports and social science
evidence in order to come to the conclusion that systemic factors played
a role in cocaine importation. Even though this evidence suggested

that systemic factors played a key role in cocaine importation, the Crown did not accept this position because they constructed Hamilton and Mason as being outside of any historical, social, and political context.

The third error outlined by the Crown (which is related to the second) also highlights the Crown's position on the introduction of evidence related to systemic factors. The Crown argued that Justice Hill "erred in substantially mitigating the sentence based on the systemic factors when the nature of the offence precluded such consideration."[88] The Crown maintained that Canadian jurisprudence dictates that if an offence is considered to be serious in nature and/or violent, considerations of systemic or background factors should be negated.[89] The Crown argued that since cocaine importation is considered to be a serious crime, Justice Hill's consideration of the issues of systemic racism and systemic disadvantage, as they relate to women conscripted as drug couriers, is simply an error of law. In the end, the Crown's position seems to be framed through two related questions: (1) is there evidence of systemic racism and (2) what is systemic racism evidence of? Obscured by this framework is the role that a "social context" analysis plays throughout the sentencing process.

Lawrence and Williams argue that the introduction of social science evidence did little to address the structural issues of racism and inequality that brought Hamilton and Mason before the courts. Instead, they suggest that such evidence merely focused to reinscribe stereotypical notions of black women drug couriers. They maintain:

> The critical question that intersectionality poses about black women – How are they constructed by the social world? How are these constructions acted upon? How are they treated by public and private decision makers who allocate benefits and assign burdens? – are not asked by Hill J.'s analysis. He focuses his intersectionality analysis on the women themselves and not on the criminal justice system as an agent of their subordination. His discussion of social context and culpability creates a causal chain passing from racism and sexism through diminished opportunities to desperation and, finally, crime.[90]

Although Lawrence and Williams note that aspects of Hill's decision do "provide a basis for questioning enforcement practices and interdiction practices," they argue that "these aspects of the decision are overshadowed by the social-context approach that dominates his justification of the disposition."[91] Indeed, it is the Crown's position that evidence entered by Justice Hill does not provide a basis for the consideration of systemic racism in sentencing. There is a need to expand the consideration of systemic racism in the sentencing process beyond a "causal chain" (which focuses on the individual ontological criminality of racialized subjects before the court) to an approach that addresses the social and historical production of criminality, racial governance, and enforcement policies as well as the global context within which drug laws have emerged domestically. For example, what would it mean in the legal process to introduce evidence that would suggest that the case of Hamilton and Mason is but one episode in a history of law enforcement practices that are devised specifically to target racialized people in Canada beginning with the *Opium Act* in 1908?[92]

The fourth error outlined by the Crown concerning Justice Hill's treatment of the social context is that Justice Hill "erred in concluding that Black women were over-represented as cocaine importers in Brampton [Ontario]." Although the Crown conceded two of Justice Hill's key findings ("black persons, men and women, are charged with cocaine importation in numbers disproportionate to their percentage in the general population and "black women, more often than not single mothers, are charged and sentenced to penitentiary sentences for cocaine importation in numbers disproportionate to their percentage in the general population"[93]), the Crown objected to the idea that Justice Hill generalized these statistics with regard to the population in Brampton. The fifth error relating to Justice Hill's treatment of the "social context" issue is that he "erred in concluding that if Black women were over-represented as cocaine importers in Brampton it was due to systemic factors rather than the predominant race of the source countries."[94] The Crown went on to state:

The only evidence explaining why there may have been some disproportion between the number of Black persons caught importing cocaine at the Pearson International Airport to their numbers in the population was that most of the cocaine imported through that airport had its origin in the Caribbean where the population was predominantly Black.[95]

The Crown argued that systemic factors related to black women conscripted as drug couriers result from the fact that the population of the Caribbean (which is identified as the global source region for drug importation) is predominantly black. In effect, this analysis obscures the systemic issues related to the transnational drug trade between nations and corporations and locates an explanation for the transnational drug trade in ideas about the innate degeneracy and criminality of black populations.

Significantly, the Ontario Court of Appeal reasoned that black peoples were overrepresented in Ontario prisons for drug offences because Jamaica "is a predominately black country."[96] As Lawrence and Williams point out,

> the court asserts that "the obvious explanation for the overrepresentation of black females among cocaine couriers" is that overseers hire women with a connection to Jamaica whose "plausible, innocent explanation ... for their trip ... [affords them] a better chance at avoiding detection. Thus, according to the Court of Appeal, the "direct cause of over-representation of black women among drug couriers is found in the selection process of those that hire them."[97]

This rationale seems to directly contradict the position of the Crown that the ideal "drug mule" is a black woman, because, as Lawrence and Williams further note, "given the suggestion that large numbers of those caught couriering drugs do have a family connection to Jamaica, might not the overseers have found a pool of couriers less likely to attract attention?"[98]

The questions and propositions advanced by the Crown ignore a number of fundamental issues that are central to understanding the broader context within which drug importation occurs. First, these questions assume that black women are the most significant conduit for drug importation in Canada and "misleadingly [suggest] that the demand for cocaine in Canada is to a significant extent satisfied by the swallowers and stuffers secreting half-kilos of drugs within their bodies."[99] Lawrence and Williams elaborate:

> No doubt some cocaine carried in these ways does reach Canadian drug markets, since officials estimate that they catch only a small percentage of couriers. But the quantities imported by couriers seem trivial compared with those that enter Canada by other means. According to RCMP estimates, "some 1-20 metric tons of cocaine enter Canada annually;" most of it does not arrive in the bellies of poor black women. It comes in huge container loads, plane loads, and boat loads, such as the "fluke" discovery of eighty-three kilos of cocaine attached to a ship arriving in Sydney, Nova Scotia, just one month before the release of the appeal court decision in *Hamilton*. The ease with which huge quantities of illicit drugs slip into Canada by plane, ship, and road exposes the absurdity of the notion that without the couriers there would be no problem.[100]

In addition, even if we were to assume that marginalized black women such as Hamilton and Mason are more likely to be targeted by small-time "drug lords" since they might receive "lighter sentences" for drug importation, this proposition ignores the material fact that conditional sanctions of house arrest are nonetheless penal sanctions with draconian restrictions on mobility that have resulted in the deaths of some women.[101]

Reduced Sentences

The Crown argued that Justice Hill "erred in reducing the sentence ordinarily imposed for this type of offence and offender due to the delay occasioned by the extended sentencing hearing."[102] One of the bases upon which Justice Hill offered reduced sentences to Hamilton and Mason was a result of the delay in the hearing owing to the fact that Hill entered a large body of evidence upon which the parties were requested to make submissions and because of the lengthy cross-examination of Doob concerning the issue of general deterrence. As a result, the Crown argued that this delay in sentencing should not act as a mitigating factor in sentencing. Employing a discourse of moral worthiness, the Crown argued that although Hamilton and Mason "claimed and received credit for pleading guilty and showing remorse," the fact that they waited "sixteen and eleven months respectively, to do so" suggests that they should not benefit from the delay in the hearing as a mitigating factor. However, the only time Hamilton and Mason were permitted to speak at their own sentencing hearing was during closing remarks – a fact that the Crown seemingly overlooked.[103]

Moreover, the rejection of the "reduced sentences" offered to Hamilton and Mason also overlooked the fact that the Crown did not object to a conditional sentence given in a previous case to "a young white man who had swallowed a slightly higher quantity of cocaine than Ms. Hamilton [and who] received a twenty-two month conditional sentence. This sentencing case involved the same judge and crown attorney as *Hamilton I* [and] the decision does not reveal any exceptional or extenuating circumstances or report significant cooperation with authorities, but the Crown did not appeal Mr. Johnston's sentence."[104] What does this fact suggest about the Crown's position? *R. v Johnston* highlights the way in which the racialized construction of black women being prone to criminality overdetermines differential treatment.[105] If the Crown were to concede the reality of systemic racism in the policing of black women in the drug importation process, it could render all criminal justice processes open to similar scrutiny.

Sentencing Guidelines and "Purity Adjusted Weight"
The Crown argued that Justice Hill "erred in distinguishing these cases from cases in which this Court [the Ontario Court of Appeal] provided clear sentencing guidelines on the basis of 'purity adjusted weight.'"[106] "Purity adjusted weight" refers to a procedural phrase for measuring drug possession and is determined by multiplying the weight of the drug by its purity, stated as a percentage.[107] The Crown maintained that Justice Hill "erred by artificially reducing the gravity of the Respondents' crimes by employing a mathematical formula entirely unrelated to their level of moral culpability."[108] This position is noteworthy for the way in

which drug possession and moral repugnancy is further interwoven as the legal test through which to determine an appropriate sentence. The "purity adjusted weight" calculation obscures yet another dimension of Canada's legal response to drug importation laws. This dimension has seen a shift from sentencing those individuals who transport small quantities of drugs into Canada to a sentencing regime that dictates that such offenders be sentenced as importers rather than traffickers. This shift occurred following *R. v Smith*, a Supreme Court of Canada decision in 1987, which

> ultimately opened up a penal space for individuals who bring small quantities of drugs into Canada to be sentenced as importers rather than as traffickers. Since Canadian courts construct importing as more serious than other drug offences, this reconfiguration of the sentencing framework rendered the small-scale importer susceptible to harsher penalties than when the same conduct was prosecuted by way of a trafficking or possession charge.[109]

Again, the recognition of this historical legal context would suggest that the history of drug enforcement law has specifically worked to target racialized peoples. This context also works to highlight that the legal determination of "purity adjusted weight" demonstrates the manner in which legal signifiers are both divested of social meaning (in favour of a mathematical calculation) and loaded with historical, legal, and racial meaning.

"Sympathetic Personal Issues" and Deterrence
The Crown argued that Justice Hill "erred in over emphasizing the sympathetic personal circumstances of the offenders and under emphasizing the need to generally deter the commission of the offence."[110] The Crown suggested that Justice Hill was overly sympathetic to the fact that Hamilton and Mason are single mothers and that a sanction of penitentiary incarceration would have placed undue stress on their parental relationships. The Crown argued that "the biological fact of parenthood in no way diminishes the moral blameworthiness of the

offender."[111] Moreover, the Crown maintained that, as a consequence of the conditional sentence that Justice Hill gave Hamilton and Mason, the court had

> effectively branded Black single mothers as the ideal courier, immune to the threat of prison and therefore least likely of all to cooperate with the police. How much easier this will make it for overseers to tempt potential couriers meeting this profile into the business is hard to estimate. That it will increase their attempts to do so is indisputable. Ironically, a result more likely to exacerbate the "over-representation" of this group before the Brampton courts can scarcely be conceived.[112]

This argument reveals a number of connections between the policing and incarceration of black women who are conscripted as drug couriers and the moral frameworks that underlie responses by the police and other Canadian legal interventions. As Sudbury points out, "[black] women are the exploited, poorly remunerated, and ultimately disposable workers of the global drug industry. Their vulnerability as primary caretakers, coupled with economic insecurity fuelled by neoliberal economic reforms, creates a gendered incentive for participation in the drug trade."[113] Furthermore, there is ample evidence to suggest that black women who are mothers are in fact doubly marginalized by the criminal justice system.[114]

Mitigation Due to Potential Deportation

The Crown argued that "to allow a sentence to be mitigated on the basis that the ordinary and otherwise appropriate sentence might expose the offender to the possibility of deportation is an error in principle."[115] In coming to his decision regarding sentencing, Justice Hill sentenced Mason to twenty-four months less a day of house arrest, noting that he granted this sentence (instead of the two-or-three-year sentence normally given for such an offence) due to the fact that Mason would have faced deportation as a "permanent resident" under Canadian law if her sentence exceeded two years. This argument bears similarities to cases of potential deportation whereby the limits of Canada's generosity in relation to working-class and poor black women reveal the moral limit of Canadian multicultural tolerance. For example, *Baker v Canada (Minister of Citizenship and Immigration)* is the case of Mavis Baker, a Jamaican woman who was "ordered deported in December 1992, after it was determined that she had worked illegally [as a live-in domestic worker] in Canada and had overstayed her visitor's visa. In 1993, Baker applied for an exemption from the requirement to apply for permanent residence outside Canada, based upon humanitarian and compassionate considerations," due to the fact that she was the sole caregiver of her Canadian-born children.[116] Lawrence and Williams reproduce the notes of the immigration officer "who recommended Baker's deportation." These notes are reproduced here in order to demonstrate that the limit of Canada's "generosity" is often exposed in the face of black women who are legally produced through racial and cultural inferiorization:

> He noted "unemployed – on Welfare ... HAS A TOTAL OF EIGHT CHILDREN ... She has FOUR CHILDREN IN JAMAICA AND ANOTHER FOUR BORN HERE. She will, of course, be a tremendous strain on our social welfare systems for (probably) the rest of her life. There are no H&C [humanitarian and compassionate] factors other than her FOUR CANADIAN CHILDREN. Do we let her stay because of that? I am of the opinion that Canada can no longer afford this type of generosity.[117]

The limit of Canada's generosity is no less at work in the Crown's contention that the sentencing judge was overly "sympathetic" to the details of the lives of Hamilton and Mason. The Crown's position on deportation reveals the way in which national responsibility for over-incarceration rates is curtailed in the context of the consideration of overincarceration rates for black women.

The Notion of a "Fit Sentence"
Finally, in outlining their response to the sentences that Justice Hill gave Hamilton and Mason, the Crown requested that they be sentenced to a term of two to three years' imprisonment and that Tracey-Ann Spencer, another black woman convicted of importing cocaine, be sentenced to

a term of four to five years.[118] The Crown argued that these sentences "reflected legal precedent in the matters of cocaine importation in Canada."[119] As noted earlier, the sentence meted out for Hamilton and Mason does not reflect legal precedent as it does in the case of *Johnston*, where the same sentencing judge offered a shorter conditional sentence to a white male who swallowed an even larger amount of cocaine than Hamilton or Mason. The Crown's position is factually incorrect and highlights the systemic racism against black women in the criminal justice system.

The Strategy of Legal Intervention

The NWAC, the ALST, and the ACLC were granted standing at the proceedings.[120] These organizations argued their respective positions by casting Aboriginal peoples and black Canadians against each other. This sections shows that the "cultural requirement" that is thinly veiled through the legal operation of section 718.2(e) demands that these legal organizations advance particular cultural difference paradigms.

NWAC

The NWAC began by noting that they strongly rejected the premise that a remedial approach to sentencing must necessarily be restricted to Aboriginal offenders. Instead, they insisted that "on its face section 718.2(e) applies to *all* offenders, including African Canadian offenders. The fact that Aboriginal offenders merit particular attention does not necessarily preclude other deserving groups from receiving a similar approach."[121] Their position in the appeal hearing challenged the Crown's perspective in three main areas: (1) the statutory interpretation of section 718.2(e) of the *Criminal Code;* (2) the misinterpretations of restorative justice; and (3) the fact that "constitutional norms protecting Aboriginal and Minority groups include *Charter* [*Canadian Charter of Rights and Freedoms*] values."[122] The NWAC did not address any other ground of the Crown's appeal. Each of these points will be discussed as they were outlined in their facta and at the hearing.

The NWAC argued that the extension of the "*Gladue* approach" to sentencing emerges directly from a straightforward reading of section 718.2(e) of the *Criminal Code*, which reads: "All available sanctions other than imprisonment that are reasonable in the circumstances should be considered for *all* offenders."[123] While the NWAC maintained that the section applies to all offenders, they emphasized the need to attend to the particularities of each offender. Borrowing from the decision in *Borde*, the NWAC maintained:

> Although there are aspects unique to Aboriginal offenders, "the principles that are generally applicable to all offenders, including African-Canadians, are sufficiently broad and flexible to enable a sentencing court in appropriate cases to consider both the systemic and background factors that may have played a role in the commission of the offence and the values of the community from which the offender comes."[124]

The NWAC used the judicial precedent set in *Borde* in order to insist that the demands of the provision enable an analysis of both the historical and systemic issues related to the individual before the court. Aboriginal people are distinct from other racialized communities in the sense that they are Canada's founding peoples. Aboriginal rights are entrenched in the Constitution of Canada, which recognizes their distinctive political communities with recognizable claims of collective rights. Significantly, it is not the politically distinct or autonomous nature of Aboriginal communities that brings them into disproportionate contact with the Canadian criminal justice system. Thus, this distinction should not be used as a way of limiting the remedial intent of section 718.2(e) to only Aboriginal peoples. It is rather the systemic racism endemic to the criminal justice system that brings racialized peoples into disproportionate contact with the law.

The NWAC argued that the "restorative approach" was not to be restricted to the Aboriginal community. Following *Gladue* and *R. v Proulx* (another decision concerning restorative justice principles in the context of sentencing), the NWAC maintained that "the dicta in *Gladue* and *Proulx* confirms that a restorative justice approach is now mandated for *all* offenders pursuant to subsections 718(d)-(f) of the *Criminal Code*."[125] Importantly, the NWAC held that the notion and practices of restorative justice are diverse, and, as a consequence, "restorative justice has different meanings in Aboriginal communities, one that transcends the criminal justice system."[126] For example, the NWAC pointed out that the rise of restorative justice programs within Aboriginal communities in Canada is directly linked to a larger movement in some Aboriginal communities for self-determination and the assertion of control over the governing functions of communities.[127] Therefore, the NWAC argued that restorative justice principles must be "properly regarded as 'an approach to remedying crime,'" rather than as a tradition that is specific to the histories and traditions present in Aboriginal communities across Canada.[128] Finally, the NWAC maintained that Justice Hill's decision was consistent with values enshrined in the *Canadian Charter of Rights and Freedoms*. It noted that Aboriginal women and African Canadian women "should be entitled to different sentencing considerations," since they experience multiple oppressions, as women and as racialized people, that converge through poverty and criminalization.[129] The NWAC attempted to move the analysis of section 718.2(e) towards a consideration of how colonization and systemic racism have together created a justice system in which Aboriginal women and other people of colour are disproportionately targeted by criminal justice processes.[130]

ALST

The ALST made three arguments at the hearing and in their facta. The first of the three arguments was that Justice Hill did not err in considering the issues of systemic discrimination and systemic racism during the sentencing proceeding. In fact, the ALST argued that courts are required to take judicial notice of the background factors related to systemic discrimination as mandated in the Supreme Court of Canada's decision in *Gladue* and elsewhere.[131] Borrowing from *Gladue*, the ALST included in their facta the following excerpt from the decision:

> As with all sentencing decisions, the sentencing of aboriginal offenders must proceed on an individual (or a case-by-case) basis: For *this* offence, committed by *this* offender, harming *this* victim, in *this* community, what is the appropriate sanction under the *Criminal Code*?

What understanding of criminal sanctions is held by the community? What is the nature of the relationship between the offender and his or her community? What combination of systemic or background factors contributed to this particular offender coming before the courts for this particular offence? How has the offender who is being sentenced been affected by, for example, substance abuse in the community, or poverty, or overt racism, or family or community breakdown? Would imprisonment effectively serve to deter or denounce crime in a sense that would be significant to the offender and community, or are crime prevention and other goals better achieved through healing? What sentencing options present themselves in these circumstances?[132]

The ALST argued that every sentencing decision must be substantiated by these questions, whether or not the defendant in question is Aboriginal. The ALST argued that the Ontario Court of Appeal (in *Borde*) reasoned that African Canadians warrant the consideration of the remedial intent of section 718.2(e) because of the overrepresentation of African Canadians in Ontario jails. As noted by Justice Rosenberg in *Borde*, "some of the same things could be said of the over-representation of African Canadians in our jails and penitentiaries. I think that in an appropriate case a sentencing judge might find assistance from the approach described by the court in *Gladue*."[133] Borrowing from the *Report of the Commission on Systemic Racism in the Ontario Criminal Justice System*, the ALST noted the following: "The Commission's findings suggest that racialized characteristics, especially those of black people, on combination with other factors, provoke police suspicion, at least in Metro Toronto."[134] The ALST noted that a sentencing judge must attend to the interaction of systemic racism and the disproportionate targeting of racialized peoples.

Second, like the NWAC, the ALST emphasized that the demand of section 718.2(e) is that it applies to all offenders. Moreover, the ALST contested the Crown's claim that "the individual circumstances of an offender must be sufficiently similar to those of Aboriginal offenders in order to justify a similar sentencing approach."[135] The ALST argued, following the *Gladue* decision, that although the Supreme Court of

Canada insisted upon the uniqueness of Aboriginal offenders in the context of sentencing as well as upon the diversity and uniqueness of traditions of restorative justice and rehabilitation within Aboriginal and Inuit communities, the court nevertheless maintained that the principles of restorative justice were enshrined in the *Criminal Code* and, therefore, applied to all offenders. As the ALST argued, "an offender need not have to point to any particular tradition of restorative justice in her ethnic, religious or cultural life in order to have the court consider restorative approaches to sentencing."[136] Furthermore, the ALST contested the Crown's argument that there must be a "causal connection" between the impact of systemic factors such as racism and discrimination and the commission of an offence. It pointed out that to track the causal connection between systemic racism and the commission of an offence would "render the judicial consideration of such factors irrelevant in most cases."[137] The ALST did point out, however, that it is precisely a result of systemic racism and systemic discrimination that brings both Aboriginal peoples and other racialized groups into disproportionate contact with the criminal justice system.

Finally, the ALST maintained that section 718 of the *Criminal Code* (the purposes and principles of sentencing section) does not place a priority on any one sentencing goal, but, rather, retribution, deterrence, denunciation, and rehabilitation should be equally measured in the application of a penal sanction.[138] While the ALST did point to studies that show that deterrence (whether general or specific) is not an effective "sentencing strategy," its position, which attempted to broaden the scope of the sentencing process, did little to dislodge the court's focus on the specific "offender" in the sentencing process. This position amounted to a lack of consideration of the historical and contemporary injustices and systemic racism that bring racialized peoples into the criminal justice system.

ACLC

The intervention by the ACLC was the most comprehensive and was a consolidated effort on the part of the ACLC, the Congress of Black Women (Ontario region), and the Jamaican Canadian Association. Their collective arguments were organized into two main areas that included:

(1) the social and historical context of anti-black racism in Canada and (2) their legal submissions that incorporated the issues of judicial notice, sentencing, the mitigating factor of the "best interests of the child," the concern of the deportation risk as a mitigating factor, and Canada's international human rights obligations. The ACLC began by contextualizing their position within both the historical context of colonization and of slavery in Canada. Like colonialism, the effect of slavery has deep-seated and far-reaching implications for every aspect of black cultural life: "The Courts and the justice system re-enforced these racist practices and perpetuated the exclusion of African Canadians from participation in society, keeping African Canadians 'in their place:' at the bottom of the socio-economic ladder in service to the dominant culture."[139]

Anti-black racism emerged through the history of colonization, slavery, and racist immigration policies that targeted black peoples and now saturates contemporary race relations.[140] The ACLC argued that the overincarceration of black Canadians is a consequence of anti-black racism. Moreover, the overincarceration of black Canadians has further contributed to the legacy of slavery, which saw the breakdown of families, communities, and kinship networks. As the ACLC argued,

> over-incarceration impacts on social networks and hence social capital, on families and children and on social norms ... When a disproportionate number of community members are placed in jail, the social capital is depleted and thus the community as a whole cannot achieve to the extent it has in the past. Prison disenfranchises large numbers of Black men and disproportionate numbers of Black women from participating in any meaningful way in society.[141]

Furthermore, racist immigration policies have had a particular effect on black Caribbean women who were "sought out as malleable, inexpensive labour at the whim of privileged white society. Later, they were subjected to large scale targeting for deportation and painted with stereotypes relating to economic and family status, and criminality."[142]

Despite a clear focus on anti-black racism in Canada and the history of slavery and colonization that produces anti-black racism, the ACLC felt obliged to also follow a cultural path owing to the way in which the courts have circumscribed the use of section 718.2(e) through paradigms of cultural difference for Aboriginal people. However, proceeding along this cultural legal course was fraught with peril. An important difficulty that this demand posed was that what seemed to be occurring in the litigation and legal reasoning surrounding section 718.2(e) was that one has to be part of a "cultural community" of individuals who are disproportionately incarcerated in order to benefit from this provision. As part of their attempt to historically contextualize anti-black racism and its effects on the relationship between the black community, the criminal justice system, and the sentencing process, the ACLC argued that, notwithstanding the violent effects of slavery and colonization in their community, certain cultural practices have survived and continue to thrive.

The ACLC pointed to the cultural system of Kwanzaa. An excerpt from their facta is reproduced here in order to highlight the manner in which the presence of Kwanzaa in African Canadian communities was articulated and entered into the Ontario Court of Appeal hearing. The ACLC argued that,

> despite slavery and the displacement of persons of African descent in the Diaspora, African Canadians have embraced Afro-Centric values such as those found in *Kwanzaa*: a shared value system. *Kwanzaa* evolved out of the civil rights movement of the 1960s and is not a religion but a celebration of African-ness and values that transcend forced separation from the homeland. The seven *Kwanzaa* values are: Umoja (unity), Kulichagulia (self-determination), Umina (collective work and responsibility), Umanmma (cooperative economics), Nia (purpose), Juumba (creativity) and Imani (faith). These values and, in particular, Kujichagulia (self-determination) are the basis for the K-Club offered by the intervener, the Jamaican Canadian Association, as an alternative, rehabilitative and reintegrative program for individuals involved in the justice system, including the respondent, Ms. Spencer. These values are consonant with the concepts of restorative justice and rehabilitation.[143]

The ACLC, along with the Congress of Black Women (Ontario region) and the Jamaican Canadian Association, privileged this use of Africanism as the (ontological) social and political ground upon which to argue that restorative justice principles are relevant to, and in, black diasporic communities. Coincidently, on the basis of this "cultural requirement," the ACLC construed section 718.2(e) in a similar manner as the Crown. This may very well be the case, because they identified the workings of culture in relation to section 718.2(e). The ACLC presented evidence relating to the existence of restorative justice principles in black diasporic communities and attempted to construct a narrative to suggest that such communities are therefore sufficiently similar to Aboriginal communities that hold restorative justice principles. This line of evidence follows two distinct lines: one that pertains to systemic racism and anti-black racism that is rooted in slavery in Canada and a second that concerns culture and cultural practices endemic to black diasporic communities. The following section will illustrate that it is this chasm that the Ontario Court of Appeal used in order to argue that black Canadians (who "commit serious offences") are outside of the legal purview of section 718.2(e). Finally, in advocating that Kwanzaa is relevant to the black community (writ large), the ACLC homogenized black diasporic practices and concomitantly narrowed the multiplicity of practices and communities that make up the black diaspora in Canada. Indeed, the Ontario Court of Appeal was critical of this homogenization.

Contextualizing their position and arguments along these historical and cultural lines, the ACLC began its legal submissions by arguing that there are a number of factors that are relevant when considering both the role of the judiciary and the question of judicial notice. It argued that "judges can and should take judicial notice of the existence and nature of racism in Canada. This is of particular import, given the near impossible task of 'proving racism.'"[144] The ACLC maintained that "African Canadian single mothers confront the unique obstacles of anti-Black racism, gender bias, profound impoverishment, lack of resources, and the stresses of being solely responsible for the care of their children."[145] It further noted that the mitigating factor of the "best interests of the child" is particularly relevant as it pertains to African

Canadian women.[146] The ACLC turned to the legal principle of the "best interests of the child" for a number of reasons. At the core of Justice Hill's decision was the fact that "he has been sentencing poor, black single mothers to penitentiary terms for these crimes for years"[147] and that the ACLC had transformed Hill's stereotypical portrayal of black single mothers into a consideration of the legal principle of the "best interests of the child."

What is at work in this legal strategy? Apart from recognizing that black women who are single mothers face unique challenges and multiple oppressions, this strategy relied upon the production of a sympathetic defendant. The law often requires that women of colour produce themselves as adequately "pitiable" in order to benefit from compassionate or compensatory legal provision. This attempt was no less at work in the case of *Hamilton*. For example, as noted earlier, the case of *R. v Spencer* was heard alongside *Hamilton* at the hearings. *Spencer* was the case of Tracy-Ann Spencer who received a conditional sentence of twenty months for drug couriering. Spencer was also a single mother, but her circumstances (having completed high school coupled with the fact that she had a job in an accounts department for a manufacturing company) did not warrant the same consideration of a remedial sentence.[148] In the latter case, the Ontario Court of Appeal noted:

> In finding that the connection between systemic racial and gender bias existed, the trial judge said at para. 59:
>
>> Her [Ms. Spencer's] post high-school educational training was incomplete due to child care responsibilities. She had after high school no marketable skills in Canada, and she had some history as an unskilled labourer through temporary agencies prior to the time of the offence. Her full-time employment now, albeit at a low income, is recent and post-dates the offence. At the time of the offence, Ms. Spencer was unskilled, on social assistance and a single mother of 2 children with little or no involvement from the father of those children.
>
> With respect, this is not an accurate description of Ms. Spencer's circumstances. She did not stop her post-high school educational

training because of child care responsibilities. While it is true that she found the nursing program difficult to complete because of her parental responsibilities, she ultimately found a different career which she prefers and which she fully intends to pursue by way of further education. The description of Ms. Spencer as having no marketable skills after completing high school is a description that would fit the vast majority of high school graduates in Canada. She was well on her way to acquiring marketable skills at the time of the offence and even further along that way by the time of sentencing. The description of Ms. Spencer as unskilled at the time of the offence ignores the fact that she was a full-time student training to be a registered nurse. The indication that Ms. Spencer was on social assistance, while accurate, ignores the fact that she had other sources of support and income and was living in her mother's home. Finally, I cannot find any indication that the father of her first two children was not involved in the raising of those children. He has a good relationship with Ms. Spencer, as does his mother, and contributes $600.00 a month towards child support.

In summary, the specific circumstances of Ms. Spencer do not support the conclusion that she was impoverished, that her race or gender contributed to her financial circumstances, or that she chose to commit the crime so as to provide for her family.[149]

The legal consideration of the "best interests of the child" entered this case to the extent that the appeal court found that "the fact that Ms. Spencer has three children and plays a very positive and essential role in their lives cannot diminish the seriousness of her crime or detract from the need to impose a sentence that adequately denounces her conduct and hopefully deters others from committing the same crime."[150] What forms of racial knowledge produced Hamilton and Mason differently from Spencer with respect to the legal consideration of the "best interests of the child"? One argument could be that the fact that Hamilton and Mason and their children lived in more "impoverished circumstances" enabled the legal principle of the "best interests of the child" to be injected into the case. They were, in Patricia Hill Collins's formulation, simply "racist stereotypes," and, as Collins poignantly argues, "race, class and gender oppression could not continue without powerful ideological justification for their existence."[151] In the end, it is clear that in all three of these cases the legal requirement to produce a black woman as being worthy of the remedial intent embedded within section 718.2(e) resulted in the manufacturing of these women within particular cultural and racial logics.

Finally, the ACLC maintained that the risk of deportation for Mason should be used as a mitigating factor in sentencing.[152] The ACLC argued that African Canadians are disproportionately subject to deportation orders and often deprived of the right to appeal under the criminality provisions of the *Immigration and Refugee Protection Act*.[153] Furthermore, in their closing arguments, the ACLC instructed the court to recognize Canada's international human rights obligations when ordering a sentence. In particular, these obligations "include the right to be free from discrimination on the basis of race, place of origin and gender, and or family status, security of the person, family preservation, and the consideration of the best interests of the child."[154]

The Ontario Court of Appeal Decision

In its rejection of section 718.2(e) being applied to groups other than Aboriginal peoples, the Ontario Court of Appeal began by noting that a sentencing hearing was not the place to right historical, systemic, and/or contemporary social problems.[155] Consequently, the court narrowed the applicability of the consideration of systemic racism and systemic discrimination in the context of sentencing. The court stated: "The imposition of a fit sentence can be as difficult a task as any faced by a trial judge. That task is particularly difficult where otherwise decent, law-abiding citizens commit very serious crimes in circumstances that justifiably attract understanding and empathy. These two cases fall within that category of cases."[156] Justice David Doherty, writing for the Ontario Court of Appeal, began the decision by admonishing Justice Hill for encouraging the parties to consider and make submissions on the issues of systemic racism and systemic discrimination as they relate to the conscription of black women as drug couriers in Ontario. The court stated:

In the two sentences under appeal, the trial judge lost that narrow focus [a focus on sentencing]. He expanded the sentencing proceedings to include broad societal issues that were not raised by the parties. A proceeding that was intended to determine fit sentences for two *specific* offenders who committed two *specific* crimes became an inquiry by the trial judge into much broader and more complex issues. In conducting this inquiry, the trial judge stepped outside of the proper role of a judge on sentencing and ultimately imposed sentences that were inconsistent with the statutory principles of sentencing and binding authorities from this court.[157]

Justice Doherty maintained that "having read and reread the transcripts, [he] must conclude that the trial judge does appear to have assumed the combined role of advocate, witness and judge."[158]

The court reasoned that Justice Hill was no longer an objective (rational) actor in a sentencing hearing. His concern about the historical and systemic issues of racialized exploitation that relate to drug importation across borders rendered him an "activist judge." The court went so far as to contest the basic premise that blacks are in fact overrepresented in Canadian prisons. It noted: "It is not apparent to me that any inference can be drawn from a single statistic indicating that black women make up six per cent of the female penitentiary population and only about two per cent of the general population."[159] Justice Doherty, writing for the court, then went on to provide (unreferenced) statistics indicating that the percentage of black women in prisons has dramatically dropped over the last eight years.[160] The overrepresentation of black peoples in prisons in Canada, as elsewhere, is well documented.[161] Studies have also shown that black women conscripted as drug "mules," like Hamilton and Mason, are disproportionately incarcerated compared to black women in prisons on any other charge.[162]

Significantly, the court chose not to apply a different and/or harsher sentence to either Hamilton or Mason as one might expect.[163] Rather, the court contested the application of a sentencing methodology that would see historical and contemporary concerns related to systemic racism and the systematic criminalization of black peoples being codified in law. While noting that the conditional sentence of house arrest was "significant but inadequate," the Ontario Court of Appeal chose not to give additional penal sanctions to Hamilton or Mason.

Competing Cultures

The Ontario Court of Appeal distinguished black people from Aboriginal people by organizing possible and competing claims to both historical disadvantage and systemic discrimination such that Aboriginal people are deemed deserving of the application of section 718.2(e), while black Canadians are understood as being outside of its possible application. The court's distinction between Aboriginal people and black Canadians is grounded in the reasoning that Aboriginal people have historically endured, and continue to endure, systemic discrimination and have culturally specific justice models that together warrant the consideration of alternative sentencing. Black Canadians, the court reasoned, experience systemic racism, but they do not as a cultural group have culturally specific justice models akin to those in Aboriginal communities. The court therefore construed the application of section 718.2(e) to be dependant upon the presence of cultural practices within Aboriginal communities and argued, effectively, that a kind of cultural justice was required in order for the application of section 718.2(e) to be warranted. A cultural explanation, then, comes to stand in place for the need for restraint or reparative justice in criminal sentencing. This distinction between systemic factors and cultural factors, as they are applied to Aboriginal people versus black Canadians, situates racial subjects within a legal paradigm of culture and worthiness (and a particular idea of Aboriginal culture), which, in turn, frames the consideration of national responsibility in criminal sentencing.

The Ontario Court of Appeal's reluctance to extend the *Gladue* principles, (and the application of section 718.2(e)), likely stemmed from the view that allowing another racial group to benefit from the sentencing principles would result in the unwieldy opening of doors to all racialized peoples who experience racism. Of course, there is no evidence to support the "floodgate" argument, and, in fact, there has been much written about the underuse of *Gladue* even in the context of Aboriginal peoples.[164] Many members of the Aboriginal community are supportive of a wide judicial interpretation of section 718.2(e), recognizing that black Canadians share characteristics and circumstances with Aboriginals that bring them into more frequent contact with the criminal justice system. The community intervention by the ALST in *Hamilton* submitted: "[The] ALST will argue that the trial judge did not err in his interpretation of s. 718.2(e) ... Systemic discrimination is a relevant circumstance and it is an error to conclude that s. 718.2(e) only applies to African Canadian offenders if their individual circumstances are similar to those of Aboriginal offenders."[165] Nonetheless, in order to narrow the sentencing paradigm of section 718.2(e), the court construed section 718.2(e) to the contrary, implying that there was a need for a particular tradition of restorative justice, or other culturally specific justice model, in the offender's ethnic, cultural, or religious life in order to justify a similar sentencing approach.

This argument is noteworthy for a number of reasons. The Ontario Court of Appeal asserted that "there was no evidence in the mass of material adduced ... to suggest that poor black women share a cultural perspective with respect to punishment akin to the aboriginal perspective."[166] This assertion may well have been quite simply because neither the parties nor the trial judge expected this evidence to be a necessary part of the *Gladue* test. Curiously, the court relied on the testimony of a single counsellor employed by the Jamaican Canadian Association in *Spencer* to emphasize the heterogeneity of the diasporic black community in Canada and to determine that Hamilton and Mason were more like the majority of Canadians than they were like Aboriginals.[167] The counsellor testified "that the black community was a diverse group with a broad range of cultures and beliefs. She also testified that to her knowledge, the Jamaican community did not have a different view about sentencing and personal responsibility for criminal conduct than did other Canadians."[168] The court followed this line and emphasized the heterogeneity of the black community as a persuasive explanation for black exclusion from section 718.2(e).

However, in *Gladue*, the Supreme Court of Canada conceded to reasoning that was in line with the reality of the diversity and heterogeneity of Aboriginal communities.[169] Furthermore, the Ontario Court of Appeal made no attempt to address the argument raised by the intervenor, the ACLC, that the devastating impact of slavery in Canada and Jamaica would have destroyed culturally specific legal practices or institutions:

> Slavery in Canada was not abolished until 1834. The history of African Canadians is one of de-facto segregation in housing, schooling, employment and exclusion from public places ... The Courts and the justice system re-enforced these racist practices and perpetuated the exclusion of African Canadians from participation in society, keeping [them] "in their place": at the bottom of the socio-economic ladder in the service of the dominant culture.[170]

Forestalling the application of section 718.2(e) for Hamilton and Mason, the court responded to this insertion of racial history and culture by offering an explanation that effectively transforms the very meaning of national responsibility and compensation in criminal sentencing. Responsibility is warranted relative only to the presence and performance of cultural justice models in particular communities. This legal demand amounts to nothing more than the fulfillment of descriptive and normative racial and cultural typologies for indigenous and racialized peoples. Culture suffocates the moral pull of national benevolence. Even if one were to engage the court and assume that it was correct in its cursory conclusion that blacks do not share a cultural perspective on punishment akin to Aboriginals, the case law is unambiguous that the concept of restorative justice is part of the new Canadian sentencing regime.[171]

The Crime Is Too Serious

Another feature of the analysis of section 718.2(e) lies in the Ontario Court of Appeal's decision to forestall its application for serious offences. Similar to the Supreme Court of Canada that refused Gladue the benefit of section 718.2(e), the Ontario Court of Appeal dismissed the appeals of Hamilton and Mason on the ground that the offences were sufficiently serious and that, as a consequence, imprisonment would be the only reasonable response regardless of the ethnic or cultural background of the offender.[172] The court justified its decision as follows:

> The use and sale of cocaine kills and harms both directly and in-directly. The direct adverse health effects on those who use the drug are enormous and disastrous. Cocaine sale and use is closely and strongly associated with violent crime. Cocaine importation begets a multiplicity of violent acts. Viewed in isolation from the conduct which inevitably follows the importation of cocaine, the act itself is not a violent one in the strict sense. It cannot however, be dis-associated from its inevitable consequences.[173]

Lawrence and Williams note that "while Hill J. labels importation *by couriers* a 'serious' crime, the Court of Appeal's judgement goes further to classify it as a 'serious and *violent* offence.'"[174] Indeed, the construct of the crimes as "serious" obliterated any possible considera-tion of the systemic racism inherent in drug importation laws and Canada's adoption of a "war on drugs" approach. It is also important to note that the *Criminal Code* does not make a distinction between serious and non-serious crimes and that there is no legal test for determining what should be considered a "serious" offence.[175] Disallowing the ap-plication of section 718.2(e) for "serious" offences essentially renders the provision useless. Section 718.2(e) is meant to direct judges to consider alternative sanctions to incarceration. Offenders who have committed offences that the court does not consider "serious" would likely not be given a sentence of incarceration in the first place.

Furthermore, Canadian sentencing legislation contains a conditional sentence option (section 742.1) that diverts cases from the justice system when, in the opinion of the investigating officers and other authorities, it is appropriate. In *Hamilton*, the Ontario Court of Appeal was con-cerned that the conditional sentences imposed by the trial judge would not have a sufficiently denunciatory or deterrent effect:

> The recruitment of young black poor women with no criminal rec-ords to carry cocaine into Canada from Jamaica could be encouraged by a sentencing policy that treats the very factors which make them

attractive as couriers as justifying a non-custodial sentence ... The conditional sentences imposed on these respondents can only reinforce in the minds of drug overseers the wisdom of their recruitment philosophy.[176]

Again, playing into the notion that Hamilton and Mason are the most ideal couriers in the "minds of drug overseers" does not take into consideration the historical context of the drug importation laws in Canada, the fact that the amount of drugs transported by individual couriers is insignificant, and the broad context of drug laws that have targeted racialized communities in Canada.

The gravest consequence of the notion of serious offences is the disproportionate impact on racialized people and blacks in particular. The war on drugs has already been documented as having a devastating effect on black communities in both the United States and Canada. As Kenneth Nunn argues, "throughout the drug war, African Americans have been disproportionately investigated, detained, searched, arrested and charged with the use, possession and sale of illegal drugs, resulting in the phenomenon of 'mass incarceration.'"[177] Similarly, African Canadian men and women have experienced significant increases in prison incarceration – in particular, between 1986 and 1993 – when there was an exponential increase in the number of African Canadians in Toronto prisons on trafficking and importing charges. The Commission on Systemic Racism in the Ontario Criminal Justice System in Ontario has noted that Canada's drug combat strategy emphasizes pursuing small-time users and dealers rather than pursuing drug overlords or pursuing the prevention and treatment of drug abuse: "Enforcement against street dealers and couriers is much easier [and] brings quick success in the form of convictions and imprisonment."[178]

The war on drugs has had a differential impact on black peoples, with prison admissions increasing threefold since 1970, but with the brunt being borne by low-income black women.[179] The drug war is a prominent example of the central role that both race and the definition of "serious crime" play in the maintenance of subjugation and oppression. The demarcation of certain crimes as being serious masks racial oppression by allowing it to be represented as a legitimate response to wrongdoing. The contention that drug importation is closely associated with violent acts and thus deserves more serious punishment is reasonable only if this logic is extended to all illegal acts with violent consequences.[180] The politics of defining a crime is merely one example of the ways in which the racial marking of crime serves to limit a consideration of national responsibility. Finally, although the use of sentencing as a means of addressing race-based discrimination is consistent with the policies that underlie Canada's sentencing procedures, the idea of "competing cultures," as evidenced in both judicial interpretation and community legal intervention, raises serious questions about the efficacy of culture claims in the field of reparative justice.

Conclusion

This chapter was motivated by a consideration of the following questions: How do different racialized communities make similar and different claims to the legal notion of "historical disadvantage" and systemic racism? What forms of historical consideration inform competing cultural and racial claims to historical injustice in the context of criminal sentencing? In response to these questions, I have offered a close reading of the legal documents that were central to the Ontario Court of Appeal's decision in *Hamilton*. This analysis reveals the ways in which cultural narratives are deployed and interpreted in the context of Canada's sentencing regime. The consequence of this deployment is that weaving race through culture does not allow for a consideration of the ways in which processes of racialization constitute the very categories of law. In this case, community intervenors used different legal and historical genealogies in the organization of their respective legal positions. For the ACLC, this legal genealogy was framed around the history of slavery and the resulting cultural devastation that has concomitantly produced systemic disadvantage and, specifically, anti-black racism. The NWAC and the ALST spoke to the history of colonization that has resulted in contemporary overincarceration rates. And yet, in the context of criminal sentencing, inserting this history into the legal narrative effectively diverts attention away from the history of colonization and slavery. As a result, the litigation demand for both the intervenors and the defendants involved certain performative requirements of law that required the offenders to produce themselves as being part of a historical community that demanded some kind of contemporary restoration as a result of colonization and slavery. That is to say, the intervenors strategically employed notions of "culture," "cultural-specificity," "tradition," "spiritual-ity," "religiosity," among other signifiers, in order to ground their respective legal claims in an appeal to a community's cultural distinctive-ness. The deployment of such concepts illuminates the manner in which the law attempts to address the multiplicity of social identities (and projects of identity formation) that constitute and circulate through the national legal archive. The pitfalls of this approach, in the context of criminal sentencing, is that racialized communities are cast against one another in such a way that the histories (both similar and disparate) of racialization and subjugation are muted and rendered legally ineffectual. The terrain of culture and cultural difference effectively strips the histor-ies of colonial and racial violence of any legal and political standing.

The legal strategy of attempting to consider "different differences," as evidenced in this context, is a troubled one at best. In the context of a "jurisprudence of reconciliation," the consideration of "different dif-ferences" is an uneasy strategy, because the nation, to position itself as multicultural, must perform its past as a singular narrative and tell a legal story of its past in the presence of (and against) subjects circum-scribed within a singular and unitary understanding of "cultural differ-ence." What results is not an adequate demonstration of "different differences" (if that is at all possible) but, rather, the story of a unified national white settler culture where the reinvention of Canada as a multicultural nation requires the disavowal of colonial violence upon which the nation and law depends. I have unravelled the basis of this approach to reparative justice in the Ontario Court of Appeal decision in order to show how claims to national responsibility come into the national/legal purview relative only to the subjects that such a practice produces.

This chapter has demonstrated that the application of section 718.2(e) sets out a kind of legal metrics for assessing national responsibility. This calculus of governance produces particular legal/national effects whereby national responsibility is warranted only relative to the combined legal operation of: (1) taking judicial notice of systemic racism experienced by the subject before the Court and the community to which they belong and (2) circumscribing claims to personhood (and, therefore, "worthiness") through race and culture and by inscribing degeneracy on racialized populations. The national and cumulative effects of this legal operation are three-fold. First, for racialized populations, legal personhood can only be recognizable within cultural/racial frames of reference where the application of remedial sentencing manifestly relies upon the criminalization of racialized populations. Second, the consideration of systemic racism in the law is a troubling strategy at best – one that, on its face, works to address (but not redress) systemic racism and merely serves to reinscribe the racialization of certain bodies that are marginalized and deemed degenerate. Finally, the application of this metrics of national responsibility highlights the manner in which mechanisms that structure gendered and racialized membership in Canada are part of evolving political and social practices that determine who is deemed a legitimate and lawful citizen.

In essence, I maintain that while the consideration of systemic racism in law is a necessary juridical process, the racial narratives at work in *Hamilton* serve a dual function for the project of law and nation building. They invite the subject before the court into a discourse of compensation by circumscribing their claims to personhood along racial and cultural lines. These racial narratives simultaneously function to inscribe notions of national responsibility for past injustice. In the Canadian context, the production of the nation works to inscribe identity-making practices, both individual and national, through the law and elsewhere, that (claim to) articulate a kind of national responsibility. In the context of a historically situated legal framework, it is imperative to analyze the systematically gendered and racialized effects of legal claims to national responsibility and identify inclusions/exclusions that are enacted through such a legal process. I have tried to illustrate that the application of section 718.2(e) in *Hamilton* requires coercive legal circumscriptions for particular subjects along racial and gendered lines. In addition, I argue that such inscriptions work through biopolitical forms of racial knowledge in order to produce racialized subjects, while engaging in a jurisprudential practice that suggests that the law and the nation are somehow detached from the very historical and political processes that both construct and sustain racial and gendered subjugation.

Conclusion

I have presented this work in academic and non-academic contexts in Canada, the United States, and Europe. Inspired by the progressive nature of this provision (and informed by ideas about "Canada, the good"), the question (variously packaged) that I have consistently received from legal practitioners, scholars, and students is the following: "What alternative would *you* propose for addressing the disproportionate incarceration of indigenous and racialized people?" These respondents acknowledge what I offer as a critique of section 718.2(e) and repeatedly challenge me to think about what is, as I duly acknowledge, a potentially progressive legal intervention on the part of the Canadian government and lawmakers. The concerns that I outline in this book invite this question. I argue that section 718.2(e) reinscribes racism in criminal justice processes, as incarceration rates continue to grow for Aboriginal people and Aboriginal women in particular. Section 718.2(e) has done little to curtail overincarceration. Incarceration rates have mushroomed not only due to the continuing racialization of crime but also because of the impact of discretionary practices on the part of police and other criminal justice officials and due to the increase of mandatory minimum sentences in Canada that often renders section 718.2(e) ineffective.

Practically and legally, however, I would not do away with provisions such as section 718.2(e) or the other restorative justice principles in the

Criminal Code. At a time when the government of Canada is proceeding through an ideological "law and order" agenda that has seen the introduction of additional mandatory minimum sentences and other punitive measures that will ultimately further contribute to gross racial disparities in the criminal justice system, there is an urgent need for provisions that, at the very least, acknowledge the disproportionate incarceration of racialized people.[1] In this book, I have pursued connections that that are often constructed as quite disparate concerns – criminal sentencing, indigenous people, racialized subjects, reparative justice – and considered the convergences of these domains in order to examine the political rationalities that underpin their connections. The intent of the book is that we must eschew simple appeals to incarceration as retribution. Instead, we must generate analyses and approaches that examine the historical relationship between moral and ethical responses to considerations of injustice as well as the impact that these responses have on aspirations for social justice.

Today there are more Aboriginal people behind bars, and encountering the criminal justice system on a daily basis, than at any other time in Canadian history. The incarceration of black Canadians is also on the rise.[2] In the years since section 718.2(e) was added to the *Criminal Code*, incarceration rates have increased and rates for Aboriginal women are at an all-time high.[3] Scholars and legal practitioners caution, however, that simply concluding that the aspirations of section 718.2(e) have been ineffective obscures a more nuanced consideration of sentencing reform, institutional legal practices, and systemic forms of racism.[4] Indeed, section 718.2(e) was not intended as a cure-all for the incarceration of indigenous peoples in Canadian prisons. However, with its simultaneous emphasis on reparation, restoration, and retribution, it provides a robust site for considering an ethics of responsibility in the context of sentencing. For black Canadians, section 718.2(e) has had little effect, and trends in case law suggest that the section remains applicable only in cases of indigenous offenders, even though the provision permits and compels the application of alternatives to incarceration for all offenders.

Tensions between the practice of individualized sentencing and the invocation of a group-based particularity ("with particular attention to the circumstances of Aboriginal offenders"), as has been shown, has resulted in the impossibility of viewing histories of systemic racism and racial governance as they are connected across racial, gendered, and cultural lines. This analysis of section 718.2(e) suggests that the underlying causes of criminalization and criminality are to be found when we examine interactions between contemporary marginalization/criminalization and historical injustice. The underlying causes of criminality, which would assist with crime prevention measures, are not revealed when we reinscribe racial ontologies premised upon cultural difference at sentencing. The "circumstances" invoked by section 718.2(e) require a robust analysis of historical injustice and processes of criminalization. Indeed, the sentencing process has thus far failed in providing this robust analysis. This book reveals that while criminalization occurs in complex, subtle, and often mundane ways, legal responses (in the form of reparative justice initiatives) often obscure connections between histories of colonial and racial governance in indigenous and other racialized communities and everyday marginalization.

Recently, the Supreme Court of Canada reconsidered section 718.2(e). In *R. v Ipeelee*, the application of the *R. v Gladue* principles was considered for two Aboriginal offenders in breach of long-term supervision orders.[5] The decision is significant not only because it reaffirmed the 1999 decision in *Gladue* that held that judges must recognize the unique historical experiences of Aboriginal offenders in the application of creative sentences, but also because it considered the application of *Gladue* in cases of serious or violent offenders in breach of long-term supervision orders. To be sure, section 718.2(e) demands a considered methodology to sentencing Aboriginal offenders. In *Gladue*, the Court held that sentencing judges must weigh case-specific information in order to assess: (1) the unique systemic and background factors that may have played a part in bringing the particular Aboriginal offender before the courts and (2) the types of sentencing procedures and sanctions that may be appropriate in the circumstances for the offender.[6] In *Ipeelee*, the court stated: "Sentencing judges (are) front-line workers in the criminal justice system (and) are in the best position to re-evaluate (sentencing) criteria to ensure that they are not contributing to ongoing systemic racial discrimination. Just sanctions are those that do not operate in a discriminatory manner."[7] The Supreme Court of Canada highlighted that sentencing judges play a central role in the *Gladue* process, and, indeed, sentencing judges must exercise creative sentences for indigenous offenders "in each and every case regardless of the seriousness of the offence."[8] The appellants, two Aboriginal men, Manasie Ipeelee and Frank Ralph Ladue, were serving long-term offender supervision orders, a form of conditional sentence that permits authorities to return the offender to custody if conditions are breached.[9]

Manasie Ipeelee is Inuk, was born and raised in Iqaluit, Nunavut; and was found at thirty-seven years old to be riding a bicycle the wrong way on a one-way street in downtown Kingston, Ontario, while intoxicated. When the police picked him up, Ipelee was in breach of the alcohol abstention condition of his long-term supervision order.[10] This offence was merely one episode in Ipeelee's experience with the criminal justice system. As a youth, he was charged with over thirty-five offences, ranging from property offences, to breach of court orders, to serious sexual assault causing bodily harm.[11] For the latest charge, Ipeelee received thirty months' imprisonment in addition to his pre-sentence custody of six months.[12] Based on the evidence from previous trials, the testimony of a forensic psychiatrist, and the determination of the trial judge, who reasoned that alcohol increased Ipeelee's risk of re-offending ("Indeed, if he has access to alcohol, it is as certain as night follows day," the trial judge said), his alcohol abstention condition was viewed as a vital component of his long-term supervision order, because intoxication was found to "play a major role in the appellant's violent offences."[14] In applying the *Gladue* principles, the Court handed down a one-year sentence to Ipeelee, replacing the three-year sentence by the appeal court. In changing Ipeelee's sentence, the court noted that he "was living in Kingston, where there are few culturally-relevant support systems in place."[15]

Frank Ralph Ladue, a residential school survivor, is a member of the Ross River Dena Council Band in Whitehorse, Yukon. At forty-nine years old, Ladue has a long history of alcohol and drug addiction as well as many encounters with the criminal justice system for serious and violent offences dating back to 1978. As the Supreme Court of Canada noted, the community of Ross River suffered a number of abuses (since) the 1940s when the United States army was building a pipeline in the region. There were reports of community members being assaulted or raped by members of the army. The community was further traumatized through the residential school experience. The effects of that collective experience continue to be evident in the high rates of alcohol abuse and violence in the community.[16]

The effects of the collective experience of Ross River form the narrative backdrop of Frank Ralph Ladue's biography. The breach of the long-term supervision order occurred due to a failed urine analysis in which he tested positive for cocaine.[17] The cases of Manasie Ipeelee and Frank Ralph Ladue highlight challenges that have occurred since 1996 in the application of section 718.2(e) in serious and violent offences, although, as the court suggests, "it would be naïve to suggest that sentencing Aboriginal persons differently, without addressing the root causes of criminality, would eliminate their overrepresentation in the criminal justice system entirely."[18] Indeed, there are limits to the role of sentencing as a criminal justice practice to undo systemic challenges, to address the underlying causes of criminalization, and to examine the histories of colonialism and racism that are central to understanding the disproportionate incarceration of indigenous and racialized people.

While the development of the legacy of section 718.2(e) and other restorative justice practices is progressing well beyond sentencing to other criminal justice processes (for instance, through the Gladue Court and Aboriginal justice projects), trends in case law in the last fifteen years suggest deep legal and systemic challenges. One of the most serious of these trends, highlighted by *Ipeelee*, is the applicability of section 718.2(e) in the context of serious and/or violent offences. In certain cases, courts have indicated that when a crime is serious and/or violent, the *Gladue* principles will not be considered or applied. Legal practitioners note that although the Supreme Court of Canada's decision in *Gladue* did not extend the provision to Jamie Tanis Gladue, section 718.2(e) was not meant to be a principle of "universal application for serious or violent offences." However, the section provides sentencing judges with "flexibility and authority" in sentencing Aboriginal offenders,[19] and judges must consider restorative justice even in serious cases.[20]

Recent and significant trends in case law suggest, however, that courts frequently take note of section 718.2(e) in serious/violent cases in the following manner: The more serious the offence, the more similar sentencing will be for Aboriginal and non-Aboriginal offenders.[21] In cases of particular acts of violence or harm, the determination of a crime as violent or serious is quite clear. In other cases, the legal determination of serious or violent offences is due to a number of factors that have worked against the aspirations of section 718.2(e), including mandatory minimum sentences, discretion by police and Crown attorneys to charge defendants with indictable or summary offences, and the interrelationship between processes of racialization and violent and serious crime.[22] Together these factors have contributed to increased incarceration rates. In *Ipeelee*, the Supreme Court of Canada has issued an "iron clad" edict that judges must be creative when sentencing Aboriginal offenders even in cases of serious and violent offenders. Failure to do so is grounds for appeal.[23] The Court further notes that lawyers for Aboriginal defendants have the duty to bring forward individualized information by way of a *Gladue* report.[24] Regional patterns and institutional constraints indicate that the applicability of section 718.2(e) has been "mixed" and that there has been a "shameful lack of background reports."[25]

Another significant trend concerning section 718.2(e) in recent case law has been the practice that seeks to determine how Aboriginal background relates to, or mitigates, the commission of an offence.[26] In this regard, some judges have sought to establish a causal link between Aboriginal identity or background factors and the commission of an offence. In some of these cases, there is an indeterminacy concerning the relationship between Aboriginal identity and the crime at issue. Similar to the analysis of *Gladue* in Chapter 3, these cases often seek to determine whether a defendant is "adequately Aboriginal," has links to their Aboriginal heritage, or whether the accused has lived in marginalized social conditions. For example, judges have cited that the "accused is not involved in cultural activities within the band" as one reason for imposing imprisonment[27] and that *Gladue* was not considered because there was no representation from "Aboriginal communities" in the case.[28] In other cases, a connection could not be drawn between a sexual assault and a defendant's Aboriginal background due to the experience of a stable upbringing,[29] or no evidence as to the applicability of background factors was provided in order to consider the *Gladue* provision.[30] In one case, the judge had difficulty applying *Gladue* because of "weak or tenuous claims to native ancestry," although the judge also found "the defendant's desire to connect with his heritage and participate in Aboriginal heritage as a path to reform to be sincere and considers rehabilitative potential in sentencing."[31] In other cases, much like *Gladue*, judges continue to place significant emphasis on whether an accused has lived on or off reserve, attempting to establish mitigating connections between race and place. In one such case where a jail term was given for violent sexual assault and sexual touching of a young person, the judge noted that the accused never lived on reserve, was not involved in Aboriginal celebrations, and experienced a good upbringing (which included the details that his parents did not drink or smoke, his father became disabled due to a brain tumour, and his family had a nice house).[32] While there is ample case law that seeks to make connections between aboriginality and crime – notably, in the recent case *R. v Collins* – the Ontario Court of Appeal has reasoned that there is no burden on an Aboriginal offender to establish a causal link between background factors and the offence.[33]

Another trend in case law suggests that there are inconsistencies and uncertainties about the role of Aboriginal justice programs and how they can function alongside the criminal justice system.[34] The role of alternative and Aboriginal justice programs also varies considerably from region to region. Aboriginal justice programs occasionally form part of sentences, are often recommended by judges, and, in a few reported cases, sentencing circles have occurred before criminal justice sentencing. In one case, the judge connected the applicability of section 718.2(e) to the defendant's personal view of restorative justice. The judge noted: "The Defendant's concept of sentencing, including restorative justice, does not seem to be informed by an aboriginal heritage. The important Gladue principles must not be diluted by weak or tenuous claims to native ancestry."[35] In yet other trends in case law, judges claim to be considering *Gladue*, but they do not specify how *Gladue* consideration bears upon the case.[36] Finally, there are cases where *Gladue* has been followed and non-carceral sentences or reduced sentences have been ordered.[37] These cases suggest that there is a need to undertake the broadening of institutionalized legal practices, including the further development of the role of Aboriginal justice programs in the determination of carceral sentences.

These trends highlight the fact that one of the most important stages for *Gladue* consideration in criminal justice processes is at the point of entry into the system. The charge/conviction and the trial stage is where discretion by the police, Crown attorneys, and trial judges is considerable. Even though the sentencing principles indicate that incarceration should be used as a last resort for all offenders, and particularly for Aboriginal offenders (in short, that section 718.2(e) should always apply for Aboriginal offenders), these trends reveal that there is a particular racial logic that permeates considerations of section 718.2(e) in sentencing processes. If we follow these racial logics to their conclusion, particular questions are embedded in recent trends in case law that expose critical fault lines in the legacy of *Gladue*. How are cultural factors and forms of indigenous subjectivity linked to an offence? How will cultural forms of justice exist alongside the criminal justice system? How are class-bound ideas about indigenousness and criminality linked in a *Gladue* methodology? Why are Aboriginal people and people of colour more readily charged with serious and violent crimes? How does the very fact of commission by an Aboriginal person or person of colour turn an act into a serious crime?

The fact that these troubling questions permeate cases for Aboriginal defendants suggests that section 718.2(e) tells us much about the ways in which liberal and progressive sentencing practices are often co-constitutive of racial and gendered social formations. Each of the recent trends in case law suggest that the racialization of culture – a particular scheme of racial governance – forms the bedrock of section 718.2(e). Section 718.2(e) is as progressive as it is organized by a distinct racial grammar. Can we harness this racial grammar in order to develop an ethical ground for reparative forms of justice? Given the limits of sentencing to reveal the underlying cause of criminalization (and the intensification of systemic challenges in recent trends in case law), what other political engagements are necessary in order to develop a deep and profound engagement with racialized and gendered forms of marginalization and violence?

Almost forty years ago, Michel Foucault pointed out that "the whole machinery that has been developing for years around the implementation of sentences ... extends its powers well beyond the sentence."[38] Foucault was concerned with tracking changes in the management of punishment in the eighteenth and nineteenth centuries that produced a range of disciplinary effects in emerging modern state formations. His insights have assisted in the development of an account of the ways in which forms of disciplinary rule are attached to the biopolitical management of certain populations. An overarching concern of biopolitics is the political rationalities that inform governmental, political, and legal practices. Foucault articulates the question of biopolitics in the following manner: "By [biopolitics] I meant the endeavor, begun in the eighteenth century by the phenomena characteristic of a group of living human beings constituted as a population: health, sanitation, birthrate, longevity, race ... It seems to be that these problems could not be dissociated from the political rationality within which they appeared."[39] Biopolitics, as the bedrock of liberal forms of governance, requires an attention to the logics that inform the political rationalities of rule.

In the context of the implementation and application of section 718.2(e), the machinery of sentencing, as this book has shown, works as a project of racial and gendered governance in which the consideration of reparative justice in criminal sentencing raises questions concerning racialized and indigenous subjectivity. Cultural difference functions as a particular technology of racial governance in the context of the criminal justice system: it works as a biopolitical tool, linking racial subjectivities to processes of reparation. For black Canadians, the "tools" of reparative justice in sentencing have been less successful, owing to the cultural ideas embedded in the application of section 718.2(e) as well as to the racialization of serious offences. Section 718.2(e) encourages us to think about the ways in which an ostensibly progressive provision in law is constituted through racial forms of governance. It invites us to think critically about how reparative justice is pursued in law in the everyday workings of the criminal justice system.

This book has been structured with the intent of examining and illustrating the specific production of the "subjects" of this provision in relation to the range of claims to historical injustice and systemic racism that can be made in the context of the criminal sentencing process. Using culture and cultural difference in sentencing ultimately strengthens the aspirations of a multicultural nation by insisting upon, and mediating, justice through a politics of cultural tolerance. In her excellent book, *Authentic Indians*, Paige Raibmon interrogates the category of authenticity as it worked through various indigenous and non-indigenous encounters along the northwest coast during the late nineteenth century. While "authenticity ... is so intensely problematic a concept," she suggests, "scholarly recognition that race and gender are constructed categories has not brought an end to the real work that these categories do in the world."[40] While cultural difference is a category that has been both maligned and embraced by groups who are differently situated, it is imperative to examine the "real work" that cultural difference accomplishes – not only in the context of considerations of reparative practices in the sentencing process but also in everyday life in the context of multicultural societies. Indeed, as indigenous and other scholars have shown, the categories of cultural difference and cultural distinctiveness need to be defined through processes of self-determination, even though self-determination practices themselves come with challenges and contestations.

As Raibmon notes, "it is disingenuous to hold Aboriginal people to a standard of social justice and equity yet to be achieved by others. So doing maintains the stranglehold of colonial paternalism ... Self-determination is more a necessary beginning than a final ending."[41] Section 718.2(e) not only requires that we address the limits of sentencing but also that we think more deeply about appeals to culture and cultural difference in the context of the range of political and legal engagements that seek to address experiences of marginalization. I have argued that section 718.2(e) reproduces the colonial, racialized, and gendered management of indigenous and racialized populations by relying upon cultural difference paradigms. This book can be read as demanding that we take seriously the temporal demand (linking past and present injustice) at the core of section 718.2(e) – not only in the everyday workings of the criminal justice system but also in the social and political worlds that we imagine.

Reparative justice and reconciliation has a particular salience in multicultural societies, whether in the context of the criminal justice system, as this book has shown, or in the context of other political, social, artistic, and commemorative practices. In Canada, for example, the politics of reconciliation and reparation are invoked in a broad range of practices concerning historical forms of injustice and contemporary forms of systemic racism. This invocation has included compensation and apology for the internment of Japanese Canadians during the Second World War, apology to Chinese Canadians for the Chinese Head Tax (a fixed fee charged to Chinese people entering Canada in the late 1800s and early 1900s), an apology to South Asian Canadians for the *Komagata Maru* incident of 1914 (the *Komagata Maru*, a ship that arrived in Vancouver with almost four hundred Indians aboard, was denied entry as part of exclusionary immigration policies designed to keep South Asians out of Canada), and reconciliation practices designed to negotiate a new relationship between indigenous peoples and the Canadian government. There are also reconciliation practices (in the form of apology, public inquiries, and monetary compensation) directed towards some victims of extraordinary rendition in light of current Canadian and global anti-terrorism practices. Each of these practices of reparative justice suggests that there is a group-based and collective logic to contemporary Canadian moral and ethical responses to injustices. One of the ideas that motivate these practices is the relationship between collective responsibility and individual responsibility. Section 718.2(e) provides a unique vantage point with which to consider the relationship between collective and individual responsibility and the importance of animating these ideas against the very real experiences of everyday racism, violence, and marginalization.

In the context of white settler and multicultural societies, scholars of reparations have shown that notions of culture inform debates regarding issues of translation that inevitably occur when there is an attempt to transform "past confrontations into contemporary restitution."[42] Cultural difference is often a ground upon which the negotiation of systemic racism, historical injustice, and other forms of human rights violations take place. The salience of cultural difference requires an assessment of the challenges involved in annexing culture-based paradigms to projects of reparative justice. This book suggests that section 718.2(e) must be understood in terms of what it reveals about the constitutive nature of cultural difference and forms of moral and ethical responsibility on the part of nations. In a multicultural context, the recognition of cultural difference itself is often thought of as a move of reparation or, at the very least, an ethical and reconciliatory one. Liberal and white settler forms of nationalism often "pivot on the question of whether and how a multitude of modern liberal nation-states should recognize the worth of their interior ethnic and indigenous cultural traditions."[43] Liberal recognition in the context of multicultural and white settler states is a process whereby "recognition is at once a formal meconnaissance of a subaltern's group *being* and of its *being worthy* of national recognition and, at the same time, a formal moment of being inspected, examined, and investigated."[44] The constitutive nature of culture, and the practices of recognition, reconciliation, and reparation, suggest that while cultural difference paradigms bear scrutiny, such frameworks are not easily unhinged from dominant ethical, legal, and political practices.

In claiming to address the need for national responsibility in sentencing, section 718.2(e) lures us with the notion that justice-seeking aspirations can be satisfied within (or by) the criminal justice system. Section 718.2(e) not only works to produce a national idea concerning ethical responses to forms of systemic racism and marginalization, but it also implores us to think about everyday action, both in the everyday workings of the criminal justice system and in everyday life. As scholars have shown, reconciliatory legal and political projects face many challenges, including the establishment of links between past injustices and contemporary realities and the motivation of a sense of outrage and complicity for violations and forms of subjugation in citizen-subjects and/or global communities. Stemming from Hannah Arendt's famous phrase "where all are guilty, nobody is," there is a flattening of responsibility at the point of recognition of injustice and violence.[45]

There is also a schism between the injustices of the past and their connections to contemporary forms of injustice and discrimination. Michel-Rolph Trouillot suggests that the linking of the past to the present "can only be made through a genealogical construction[;] that is, on a particular composition of subjects involved and on a particular interpretation of history."[46] The challenge of recognizing historical forms of injustice stems from attempting to recreate a spatial and temporal link between collective groups of the past and collective groups in the present.[47] In each of the cases examined, this challenge has been negotiated in the form of specific genealogical constructions – with varying effects and varying levels of success – by defendants, prosecutors, and legal intervenors. Projects of legal and political reparation, in the form of formal apologies, commemorative projects, affirmative action policies, or reparative sentencing guidelines – and the very real and difficult contestations and challenges inherent in each of these projects – compel us to reflect upon a new route through injustice.

Farid Abdel-Nour's account of national responsibility, noted briefly in the introduction of this book, involves thinking about the idea of individual national responsibility. Abdel-Nour develops an account of national responsibility that is anchored in the individual citizen-subject who is the direct beneficiary (in the case of white settler societies) of the economic, political, and racial entitlements that result from colonialism, genocide, and slavery. I quote Abdel-Nour at length in order to encapsulate his account of individual national responsibility:

> If by dint of her national belonging an individual can "win wars," "civilize barbarians," "build empires," and so on, is it not only logical to ask whether corresponding to these her imagined exploits that she does not incur a responsibility for all of the bad states of affairs that

these same actions have brought about? Like all complex political actions, those with which she identifies as agent have probably had other less heroic outcomes. Presumably the action with which "barbarians" were civilized also exterminated large numbers of them on the way, and what won the war are presumably the same actions that brought about destruction. In short, if the national bond creates imagined agents, ought these same agents be imagined as responsible? My core claim is this: *national responsibility is actively incurred by individuals with every proud thought they have and every proud statement they make about the achievements of their nation* ... The consequence of this argument for every person who takes her national responsibility seriously are at the very least the following: when arguments are made establishing a causal link between a bad state of affairs and actions that have also brought about some of the objects of one's national pride, a *potential* path of responsibility between oneself and the bad state of affairs in question is established. Under such circumstances, one cannot simply dismiss all talk of responsibility by simply pointing to one's date of birth.[48]

Abdel-Nour argues that the "potential path to responsibility" is secured when there is a narrative link between a nation's destructive past and contemporary signs of national "pride" and belonging. In national discussions relating to the implementation of section 718.2(e), this narrative link was established in pronouncements made by the minister of justice (and others) who celebrated that the bill, of which section 718.2(e) was a part, was a reflection of the "values that Canadians have told us are important to them in the treatment of offenders."[49] Bill C-41 imagined "heroic outcomes" for Canada in the face of a national incarceration crisis. Can an account of individual national responsibility be applicable to Canada's sentencing regime?

Abdel-Nour's account of individual national responsibility helps us to think about the ways in which the law carves out identities for the various players in the legal process and, thus, ultimately bolsters "a national bond" of "imagined agents." The task, Abdel-Nour maintains, is to "implicate" ourselves "with the causes of these horrors," even though his "conclusion is simple[:] Where there is national pride, there is national responsibility."[50] Abdel-Nour's account suggests that one crucial element to national responsibility is to draw connections between individual histories, subject-making practices, and the broader historical and national context. The temporal linking of justice and responsibility requires that we consider how particular citizens benefit from the production of racial and gendered knowledge about cultural forms of difference and, importantly, the role that law plays in securing these benefits.

Notes

Preface and Acknowledgments

1 *Criminal Code*, RSC 1985, c C-46.
2 *R v Ipeelee*, 2012 SCC 13, [2012] 1 SCR 433 at para 60.
3 Alison Crawford, "Prison Watchdog Probes Spike in Number of Black Inmates," *CBC News*, 15 December 2011, http://www.cbc.ca/news/canada/story/2011/12/14 /crawford-black-prison.html.
4 Mark Gibney et al, eds, *The Age of Apology: Facing Up to the Past* (Philadelphia, PA: University of Philadelphia Press, 2008); Elazar Barkan and Alexander Karn, *Taking Wrongs Seriously: Apologies and Reconciliation* (Stanford, CA: Stanford University Press, 2006); Roy L Brooks, *When Sorry Isn't Enough: The Controversy over Apologies and Reparations for Human Injustice* (New York: New York University Press, 2005).
5 Elazar Barkan, *The Guilt of Nations: Restitution and Negotiating Historical Injustices* (New York: Norton, 2000), xvii; Martha L Minow, *Between Vengeance and Forgiveness: Facing History after Genocide and Mass Violence* (Boston, MA: Beacon Press, 1998); John Torpey, *Politics of the Past: On Repairing Historical Injustice* (New York: Rowman and Littlefield, 2003).
6 *Criminal Code.*
7 Stephen Best and Saidiya Hartman, "Fugitive Justice," *Representations* 92 (2005): 4.

Introduction

1 *Criminal Code*, RSC 1985, c C-46.
2 I vacillate between the terms "Aboriginal" and "Aboriginal peoples." Occasionally, I utilize the phrase "indigenous people." In Canada, the term "Aboriginal" or "Aboriginal people," which is largely a term of nation/state governance, came into

use in the 1980s. While contested, it is meant to be an inclusive term to refer to peoples who have been historically defined through white settler governance as status Indians, non-status Indians, Inuit, and Métis. The term "indigenous peoples" "is a relatively recent term which emerged in the 1970s out of the struggles primarily of the American Indian Movement (AIM), and the Canadian Indian Brotherhood." See Linda Tuhiwai Smith, *Decolonizing Methodologies: Research and Indigenous Peoples* (London: Zed Books, 1999), 7.

3 Martha Flaherty, president of Pauktuutit, also pointed out to the Standing Committee on Justice and Legal Affairs that in utilizing the phrase "Aboriginal peoples" throughout the proceedings (and in the proposal), they were collapsing Inuit peoples with Aboriginal peoples without recognizing regional distinctions and the fact that Inuit peoples are not Aboriginal peoples. House of Commons, Standing Committee on Justice and Legal Affairs, "Respecting Bill C-41, An Act to Amend the Criminal Code (Sentencing) and Other Acts in Consequence thereof" in *Minutes of Proceedings*, No 85 (28 February 1995).

4 Ibid, 1040.

5 Ibid, 0950.

6 Ibid. For the ways in which Aboriginal women are particularly at risk as a result of the sentencing process, see Elizabeth Adjin-Tettey, "Sentencing Aboriginal Offenders: Balancing Offenders' Needs, the Interests of Victims and Society and the Decolonization of Aboriginal Peoples," *Canadian Journal of Women and the Law* 19, no 1 (2007): 179-216.

7 *Criminal Code.*

8 Mariana Valverde points out that there exists a large body of literature that links criminal justice with other "regulatory systems," such as citizenship and migration. A consideration of "Aboriginal difference" at the point of sentencing, therefore, "creat[es] an interesting assemblage of citizenship" in which "the verdict continues to constitute the nation-state." Mariana Valverde, "Practices of Citizenship and Scales of Governance," *New Criminal Law Review* 13, no 2 (2010): 224.

9 Mark D Walters, "The Jurisprudence of Reconciliation: Aboriginal Rights in Canada," in Will Kymlicka and Bashir Bashir, eds, *The Politics of Reconciliation in Multicultural Societies* (Oxford: Oxford University Press, 2008), 166.

10 Ibid.

11 For examples, see David Daubney and Gordon Perry, "An Overview of Bill C-41," in Julian V Roberts and David P Cole, eds, *Making Sense of Sentencing* (Toronto: University of Toronto Press, 1999), 31-47; David Daubney, *Taking Responsibility: Report of the Standing Committee on Justice and Solicitor General on Its Review of Sentencing, Conditional Release and Related Aspects of Corrections* (Ottawa: Canadian Government Publishing Centre, 1988); Ross Green, "Treat *Gladue* as a Call to Action," *Lawyers Weekly* 42 (2000): 12; Susan Haslip, "Aboriginal Sentencing Reform in Canada – Prospects for Success: Standing Tall with Both Feet Planted Firmly in the Air," *Murdoch University Electronic Journal of Law* 7, no 1 (2000), http://www

.murdoch.edu.au/elaw/issues/v7n1/haslip71nf.html; Kent Roach and Jonathan Rudin, "*Gladue:* The Judicial and Political Reception of a Promising Decision," *Canadian Journal of Criminology* 42 (2000): 355-88; Julian V Roberts, "Sentencing Reform: The Canadian Approach," *Federal Sentencing Reporter* 9, no 5 (1997): 245. See also the recent special issue of *Criminal Law Quarterly* 54 (2009).

12 Carol LaPrairie, "The Role of Sentencing in the Over-Representation of Aboriginal People in Correctional Institutions," *Canadian Journal of Criminology* 32 (1990): 429-40; Carol LaPrairie, "Community Types, Crime and Police Services on Canadian Indian Reserves," *Journal of Research in Crime and Delinquency* 25, no 4 (1988): 375-91; Tim Quigley, "Are We Doing Anything about the Disproportionate Jailing of Aboriginal People?" *Criminal Law Quarterly* 42 (1999): 133-34, n 11; Philip Stenning and Julian V Roberts, "Empty Promises: Parliament, the Supreme Court and the Sentencing of Aboriginal Offenders," *Saskatchewan Law Review* 64 (2001): 137-68; Jennifer J Llewellyn, "Restorative Justice in *Borde and Hamilton:* A Systemic Problem?" *Criminal Reports* 8 (2003): 308; Renee Pelletier, "The Nullification of Section 718.2(e): Aggravating Aboriginal Over-Representation in Canadian Prisons," *Osgoode Hall Law Journal* 39 (2001), http://www.ohlj.ca/archive/vol39.htm.

13 Carol LaPrairie and Jane Dickson-Gilmore, *Will the Circle Be Unbroken? Aboriginal Communities, Restorative Justice and the Challenge of Conflict and Change* (Toronto: University of Toronto Press, 2005); Josephine Savarese, "Gladue Was a Woman: The Importance of Gender in Restorative-Based Sentencing," in Elizabeth Elliot and Robert Gordon, eds, *New Directions in Restorative Justice: Issues, Practice, Evaluation* (Vancouver: Willan Publishing, 2005), 135-50.

14 See, for example, Sonia Lawrence and Toni Williams, "'Swallowed Up': Drug Couriers at the Borders of Canadian Sentencing," *University of Toronto Law Journal* 56, no 4 (2006): 285-332.

15 Ibid. See also Jonathan Rudin, "Addressing Aboriginal Overrepresentation Post-*Gladue:* A Realistic Assessment of How Social Change Occurs," *Criminal Law Quarterly* 54 (2009): 460; Kent Roach, "One Step Forward, Two Steps Back: *Gladue* at Ten and in the Courts of Appeal," *Criminal Law Quarterly* 54 (2009): 471.

16 Walters, "The Jurisprudence of Reconciliation," 166.

17 *R v Hamilton*, [2004] OJ no 3252 at para 1 (Ont CA) (QL) [emphasis in original].

18 Toni Williams, "Punishing Women: The Promise and Perils of Contextualized Sentencing for Aboriginal Women in Canada," *Cleveland State Law Review* 55, no 3 (2007): 269, 274. See also Daubney and Perry, "An Overview of Bill C-41," 31.

19 Haslip, "Aboriginal Sentencing Reform in Canada."

20 Williams notes that other significant changes in the last twenty-five years include the "transformation of complainants into 'victims' and the apparent empowerment of this new juridical subject with standing and participation rights in sentencing and parole hearings; the re-emergence of penal practices that link criminality more to character than to capacity, and the development or, perhaps revival, of a risk-based model of law enforcement practice." Williams, "Punishing Women," 270.

21 Ibid, 270.

22 *R v Gladue*, 1999 SCC 1, [1999] 1 SCR 688.

23 See a reproduction of the cases *R v Bain*, [1992] 1 SCR 91, and *R v Crawford*, [1995] 1 SCR 858, at Aboriginal Legal Services of Toronto, "Gladue (Aboriginal Persons) Court," http://www.aboriginallegal.ca/gladue.php.

24 See Rudin, "Addressing Aboriginal Overrepresentation," 460. *Youth Criminal Justice Act*, SC 2002, c 1.

25 Rudin, "Addressing Aboriginal Overrepresentation," 457.

26 Roach, "One Step Forward," 471.

27 Ibid, 271. To be specific, "132 prisoners per 100,000 adults in 1995, to 107 per 100,000 in 2006, a drop of almost 20 percent." Williams, "Punishing Women," 279.

28 There are important regional distinctions to these numbers. For example, the percentage of Aboriginal people in custody is higher in Western provinces, with Saskatchewan presenting the most disproportionate numbers: "81% of the admissions to provincial sentenced custody while they represent 11% of the general population." Samuel Perreault, "The Incarceration of Aboriginal People in Adult Correctional Services," Statistics Canada, *Juristat* 29, no 3 (2009): 5, http://www.statcan.gc.ca/pub/85-002-x/2009003/article/10903-eng.pdf.

29 Williams, "Punishing Women," 279.

30 Perreault, "The Incarceration of Aboriginal People," 5.

31 These observations were noted by Jonathan Rudin (Program Director, Aboriginal Legal Services), Judy L Mungovan (Counsel, Aboriginal Justice Leadership Team, Criminal Law Division, Ministry of Attorney General [Ontario]), Erin Winocour (Assistant Crown Attorney, Criminal Law Policy Division, Ministry of Attorney General [Ontario]) at the second National Conference on Aboriginal Criminal Justice Post-*Gladue*, Toronto, 24 April 2010.

32 John Torpey, *Politics of the Past: On Repairing Historical Injustices* (New York: Rowman and Littlefield, 2003), 5. For other examples, see Elazar Barkan, *The Guilt of Nations: On Repairing Historical Injustices* (Baltimore, MD: Johns Hopkins University Press, 2000); Martha Minow, *Between Vengeance and Forgiveness: Facing History after Genocide and Mass Violence* (Boston, MA: Beacon Press, 1998).

33 Janna Thompson, "From Slaughter to Abduction: Coming to Terms with the Past in Australia," Centre for Applied Philosophy and Public Ethics Working Paper (2003), http://www.cappe.edu.au/docs/working-papers/Thompson6.pdf.

34 John Borrows, *Recovering Canada: The Resurgence of Indigenous Law* (Toronto: University of Toronto Press, 2002); Patricia Monture, *Thunder in My Soul: A Mohawk Woman Speaks* (Halifax, NS: Fernwood Publishing, 1995); Andrea Smith, *Conquest: Sexual Violence and the American Indian Genocide* (Cambridge, MA: South End Press, 2005).

35 Taiaiake Alfred, "Sovereignty," in Philip J Deloria and Neal Salisbury, eds, *A Companion to American Indian History* (New York: Blackwell Publishers, 2002), 460.

36   Ibid, 460-74; Borrows, *Recovering Canada.*

37   Alfred, "Sovereignty," 465.

38   Ibid, 469

39   Jennifer Nelson, *Razing Africville: A Geography of Racism* (Toronto: University of Toronto Press, 2008), 8.

40   Afua Cooper, *The Hanging of Angelique: The Untold Story of Canadian Slavery and the Burning of Old Montreal* (Toronto: Harper Collins, 2006); Renisa Mawani, *Colonial Proximities: Crossracial Encounters and Juridical Truths in British Columbia, 1871-1921* (Vancouver: UBC Press, 2009).

41   Edward Said, *Culture and Imperialism* (New York: Vintage Books, 1994); Ann Laura Stoler and Frederick Cooper, "Between Metropole and Colony: Rethinking a Research Agenda," in Ann Laura Stoler and Frederick Cooper, eds, *Tensions of Empire: Colonial Cultures in a Bourgeois World* (Berkeley, CA: University of California Press, 1997), 1-58; Anne McClintock, *Imperial Leather: Race, Gender and Sexuality in the Colonial Contest* (London: Routledge, 1995); Homi Bhabha, *The Location of Culture* (London: Routledge, 1994); David Scott, *Refashioning Futures: Criticism after Postcoloniality* (Princeton, NJ: Princeton University Press, 1999), 23-52.

42   Sherene H Razack, "Introduction: When Place Becomes Race," in Sherene H Razack, ed, *Race, Space and the Law: Unmapping a White Settler Society* (Toronto: Between the Lines, 2002), 1-2 [emphasis in original].

43   Hannah Arendt, *Responsibility and Judgment*, edited by Jerome Kohn (New York: Schocken Books, 2003), 149.

44   Ibid.

45   Andrew Schaap offers a useful explanation of the Foucaultian relationship between responsibility and power. He writes "that power is immanent in all our social relations and mediated through knowledge. Everyone both has power and is subject to power. Moreover, [Foucault] inverts the liberal understanding of responsibility as contingent on an agent's 'power to.' Instead, Foucault's analysis suggests that the extent to which an individual is 'in power,' and hence responsible, is an indication of his subjection." See Schaap, "Power and Responsibility: Should We Spare the King's Head?" *Politics* 20, no 3 (2000): 130.

46   David Miller, *National Responsibility and Global Justice* (Oxford: Oxford University Press), 9.

47   Ibid, 1-22

48   Farid Abdel-Nour, "National Responsibility," *Political Theory* 31, no 5 (2003): 694.

49   Ibid, n 7.

50   See, for examples, Barkan, *The Guilt of Nations*; Sherene H Razack, "Making Canada White: Law and the Policing of Bodies of Colour in the 1990s," *Canadian Journal of Law and Society* 14, no 1 (1999): 159-84; and Sherene H Razack, "'Simple Logic': Race, the Identity Documents Rule and the Story of a Nation Besieged and Betrayed," *Journal of Law and Social Policy* 15 (2002): 199-220.

51   For other examples, see Barkan, *The Guilt of Nations*, xxxi.

52 Some examples from this expansive literature include Steven Price and Anupama Rao, eds, *Discipline and the Other Body: Correction, Corporeality and Colonialism* (Durham, NC: Duke University Press, 2006); Frederick Cooper and Ann Laura Stoler, eds, *Tensions of Empire* (Berkeley, CA: University of California Press, 1997); Ann Laura Stoler, ed, *Haunted by Empire* (Durham, NC: Duke University Press, 2006); McClintock, *Imperial Leather*; Andrea Smith, *Conquest: Sexual Violence and the American Indian Genocide* (Cambridge, MA: South End Press, 2005); Thomas Biolsi, *Deadliest Enemies: Law and Race Relations on and off Rosebud Reservations* (Minneapolis, MN: University of Minnesota Press, 2001); Achille Mbembe, *On the Postcolony* (Berkeley, CA: University of California Press, 2001); Gillian Cowlishaw, *Blackfellas, Whitefellas and the Hidden Injuries of Race* (Oxford: Blackwell Publishers, 2004); Constance Backhouse, *Colour-Coded: A Legal History of Racism in Canada, 1900-1950* (Toronto: University of Toronto Press, 1999).

53 Jean and John L Comaroff, "Introduction," in Jean and John L Comaroff, eds, *Law and Disorder in the Postcolony* (Chicago: University of Chicago Press, 2006), 7.

54 Ibid, 5.

55 My use of the terms "racialized"/"racialization" is meant to refer to race and racial classification as historical processes and not as entities that are fixed through space and time. Furthermore, I am cognizant throughout of David Goldberg's important reminder that Frantz Fanon utilized the notion "to racialize" when contrasting it from the phrase "to humanize," thereby signalling the ways in which processes of racialization eject certain peoples from the very category of the human in the moment of iteration. See David Goldberg, *The Racial State* (Oxford: Blackwell Publishers, 2002), 12. My use of the term "racialized" is meant to anchor these two usages and meanings. I am also aware of recent critiques of the notion of racialization that suggest that the concept has been emptied of its conceptual and paradigmatic utility owing to its pervasiveness and facile use in the social sciences. Instead, we should examine what Goldberg describes as "racial regionalisms," the many and complicated ways in which notions of racial difference emerge spatially and geographically across different and simultaneous temporalities. See David Goldberg, *The Threat of Race: Reflections on Racial Neoliberalism* (Oxford: Blackwell Publishers, 2008).

56 Angela Davis, *Are Prisons Obsolete?* (New York: Seven Stories Press, 2003).

57 Gayatri Spivak, *Outside the Teaching Machine* (New York: Routledge, 1993), 45-46.

58 Wendy Brown, "Suffering Rights as Paradoxes," *Constellations* 7, no 2 (2000): 230. Brown notes that critical race scholars Drucilla Cornell and Patricia Williams offer "a very different register," one in which there is a "tacit confession that recalls Spivak's own weary recognition of the historical limits of our political imagination" of the need to yield to an "imaginary domain in which a future anterior is not beyond women's grasp, [as] the surest way to finesse the tradeoff between liberty and equality" Ibid, 230-31.

59 Michel Foucault, cited in Paul Rabinow, *The Foucault Reader* (New York: Pantheon, 1984), 7.

60 Michel Foucault, *The History of Sexuality,* volume 1 (New York: Vintage Books, 1990), 149.

61 Ibid, 143. It is perhaps in *Discipline and Punish* that Foucault fully articulates the centrality of biopower to his oeuvre on the genealogy of modern state formation. Michel Foucault, *Discipline and Punish: The Birth of the Prison*, translated by Alan Sheridan (London: Allen Lane, 1977).

62 Foucault explains that governance and biopower "is a form of activity which attempts or aims at the conduct of persons; it is the attempt to shape, to guide, or to affect not only the conduct of people but, also, the attempt to constitute people in such ways that they can be governed." Foucault, cited in Ann Laura Stoler, *Race and the Education of Desire: Foucault's History of Sexuality and the Colonial Order of Things* (Durham, NC: Duke University Press, 1995), 33. In order to better conceptualize this dual process, Foucault proposed the notion of governmentality. As Colin Gordon explains, Foucault "proposed the term 'government' in general as meaning 'the conduct of conduct': that is to say, a form of activity aiming to shape, guide or affect the conduct of some person or persons." Colin Gordon, "Governmental Rationality: An Introduction," in Graham Burchell, Colin Gordon, and Peter Miller, eds, *The Foucault Effect: Studies in Governmentality* (Chicago: University of Chicago Press, 1991), 2. Gail Lewis points out, "governmentality refers to the encompassing of (certain) populations within the net of the nation," and as a result, "racialized populations are introduced and subjected to differential racializations" based upon ideological demarcations meant to control and manage them." Gail Lewis, *"Race," Gender, Social Welfare: Encounters in a Postcolonial Society* (Cambridge: Polity Press, 2000), 41. Such techniques of power are employed as a technology of government and are linked to the programmatic elements of governance concerning "a complex body of knowledges and 'know-how' about government, the means of its exercise and the nature of those over whom it was [is] to be exercised." Nikolas Rose and Peter Miller "Political Power beyond the State," *British Journal of Sociology* 43, no 2 (1992): 174. There is a tendency in studies inspired by a governmentality approach to avoid positive or normative claims that bring with them narrative coherence. As Duncan Ivison asks, "why do most studies of governmentality eschew all form of 'positive' claims? Are there not 'authorities' or individualizations that work on the capacities of individuals and groups that we might want to defend, for example, those which allow for critical reflection on, or engagement with, the particular forms of government or regularization shaping our lives in various contexts?" Duncan Ivison, "The Technical and the Political: Discourse of Race, Reasons of State," *Social and Legal Studies* 7, no 4 (1998): 562.

63 Stoler, *Race and the Education of Desire*, 28.

64 Stoler maintains that for Foucault the term "racism" encompassed the management of bodies that served a productive function in colonialism, in relation to the regulation of internal/external enemies in the creation of bourgeois society: "[Racism]

gives credence to the claim that the more 'degenerates' and 'abnormals' are eliminated, the lives of those who speak will be stronger, more vigorous, and improved. The enemies are not political adversaries, but those identified as internal threats to the population." Ibid, 85.

65 Michel Foucault, "Society Must Be Defended," in Mauro Bertani et al, eds, *Lectures at the College de France 1975-1976* (New York: Picador, 1997), 254-56. Foucault's formulation of biopolitics was inspired by the Nazi regime that required biopolitical forms of power to become "a racist State, a murderous State and a suicidal State." In the Nazi state, "disciplinary power and biopower: all of this permeated, underpinned, Nazi society (control of the biological, of procreation and heredity; control over illness and accidents too)" (259-60).

66 Ibid, 48. Simona Forti describes state racism in the following manner: "When racism turns into 'state doctrine,' it also becomes the theoretical point of reference for a practice that (to make 'productive') is able to organize in a hierarchical manner and differentiate, to include and exclude beings from the human field, making death of one necessity for life at all." Simona Forti, "The Biopolitics of Souls: Racism, Nazism, and Plato," *Political Theory* 34, no 9 (2006): 11.

67 Rose and Miller, "Political Power beyond the State," 178-79.

68 Ibid.

69 Discourse, as defined by Foucault, refers to ways of constituting knowledge, together with the social practices, forms of subjectivity, and power relations that are inherent in such knowledges and relations between them. Discourses are more than ways of thinking and producing meaning. They constitute the "nature" of the body, the unconscious and conscious mind, and the emotional life of the subjects they seek to govern. Chris Weeden, *Feminist Practice and Poststructuralist Theory* (New York: Blackwell Publishers, 1987), 108.

70 Race/modernity studies "uncovers the much-neglected relation between *modern philosophy and the discourse of race*. It interrogates the indebtedness of eighteenth- and nineteenth-century modern thought through ideas of liberty, rationality and superiority shaped by the cultivation of *Europeanness*, while postulating an invented 'non-Europeanness' as its antithesis." The second tradition "argue[s] for understanding the significance of the social, economic, political and cultural formation of the modern world since the sixteenth century within the colonial *and liberal* system in which race was gestated and elaborated." Barnor Hesse, "Racialized Modernity: An Analytics of White Mythologies," *Racial Studies* 30, no 4 (2007): 663, n 7 [emphasis added].

71 Ibid, 643.

72 Said, *Culture and Imperialism*, 7.

73 Ibid, 12.

74 Anthony Kwame Appiah, "Race," in Frank Lentricchia and Tom McLaughlin, eds, *Critical Terms for Literary Study* (Chicago: University of Chicago Press, 1990), 274-87;

Paul Gilroy, *Against Race: Imagining Political Culture beyond the Color Line* (Cambridge, MA: Harvard University Press, 2000); Goldberg, *Racist Culture: Philosophy and the Politics of Meaning* (Cambridge, MA: Blackwell Publishers, 1993); Mary-Ellen Kelm, *Colonizing Bodies: Aboriginal Health and Healing in British Columbia 1900-50* (Vancouver: UBC Press), 1998.

75 Gilroy, *Against Race.*

76 Nasser Hussain, "Towards a Jurisprudence of Emergency," *Law and Critique* 10, no 3 (1999): 93-115.

77 Homi Bhabha, "'Race' Time and the Revision of Modernity," in Les Back and Jon Solomos, eds, *Theories of Race and Racism: A Reader* (London: Routledge, 2000), 355.

78 Hesse suggests that social construction analyses of cultural difference "ten[d] to encourage a reading of race through some exclusive attachment or attribution to the body as a discrete entity." Hesse, "Racialized Modernity," 645.

79 For examples, see Paige Raibmon, *Authentic Indians: Episodes of Encounter from the Late Nineteenth Century Northwest Coast* (Durham, NC: Duke University Press, 2005); Jo-Anne Fiske and Betty Patrick, *Cis Dideen Kat, When the Plumes Rise: The Way of the Lake Babine Nation* (Vancouver: UBC Press, 2000); Borrows, *Recovering Canada*; Ronald Niezen, *The Rediscovered Self: Indigenous Identity and Cultural Justice* (Montreal and Kingston: McGill-Queen's University Press, 2009); Elizabeth Furniss, *The Burden of History: Colonialism and the Frontier Myth in a Rural Canadian Community* (Vancouver: UBC Press, 1999); Justin B Richland, *Arguing with Tradition: The Language of Law in the Hopi Tribal Court* (Chicago: University of Chicago Press, 2008); Biolsi, *Deadliest Enemies.*

80 Raibmon, *Authentic Indians*, 6-7.

81 Ibid.

82 Stoler and Cooper, "Between Metropole and Colony," 3-4.

83 David Scott, "Colonial Governmentality," *Social Text* 43 (1995): 193 [emphasis in original].

84 Ibid. Inspired by Foucault's conception of biopower, Scott suggests an analytics that examines "the *targets* of colonial power (the point or points of power's application; the object or objects it aims at; and the means and instrumentalities it deploys in search of these targets, points and objects) and the *field* of its operation (the *zone* that it actively constructs for its functionality)." [emphasis in original]. David Scott, "Colonial Governmentality," *Social Text* 43 (1995): 193.

85 Razack, *Looking White People in the Eye: Gender, Race, and Culture in Courtrooms and Classrooms* (Toronto: University of Toronto Press, 1998), 59.

86 Ibid, 60.

87 Ibid.

88 Val Napoleon, "Delgamuukw: A Legal Straitjacket for Oral Histories?" *Canadian Journal of Law and Society* 20, no 2 (2005): 123-55; Richland, *Arguing with Tradition*; Emma LaRocque, "Re-examining Culturally Appropriate Models in Criminal

Justice Applications," in M Asch, ed, *Aboriginal and Treaty Rights in Canada: Essays on Law, Equity and Respect for Difference* (Vancouver: UBC Press, 1997), 75-96; Biolsi, *Deadliest Enemies*.

89 Royal Commission on Aboriginal Peoples, *Bridging the Cultural Divide: A Report on Aboriginal People and Criminal Justice in Canada* (Ottawa: Minister of Supply and Services, 1996); Aboriginal Justice Implementation Commission, *Report of the Aboriginal Justice Inquiry of Manitoba* (1991), http://www.ajic.mb.ca/volume.html; Government of Ontario, *Report of the Commission on Systemic Racism in the Criminal Ontario Justice System* (Toronto: Queen's Printer, 1995).

Chapter 1: Culture and Reparative Justice

1 *R v Ipeelee*, 2012 SCC 13, [2012] 1 SCR 433 at para 77.

2 Royal Commission on Aboriginal Peoples, *Bridging the Cultural Divide: A Report on Aboriginal People and Criminal Justice in Canada* (Ottawa: Minister of Supply and Services, 1996); Aboriginal Justice Implementation Commission, *Report of the Aboriginal Justice Inquiry of Manitoba* (1991), http://www.ajic.mb.ca/volume.html; Government of Ontario, *Report of the Commission on Systemic Racism in the Criminal Ontario Justice System* (Toronto: Queen's Printer, 1995). In addition to the reports under examination, Michael Jackson's study "Locking Up Natives in Canada" is also often used by courts. See Michael Jackson, "Locking Up Natives in Canada," *UBC Law Review* 23 (1989): 215-300. See also Jonathan Rudin, "Addressing Aboriginal Overrepresentation Post-*Gladue*: A Realistic Assessment of How Social Change Occurs," *Criminal Law Quarterly* 54 (2009): 458.

3 Margaret Urban Walker, *What Is Reparative Justice?* (Milwaukee, WI: Marquette University Press, 2011); Janna Thompson, *Taking Responsibility for the Past: Reparation and Historical Injustice* (Oxford: Blackwell Publishers, 2002); Elazar Barkan, *The Guilt of Nations: Restitution and Negotiating Historical Injustices* (New York: Norton, 2000); Martha L Minow, *Between Vengeance and Forgiveness: Facing History after Genocide and Mass Violence* (Boston, MA: Beacon Press, 1998).

4 Thompson, *Taking Responsibility*, xi.

5 Walker, *Reparative Justice*, 13; see also Annalise Acorn, *Compulsory Compassion: A Critique of Restorative Justice* (Vancouver: UBC Press, 2004); George Pavlich, *Governing Paradoxes of Restorative Justice* (London: Glasshouse Press, 2005).

6 Thompson, *Taking Responsibility*; Janna Thompson, "Historical Responsibility and Liberal Societies," *Intergenerational Justice Review* 9 (2009): 13-18; Barkan, *Guilt of Nations*; Minow, *Between Vengeance and Forgiveness*; Priscilla B Hayner, *Unspeakable Truths: Facing the Challenges of Truth Commissions* (London: Routledge, 2002); Andrew Schaap, *Political Reconciliation* (London: Routledge, 2005); Stanley Cohen, "State Crimes of Previous Regimes: Knowledge, Accountability, and the Policing of the Past," *Law and Social Inquiry* 20, no 1 (1995): 7-50.

7 Mark Gibney et al, eds, *The Age of Apology: Facing Up to the Past* (Philadelphia, PA: University of Philadelphia Press, 2008); John Torpey, ed, *Politics of the Past: On*

Repairing Historical Injustice (Oxford: Rowman and Littlefield, 2003); Michel-Rolph Trouillot, "Abortive Rituals: Historical Apologies in a Global Era," *Interventions* 2, no 2 (2000): 171-86; Janna Thompson, "Apology, Historical Obligations and the Ethics of Memory," *Memory Studies* 2, no 2 (2009): 195-210; Melissa Nobles, *The Politics of Official Apologies* (New York: Cambridge University Press, 2008).

8 Hayner, *Unspeakable Truths*; Will Kymlicka and Bashir Bashir, eds, *The Politics of Reconciliation in Multicultural Societies* (Oxford: Oxford University Press, 2008); Trudy Govier and Wilhelm Verwoerd, "Trust and the Problem of National Reconciliation," *Philosophy of the Social Sciences* 32 (2002): 178-205; Leigh A Payne, *Unsettling Accounts: Neither Truth Nor Reconciliation in Confessions of State Violence* (Durham, NC: Duke University Press, 2008).

9 Ifi Amadiume and Abdullahi An-Na'im, *The Politics of Memory: Truth, Healing and Social Justice* (New York: Zed Books, 2000); Henri Bergson, *Matter and Memory*, translated by NM Paul and WS Palmer (New York: Zone Books, 1988); Paul Ricoeur, *Memory, History, Forgetting*, translated by K Blamey and D Pellauer (Chicago: University of Chicago Press, 2004).

10 Barkan, *Guilt of Nations*; Roy L Brooks, *When Sorry Isn't Enough: The Controversy over Apologies and Reparations for Human Injustice* (New York: New York University Press, 2005); Mayo Moran and David Dzyenhaus, eds, *Calling Power to Account: Law, Reparations and the Chinese Canadian Head Tax Case* (Toronto: University of Toronto Press, 2005).

11 Thompson, *Taking Responsibility*, 47.

12 Ibid, 48.

13 Ibid.

14 *Indian Act*, RS 1951, c I-5.

15 Pavlich, *Governing Paradoxes*, 3.

16 Ibid.

17 Andrew Woolford, *The Politics of Restorative Justice* (Toronto: Fernwood Publishing, 2009), 12.

18 Ibid, 13-18.

19 Ibid, 15.

20 Ibid, 16; Pavlich, *Governing Paradoxes*. See also Emma Cunliffe and Angela Cameron, "Writing the Circle: Judicially Convened Sentencing Circles and the Textual Organization of Criminal Justice," *Canadian Journal of Women and the Law* 19, no 1 (2007): 13.

21 Cunliffe and Cameron, "Writing the Circle," 13.

22 *Constitution Act, 1982* (UK), 1982, c 11, s 59. John Borrows, *Recovering Canada: The Resurgence of Indigenous Law* (Toronto: University of Toronto Press, 2002); Val Napoleon, "Delgamuukw: A Legal Straightjacket for Oral Histories?" *Canadian Journal of Law and Society* 20, no 2 (2005): 123-55; Taiaiake Alfred, "Sovereignty," in Philip J Deloria and Neal Salisbury, eds, *A Companion to American Indian History*

(London: Blackwell Publishers, 2002), 460-74. A key difference between racialized populations is that Aboriginal peoples arguably have the right to self-government as an existing Aboriginal right under section 35 of the *Constitution Act, 1982.*

23 John Braithwaite, "Restorative Justice: Assessing Optimistic and Pessimistic Accounts," in M Tonry, ed, *Crime and Justice: A Review of Research* (Chicago: University of Chicago Press, 1999), 1-127.

24 David Lerman,"Restoring Justice," *Tikkun: A Bimonthly Jewish and Interfaith Critique of Politics, Culture and Society* (September/October 1999), http://www.tikkun.org/article.php?story=sep1999_lerman.

25 *R Gladue*, 1999 SCC 1, [1999] 1 SCR 688 at para 74 [*Gladue*].

26 Jennifer J Llewellyn, "Restorative Justice in *Borde* and *Hamilton:* A Systemic Problem?" *Criminal Reports* 8 (2003): 308. See also Cunliffe and Cameron, "Writing the Circle," 12.

27 Ibid, 4.

28 See Angela Cameron, "Stopping the Violence: Canadian Feminist Debates on Restorative Justice and Intimate Violence," *Theoretical Criminology* 10, no 1 (2006): 40.

29 Ibid, 59 [emphasis in original].

30 Ibid.

31 Emma LaRocque, "Re-examining Culturally Appropriate Models in Criminal Justice Applications," in M Asch, ed, *Aboriginal and Treaty Rights in Canada: Essays on Law, Equity, and Respect for Difference* (Vancouver: UBC Press, 1997), 87.

32 Jarem Sawatsky, *The Ethic of Traditional Communities and the Spirit of Healing Justice: Studies from Hollow Water, the Iona Community and Plum Village* (London: Jessica Kingsley Publishers, 2009), 97-98.

33 Berma Bushie, "Community Holistic Circle Healing" (1999), International Institute for Restorative Practices, http://www.iirp.edu/article_detail.php?article_id=NDc0. See also Native Counselling Services of Alberta, "A Cost-Benefit Analysis of Hollow Water's Community Holistic Circle Healing" (2001), Public Safety Canada, http://www.publicsafety.gc.ca/res/cor/apc/apc-20-eng.aspx; James Ptacek, ed, *Restorative Justice and Violence against Women* (Oxford: Oxford University Press, 2010); Heather Strang and John Braithwaite, eds, *Restorative Justice and Family Violence* (Cambridge: Cambridge University Press, 2002); Anne McGillivray and Brenda Comasky, *Black Eyes All of the Time* (Toronto: University of Toronto Press, 1999).

34 Royal Commission on Aboriginal Peoples, *Bridging the Cultural Divide*, 159.

35 Ibid, 160.

36 LaRocque, "Re-examining Culturally Appropriate Models," 75.

37 Ibid, 75.

38 Ibid, 77.

39 Ibid, 84.

40 Ibid, 85.

41   Ibid, 93.
42   Elizabeth Povinelli, *The Cunning of Recognition: Indigenous Alterities and the Making of Australian Multiculturalism* (Durham, NC: Duke University Press, 2002), 8.
43   One model for this approach is the practice of peacemaking circles, which began in the early 1980s in Yukon, under the tutelage of Justice Barry Stuart: "While not designed to replicate the culturally steeped rituals of First Nations culture, peacemaking circles are profoundly indebted to First Nations teachings." Barry Stuart and Kay Pranis, "Peacemaking Circles: Reflections on Principal Features and Primary Outcomes," in Dennis Sullivan and Larry Tifft, eds, *Handbook of Restorative Justice: A Global Perspective* (New York: Routledge, 2006), 121. In addition to addressing ideas about punishment through restorative measures, peacemaking circles have been used for a broad range of issues including resolving conflicts and developing new visions for communities. See also Kay Pranis, Barry Stewart, and Mark Wedge, *Peacemaking Circles: From Crime to Community* (St Paul, MN: Living Justice Press, 2003).
44   Michael Tonry, "The Fragmentation of Sentencing and Corrections in America" (September 1999), National Institute of Justice, http://www.ojp.usdoj.gov/nij/pubs -sum/175721.htm.
45   Mark Harris, "From Australian Courts to Aboriginal Courts in Australia: Bridging the Gap?" *Current Issues in Criminal Justice* 16, no 1 (2004): 26-41.
46   Elena Marchetti and Kathleen Daly, "Indigenous Courts and Justice Practices in Australia," *Trends and Issues in Crime and Criminal Justice* 277 (May 2004), http://www.aic.gov.au/documents/0/8/3/%7B08326CEA-3B11-4759-A25B-02C1764 BCB8A%7Dtandi277.pdf.
47   Kate Auty, "Koori Court Victoria: Magistrates Court (Koori Court) Act 2002" (paper presented at the Law and Society Conference, Chicago, 27-30 May 2004).
48   Council for Aboriginal Reconciliation, "Final Report of the Royal Commission into Aboriginal Deaths in Custody" (1998), Indigenous Law Resources, http://www .austlii.edu.au/au/other/IndigLRes/rciadic/.
49   Harris, "From Australian Courts."
50   Acorn, *Compulsory Compassion*, 16.
51   Ann Laura Stoler and Frederick Cooper, "Between Metropole and Colony: Rethinking a Research Agenda," in Ann Laura Stoler and Frederick Cooper, eds, *Tensions of Empire: Colonial Cultures in a Bourgeois World* (Berkeley, CA: University of California Press, 1997), 7.
52   See Jackson, "Locking up Natives in Canada"; see also Rudin, "Addressing Aboriginal Overrepresentation," 458.
53   Patricia A Monture-Okanee, "Justice as Healing: Thinking about Change" (1995), Native Law Centre, http://www.usask.ca/nativelaw/publications/jah/1995/JAH _Thinking_Change.pdf.
54   Ibid.

55 Patricia A Monture-Okanee, interviewed by *CBC National News* (Television), 16 October 2006 [on file with author].

56 *House of Commons Debates*, 41st Parliament, 1st Session, No 62 (16 October 2006) at 1510 (Hon Stockwell Day, Minister of Public Affairs).

57 Alan Cairns, "Coming to Terms with the Past," in Torpey, *Politics of the Past.*

58 John Torpey, *Making Whole What Has Been Smashed: On Reparation Politics* (Cambridge, MA: Harvard University Press, 2006), 5 [emphasis in original].

59 Indian and Northern Affairs Canada, "Volume 1: Looking Forward, Looking Back," *Royal Commission on Aboriginal Peoples* (2006), http://www.collectionscanada .gc.ca.

60 Thompson, *Taking Responsibility*, ix-x.

61 David Goldberg asserts, "morality is the scene of [the] legitimation and justification" for the racial violence that enabled colonial/racial projects. Goldberg, *Racist Culture: Philosophy and the Politics of Meaning* (Cambridge, MA: Blackwell Publishers, 1993), 14.

62 Mary Ellen Turpel, "On the Question of Adapting the Canadian Criminal Justice System for Aboriginal Peoples: Don't Fence Me In," in Royal Commission on Aboriginal Peoples, ed, *Aboriginal Peoples and the Justice System, Report from the National Round Table on Aboriginal Justice Issues* (Ottawa: Supply and Services, 1997), 166-67. The commission was established on 26 August 1991, when the future of the Canadian federation was being debated. It came to fruition in the months following the demise of the Meech Lake Accord and the confrontation, in the summer of 1990, between Mohawks and the power of the Canadian state at Kanesatake (Oka), Quebec. "Highlights from the Report of the Royal Commission on Aboriginal Peoples" (28 April 2010), Indian and Northern Affairs Canada, http:// www.ainc-inac.gc.ca/ap/pubs/rpt/rpt-eng.asp.

63 Royal Commission on Aboriginal Peoples, *Bridging the Cultural Divide.*

64 Jonathan Rudin and Kent Roach, "Colloquy on 'Empty Promises: Parliament, the Supreme Court, and the Sentencing of Aboriginal Offenders': Broken Promises: A Response to Stenning and Roberts' 'Empty Promises,'" *Saskatchewan Law Review* 65 (2002): 16.

65 Ibid, 7. Some Indigenous practices require people to take responsibility for their actions. As has often been noted, terms such as "guilt" and "innocence" may not be concepts that are relevant in some Indigenous languages. See Ross Green, *Justice in Aboriginal Communities: Sentencing Alternatives* (Saskatoon, SK: Purich Publishing, 1998).

66 Royal Commission on Aboriginal Peoples, *Bridging the Cultural Divide*, 17.

67 Rudin and Roach, "Broken Promises," 17.

68 Ibid, 18-19.

69 *Gladue*, para 74.

70 Royal Commission on Aboriginal Peoples, *Bridging the Cultural Divide*, 309 [emphasis added].

71 "Stolen Sisters: Helen Betty Osborne." Amnesty International, 4 October 2007, http://www.amnesty.ca/research/reports/no-more-stolen-sisters-the-need-for-a -comprehensive-response-to-discrimination-and-.

72 Aboriginal Justice Implementation Commission, "Report of the Aboriginal Justice Inquiry of Manitoba" (1991), http://www.ajic.mb.ca/volume.html.

73 Ibid.

74 Carole LaPrairie, cited in Allan Manson, Patrick Healy, and Gary Trotter, *Sentencing and Penal Policy in Canada: Cases, Materials and Commentary* (Toronto: Emond Montgomery Publications, 2000), 578.

75 Joyce Green, "From Stonechild to Social Cohesion: Anti-Racist Challenges for Saskatchewan" (paper presented to the Canadian Political Science Association, London, ON, 2-4 June 2005), 15. http://www.cpsa-acsp.ca/papers-2005/Greene.pdf.

76 Government of Ontario, *Report of the Commission on Systemic Racism.*

77 Similar studies are included in the following collections: Robynne Neugebauer, ed, *Criminal Injustice: Racism in the Criminal Justice System* (Toronto: Canadian Scholars Press, 2000); Wendy Chan and Kiran Mirchandani, eds, *Crimes of Colour: Racialization and the Criminal Justice System in Canada* (Peterborough, ON: Broadview Press, 2002); David Tanovich, *The Colour of Justice: Policing and Race in Canada* (Toronto: Irwin Law, 2006).

78 Government of Ontario, *Report of the Commission on Systemic Racism*, 11.

79 See Kent Roach, "Systemic Racism and Criminal Justice Policy," *Windsor Yearbook of Access to Justice* 15 (1995): 239; Frances Henry, "Review of the Report of the Commission on Systemic Racism in the Ontario Criminal Justice System," *Windsor Yearbook of Access to Justice* 15 (1996): 231.

80 Government of Ontario, *Report of the Commission on Systemic Racism*, 17.

81 Roach, "Systemic Racism and Criminal Justice Policy," 239.

82 Henry, "Review of the Report of the Commission on Systemic Racism," 231.

83 Kay Anderson, *Vancouver's Chinatown: Racial Discourse in Canada, 1875-1980* (Montreal and Kingston: McGill-Queen's University Press, 1991), 19.

84 Ibid.

85 Government of Ontario, *Report of the Commission on Systemic Racism*, 11.

86 Gibney, *The Age of Apology*; Elazar Barkan and Alexander Karn, *Taking Wrongs Seriously: Apologies and Reconciliation* (Stanford, CA: Stanford University Press, 2006); Brooks, *When Sorry Isn't Enough.*

87 Will Kymlicka, *Multicultural Citizenship: A Liberal Theory of Minority Rights* (Oxford: Oxford University Press, 1995); Will Kymlicka, *Multicultural Odysseys: Navigating the New International Politics of Diversity* (Oxford: Oxford University Press, 2007); Himani Bannerji, *The Dark Side of the Nation: Essays on Multiculturalism, Nationalism and Gender* (Toronto: Canadian Scholars Press, 2000); Wendy Brown, *States of Injury: Power and Freedom in Late Modernity* (Princeton, NJ: Princeton University Press, 1995).

88 Povinelli, *Cunnning of Recognition*, 24-25.

89 Schaap, *Political Reconciliation*; Minow, *Between Vengeance and Forgiveness*; Stanley Cohen, "State Crimes of Previous Regimes: Knowledge, Accountability, and the Policing of the Past," *Law and Social Inquiry* 20 (1995): 7-50.

90 Minow, *Between Vengeance and Forgiveness*, 90.

91 Charles Villa-Vicencio and Erik Doxtader, "Introduction: Provocations at the End of Amnesty," in Charles Villa-Vicencio and Erik Doxtader, eds, *The Provocations of Amnesty: Memory, Justice and Impunity* (Trenton, NJ: Africa World Press, 2004), xi.

92 Minow, *Between Vengeance and Forgiveness*, 56.

93 Kymlicka and Bashir, *Politics of Reconciliation*, 15.

94 Steven Price and Anupama Rao, *Discipline and the Other Body: Correction, Corporeality, Colonialism* (Durham, NC: Duke University Press, 2006), 19.

95 Ibid.

96 Ibid, 19.

97 *Criminal Code*, RSC 1985, c C-46.

98 "A Long-Awaited Apology" (11 June 2008), CBC Digital Archives, http://rc-archives .cbc.ca/programs/2345-15394/page/1/; "Inuit Get Federal Apology for Relocation" (18 August 2010), *CBC News*, http://www.cbc.ca/news/canada/north/story/2010 /08/18/apology-inuit-relocation.html.

99 "Ipperwash Report Released," *Maclean's*, 31 May 2007, http://www.macleans .ca/canada/national/article.jsp?content=20070531_165856_1396; "RCMP Apologizes for B.C. Pepper Spray Incident" (5 July 2007), *CBC News*, http://www.cbc.ca /canada/british-columbia/story/2007/07/05/pepper-spray.html; "Health Canada Apologizes for Body Bags" (17 September 2009), *CBC News*, http://www.cbc.ca /news/canada/manitoba/story/2009/09/17/mb-body-bags-butler-jones-manitoba .html.

100 Moran and Dzyenhaus, *Calling Power to Account*; Renisa Mawani, "'Cleansing the Conscience of the People': Reading Head Tax Redress in Multicultural Canada," *Canadian Journal of Law and Society*, 19, no 2 (2004): 127-51; Matt James, "Recognition, Redistribution and Redress: The Case of the 'Chinese Head Tax,'" *Canadian Journal of Political Science* 37, no 4 (2004): 883-902; "Harper Apologizes in B.C. for 1914 *Komagata Maru* Incident" (3 August 2008), *CBC News*, http://www .cbc.ca/news/canada/british-columbia/story/2008/08/03/harper-apology.html; Kirsten Emiko McAllister, *Terrain of Memory: A Japanese Canadian Memorial Project* (Vancouver: UBC Press, 2010); Lubomyr Luciuk, ed, "Righting an Injustice: The Debate over Redress for Canada's First National Internment Operations" (1994), http://www.infoukes.com/history/internment/booklet02/; "Apology to Interned Italian-Canadians Questioned" (6 May 2010), *CBC News*, http://www.cbc.ca/canada /ottawa/story/2010/05/06/internment-ww2-italian-candians-apology.html; "Life after Auschwitz" (July 2009), CBC Digital Archives, http://archives.cbc.ca/war _conflict/ second_world_war/topics/1579-10644/.

101 Trouillot, "Abortive Rituals," 174.
102 Kymlicka and Bashir, *Politics of Reconciliation.*
103 Barkan, *Guilt of Nations,* xi.
104 Kymlicka and Bashir, *Politics of Reconciliation,* 4.
105 Ibid.
106 Thompson, *Taking Responsibility*; Schaap, *Political Reconciliation*; Torpey, *Politics of the Past.*
107 Mark D Walters, "The Jurisprudence of Reconciliation: Aboriginal Rights in Canada," in Bashir Bashir and Will Kymlicka, eds, *The Politics of Reconciliation in Multicultural Societies* (London: Oxford University Press, 2008), 165.
108 Mary-Ellen Kelm, *Colonizing Bodies: Aboriginal Health and Healing in British Columbia, 1900-50* (Vancouver: UBC Press, 1998), 101.

Chapter 2: From Incarceration to Restoration

1 *Criminal Code*, RSC 1985, c C-46.
2 Carmela Murdocca, "National Responsibility and Systemic Racism in Criminal Sentencing: The Case of *R. v. Hamilton*," in Law Commission of Canada, ed, *The "Place" of Justice* (Black Point, NS: Fernwood Publishing, 2006), 68.
3 It is worth noting that efforts to consult with indigenous groups have decreased in recent years. See Idle No More, http://idlenomore.ca/.
4 Gillian Cowlishaw, "Disappointing Indigenous People: Violence and the Refusal to Help," *Public Culture* 15, no 1 (2003): 107.
5 Bill C-41 received royal assent on 13 July 1995 and was enforced at the beginning of September 1996.
6 *Criminal Code.*
7 Ibid.
8 See Jonathan Rudin, "Addresing Aboriginal Overrepresentation Post-*Gladue*: A Realistic Assessement of How Social Change Occurs," *Criminal Law Quarterly* 54 (2009): 448.
9 See Julian V Roberts and David P Cole, "Introduction to Sentencing and Parole," in Julian V Roberts and David P Cole, eds, *Making Sense of Sentencing* (Toronto: University of Toronto Press, 1999), 2-30.
10 Ibid, 10.
11 See Tim Quigley, "Are We Doing Anything about the Disproportionate Jailing of Aboriginal People?" *Criminal Law Quarterly* 42 (1999): 133-34, n 11.
12 Honorable Allan Rock moved for leave to introduce Bill C-41, *An Act to Amend the Criminal Code (Sentencing) and Other Acts as a Consequence thereof*, SC 1995, c 22. *House of Common Debates*, 35th Parliament, 1st Session, No 84 (13 June 1994) at 1155 (Hon Allan Rock, Minster of Justice and the Attorney General of Canada).
13 Ibid, 5871.

14 Ibid, 5876 (Hon Pierrette Venne, Parti Québécois, Saint-Hubert).

15 *War Measures Act,* George V, c 2.

16 I am grateful to Fenn Stewart for this observation.

17 *House of Common Debates,* 35th Parliament, 1st Session, No 84 (13 June 1994) at 5878 (Hon Paul E Forseth, Reform Party, Burnaby-New Westminster).

18 House of Commons, Standing Committee on Justice and Legal Affairs, "Respecting Bill C-41, An Act to Amend the Criminal Code (Sentencing) and Other Acts in Consequence Thereof," in *Minutes of Proceedings,* No 62 (17 November 1994) (Hon Allan Rock, Minister of Justice and Attorney General of Canada).

19 Philip Stenning and Julian V Roberts, "Empty Promises: Parliament, the Supreme Court, and the Sentencing of Aboriginal Offenders," *Saskatchewan Law Review* 64 (2001): 137.

20 Talal Asad, "Ethnographic Representation, Statistics and Modern Power," *Social Research* 61, no 1 (1994): 62.

21 George Pavlich, *Governing Paradoxes of Restorative Justice* (London: Glasshouse Press, 2005), 83.

22 Emma LaRocque, "Re-examining Culturally Appropriate Models in Criminal Justice Applications," in Michael Asch, ed, *Aboriginal and Treaty Rights in Canada: Essays on Law, Equity, and Respect for Difference* (Vancouver: UBC Press, 1997), 75-96.

23 Uma Narayan, *Dislocating Cultures: Identities, Tradition and Third World Feminism* (London: Routledge, 1997).

24 Justin B Richland, *Arguing with Tradition: The Language of Law in the Hopi Tribal Court* (Chicago: University of Chicago Press, 2008), 157.

25 In highlighting Pauktuutit's submissions, I do not intend to homogenize Aboriginal women's groups. See, for example, Jocelyn Proulx and Sharon Perrault, eds, *No Place for Violence* (Toronto: Fernwood Publishing, 2000).

26 Emma Cunliffe and Angela Cameron, "Writing the Circle: Judicially Convened Sentencing Circles and the Textual Organization of Criminal Justice," *Canadian Journal of Women and the Law* 19, no 1 (2007): 1-35.

27 Ibid, 3.

28 Ibid, 12.

29 House of Commons, Standing Committee on Justice and Legal Affairs, "Respecting Bill C-41: An Act to Amend the Criminal Code (Sentencing) and Other Acts in Consequence Thereof," in *Minutes of Proceedings,* No 85 (28 February 1995) at 0955 (Martha Flaherty, President of Pauktuutit, Inuit Women's Association of Canada).

30 Ibid, 1000 (Ruby Arngna'naaq, Pauktuutit, Inuit Women's Association of Canada).

31 Ibid, 1045 (Jeanne Sala, Pauktuutit, Inuit Women's Association of Canada).

32 LaRocque, "Re-examining Culturally Appropriate Models," 87.

33 House of Commons, *Minutes of Proceedings,* 0945 (Martha Flaherty).

34 Ibid, 1050 (Jeanne Sala).

35   Elizabeth A Povinelli, *The Cunning of Recognition: Indigenous Alterities and the Making of Australian Multiculturalism* (Durham, NC: Duke University Press, 2002), 150.
36   Ibid.
37   House of Commons, *Minutes of Proceedings*, 1055 (Jeanne Sala).
38   Ibid.
39   Pavlich, *Governing Paradoxes*, 83.
40   This point is similar to Sherene Razack's insistence upon the dangers of cultural difference approaches to sexual violence against Aboriginal women, and women of colour, that fail to take history into account. Sherene H Razack, *Looking White People in the Eye: Gender, Race and Culture in Courtrooms and Classrooms* (Toronto: University of Toronto Press, 1998), 61.
41   Cunliffe and Cameron, "Writing the Circle," 3.
42   James Ptacek, ed, *Restorative Justice and Violence against Women* (London: Oxford University Press, 2010); Heather Strang and John Braithwaite, eds, *Restorative Justice and Family Violence* (London: Cambridge University Press, 2002); Anne McGillivray and Brenda Comasky, *Black Eyes All the Time* (Toronto: University of Toronto Press, 1999).
43   Aboriginal Women's Action Network, *The Implications of Restorative Justice for Aboriginal Women and Children Survivors of Violence: A Comparative Overview of Five Communities in British Columbia* (Vancouver: Aboriginal Women's Action Network, 2001).
44   Razack, *Looking White People in the Eye*.
45   *House of Common Debates*, 1615 (Pierrette Venne).
46   *House of Commons Debates*, 35th Parliament, 1st Session, No 84 (13 June 1994) at 2045 (Hon Dick Harris, Reform, Prince George, Bulkley Valley).
47   Sentencing Project, "Executive Summary: Does the Punishment Fit the Crime? Drug Users and Drunk Drivers, Questions of Race and Class" (1993), http://www.sentencingproject.org.
48   House of Commons, Standing Committee on Justice and Legal Affairs, "Respecting Bill C-41: An Act to Amend the Criminal Code (Sentencing) and Other Acts in Consequence Thereof," in *Minutes of Proceedings*, No 75 (7 February 1995) at 1545 (Julian V Roberts, Professor of Criminology, Individual Witness).
49   *R v Hamilton*, [2004] OJ no 3252 (QL) (Ont CA).
50   House of Commons, Standing Committee on Justice and Legal Affairs, "Respecting Bill C-41: An Act to Amend the Criminal Code (Sentencing) and Other Acts in Consequence Thereof," in *Minutes of Proceedings*, No 79 (14 February 1995) at 1550 (Chief Blaine Favel, Federation of Saskatchewan Indian Nations).
51   Ibid.
52   Institutionalized practices of self-determination among Indigenous people are always mediated through colonial law. However, this does not preclude the possibility/inevitability that Indigenous people manoeuvre within and through such colonial determinations.

Chapter 3: Her Aboriginal Connections

1 *R v Gladue*, 1999 SCC 1, [1999] 1 SCR 688 at para 3 [*Gladue*].

2 Ibid, para 4.

3 There was additional evidence that indicated that Gladue stabbed Beaver before they left their townhouse unit. Ibid, para 6.

4 Ibid, para 9.

5 Other aggravating factors included that Gladue intended to seriously harm Beaver, that she was not afraid of him, and that she had committed what is legally considered a "serious crime." See Jean Lash, "Case Comment: *R v Gladue,*" *Canadian Woman Studies* 20, no 3 (2000): 86; *Gladue*, para 10.

6 *Gladue.* Kim Pate (Executive Director, Canadian Association of Elizabeth Fry Societies), "Aboriginal Women and Their Over-Representation in Prisons" (paper presented at the Third National Conference on Aboriginal Criminal Justice Post-*Gladue*, Osgoode Hall, York University, Toronto, 30 April 2011).

7 *Gladue*, para 10.

8 Ibid, para 47.

9 *Criminal Code*, RSC 1985, c C-46.

10 Ibid.

11 While on bail for seventeen months awaiting trial, Gladue entered a drug and alcohol counselling program and completed Grade 10. See *Gladue*.

12 Lash, "Case Comment."

13 Although *Gladue* is one of the most significant cases, there were others that considered section 718.2(e) soon after 1996. In a case involving the sentencing hearing of Lori Morin, an Aboriginal woman found guilty of theft and possession of $120,000, the Ontario Court of Appeal insisted on the concept of general deterrence in sentencing and reasoned that there was "no reason to think that Parliament has abandoned any concept of general deterrence" in the new sentencing provisions that were described in the decision as 'radical.'" *R v Morin*, [1997] OJ no 2413 at para 38 (QL). This decision is significant to the extent that it reaffirms the principle of general deterrence in sentencing, even in light of new sentencing guidelines. Elizabeth Comack and Gillian Balfour note that section 718.2(e) also appeared in cases before the Manitoba Court of Queen's Bench in the years after 1996. See Elizabeth Comack and Gillian Balfour, "Racializing Violent Crime," in Elizabeth Comack and Gillian Balfour, eds, *The Power to Criminalize: Violence, Inequality and the Law* (Black Point, NS: Fernwood Publishing, 2004), 106-8. In addition, *R v Wells*, 2000 SCC 10, [2000] 1 SCR 207, a case concerning the use of conditional sentences for an Aboriginal offender charged with a sexual offence, is often considered the "companion" decision to *Gladue*. Yet another case (*R v Williams*, 2003 SCC 41, [2003] 2 SCR 134) also predated *Gladue* in its indictment of the connection between systemic racism in the criminal justice system and disproportionate incarceration rates. See Jonathan Rudin, "Addressing Aboriginal Overrepresentation Post-*Gladue*: A Realistic Assessment of How Social Change Occurs," *Criminal Law Quarterly* 54 (2009): 447.

14 Jonathan Rudin, "Justice, Race and Time," *Toronto Star,* 17 February 2003, A21.

15 Rudin, "Addresing Aboriginal Overrepresentation," 448.

16 Kent Roach and Jonathan Rudin, "*Gladue:* The Judicial and Political Reception of a Promising Decision," *Canadian Journal of Criminology* 42, no 3 (2000): 355-88.

17 Ross Gordon Green, "Treat *Gladue* as a Call to Action," *Lawyers Weekly* 42 (2000): 12.

18 There are a number of scholars in Canada who have examined the operation of "national innocence" in Canadian law. For example, Sherene Razack argues that "white settler innocence" underscores Canadian national mythologies in the law. See Sherene H Razack, "When Place Becomes Race," in Sherene H Razack, ed, *Race, Space and the Law: Unmapping a White Settler Society* (Toronto: Between the Lines, 2002), 5. In her examination of the legal history of race and racism in the first half of the twentieth century, Constance Backhouse utilizes the idea of "stupefying innocence" embedded within what she calls the "mythology of racelessness," which together produce national innocence in Canada. See Constance Backhouse, *Colour-Coded: A Legal History of Racism in Canada, 1900-1950* (Toronto: Osgoode Society for Canadian Legal History, 1999).

19 *Jamie T. Gladue v. Queen,* transcripts from the Supreme Court Proceedings (VHS recording) (10 December 1998) (Defence Counsel Gil D McKinnon).

20 Ibid [emphasis added].

21 In the Australian context, Elizabeth Povinelli describes similar examples ("clitori-dectomy and bride murder") where sexuality and culture function "to expand the field of shame and cast a pall over unnamed subaltern practices where no national popular collective will would be possible." Elizabeth A Povinelli, *The Cunning of Recognition: Indigenous Alterities and the Making of Australian Multiculturalism* (Durham, NC: Duke University Press, 2002), 27; Michel Foucault, *The History of Sexuality: An Introduction, volume 1.* New York: Vintage, 1978, 103.

22 Ibid.

23 *Jamie T. Gladue v. Queen,* transcripts (Defence Counsel Gil D McKinnon).

24 Emma LaRocque, *Defeathering the Indian* (Agincourt, ON: Book Society of Canada, 1975), 8.

25 Elizabeth Furniss, *The Burden of History: Colonialism and the Frontier Myth in a Rural Canadian Community* (Vancouver: UBC Press, 2000), 12.

26 *Indian Act,* RS 1951, c I-5.

27 *Jamie T. Gladue v. Queen,* transcripts (Defence Counsel Gil D McKinnon) [emphasis added].

28 *Gladue,* paras 9 and 11 (Factum of Intervenor Aboriginal Legal Services of Toronto (ALST)). The ALST was formed in 1990: "[The] ALST was formed following a needs assessment by the Native Canadian Centre of Toronto in the mid-1980s. The Centre had been operating legal-related programs for Aboriginal people in Toronto but concluded an agency dedicated to this issue was needed." See "Aboriginal Legal Services of Toronto," ALST, http://www.aboriginallegal.ca/.

29 *Jamie T. Gladue v. Queen,* transcripts (Defence Counsel Gil D McKinnon).

30 *Gladue*, para 7.
31 Ibid, para 8 (Factum of Intervenor ALST).
32 Ibid, para 28.
33 Ibid, para 30.
34 Ibid, para 31.
35 The ALST notes that "this myth is best exemplified in cases where the trial judge refuses to consider the circumstances of Aboriginal offenders in general because the offence for which the specific Aboriginal offender is convicted of is not an 'Aboriginal offence' such as hunting or fishing." Ibid, para 32.
36 It is important to note that the "ALST does not take issue with accommodation in such circumstances, but it does object to the implication that all Aboriginal people ... are not worthy of consideration as Aboriginal persons during sentencing." Ibid, para 35.
37 Ibid, para 36.
38 Furthermore, the ALST reminds the Court that the presence of off-reserve programs is minimal: "There are eleven off reserve justice programs across Canada, eight of which are in the province of Saskatchewan. Only three other urban centres in Canada have alternative justice programs – Toronto, Thunder Bay and Winnipeg. Other types of justice programs are in place for approximately 182 reserve communities." Ibid, para 37.
39 Ibid, para 30.
40 Marilyn Dumont, cited in Chris Anderson, "Governing Aboriginal Justice in Canada: Constructing Responsible Individuals and Communities through 'Tradition,'" *Crime, Law and Social Change* 31, no 4 (1999): 303.
41 *Gladue*, paras 40-41 (Factum of Intervenor ALST).
42 Ibid, para 64.
43 Ibid.
44 Ibid, para 61. Royal Commission on Aboriginal Peoples, *Bridging the Cultural Divide: A Report on Aboriginal People and Criminal Justice in Canada* (Ottawa: Minister of Supply and Services, 1996).
45 *Gladue*, para 89.
46 Ibid.
47 Ibid.
48 Ibid, paras 90-92.
49 *Canadian Charter of Rights and Freedoms*, Part 1 of the *Constitution Act, 1982*, being Schedule B to the *Canada Act 1982* (UK), 1982, c 11.
50 Val Napoleon, "*Delgamuukw*: A Legal Straightjacket for Oral Histories?" *Canadian Journal of Law and Society* 20, no 2 (2005): 123-24. *Delgamuukw v British Columbia*, [1997] 3 SCR 1010.
51 Carole LaPrairie, "The Role of Sentencing in the Over-Representation of Aboriginal Peoples in Correctional Institutions," *Canadian Journal of Criminology* 132, no 3 (1990): 436.

52   Royal Commission on Aboriginal Peoples, *Bridging the Cultural Divide*, 309.

53   Jane Dickson-Gilmore and Carole LaPrairie, *Will the Circle Be Unbroken? Aboriginal Communities, Restorative Justice and the Challenges of Conflict and Change* (Toronto: University of Toronto Press, 2005).

54   Jennifer J Llewellyn, "Restorative Justice in *Borde* and *Hamilton:* A Systemic Problem?" *Criminal Reports* 8 (2003): 308; Anderson, "Governing Aboriginal Justice in Canada," 303.

55   Susan Haslip, "Aboriginal Sentencing Reform in Canada – Prospects for Success: Standing Tall with Both Feet Planted Firmly in the Air," *Murdoch University Electronic Journal of Law* 7, no 1 (2000): 29.

56   Llewellyn, "Restorative Justice," 308.

57   George Pavlich, *The Governing Paradoxes of Restorative Justice* (London: Glasshouse Press, 2005).

58   Llewellyn, "Restorative Justice," 137.

59   Emma LaRocque, "Re-examining Culturally Appropriate Models in Criminal Justice Applications," in M Asch, ed, *Aboriginal Treaty Rights in Canada: Essays on Law, Equity and Respect for Difference* (Vancouver: UBC Press, 1997), 76.

60   For examples, see Jo-Anne Fiske and Betty Patrick, *Cis Dideen Kat, When the Plumes Rise: The Way of the Lake Babine Nation* (Vancouver: UBC Press, 2000); Bruce G Miller, *The Problem of Justice: Tradition and Law in the Coast Salish World* (Lincoln, NE: University of Nebraska Press, 2000); Justin R Richland, *Arguing with Tradition: The Language of Law in the Hopi Tribal Court* (Chicago: University of Chicago Press, 2008).

61   Judges consulted with the Aboriginal community in Toronto to create this specially structured court, which deals specifically with Aboriginal offenders. The objective of the court is to facilitate the trial court's ability to consider the unique circumstances of Aboriginal defendants and Aboriginal offenders. To assist the court, the ALST has designated court workers to deal with the initial problem of identifying Aboriginal people, should they wish to be identified. Participation of an accused in the court is voluntary. A distinguishing feature of the Gladue Court is that all persons working in the court, including prosecutors, duty counsel, case workers, defence counsel, probation workers, and judges have the relevant expertise and training concerning the range of programs and services available to Aboriginal people in Toronto. These services are linked to the court through the presence of ALST court workers. Both the Aboriginal court worker and the Gladue Aboriginal person court case worker play critical roles in the operation of the court by securing residence beds for defendants when needed and arranging any treatment resources. Sherry L Van de Veen, "Some Canadian Problem Solving Court Processes" (2003), 12 [unpublished manuscript, on file with the National Judicial Institute]. For more information, see "Gladue (Aboriginal Persons) Court," ALST, http://www.aboriginallegal.ca/gladue.php. For more information about the Gladue Court

process, see "Aboriginal Legal Services of Toronto." The following sites offer more information about various Aboriginal justice initiatives across Canada:

Federal: "The Aboriginal Justice Strategy," Department of Justice Canada, http:// www.justice.gc.ca/eng/pi/ajs-sja/index.html.

Alberta: "Aboriginal Justice," Government of Alberta Justice and Attorney General, http://justice.alberta.ca/programs_services/aboriginal/Pages/default.aspx.

British Columbia: "Aboriginal Justice Programs and Services," Justice British Columbia, http://www.justicebc.ca/en/cjis/understanding/aboriginal/programs. html.

Manitoba: "Aboriginal Justice Initiatives," Manitoba Justice, http://www.gov.mb.ca /justice/aboriginal/index.html. This site links to the Aboriginal Justice Implementation Commission.

New Brunswick: "Report of the Task Force on Aboriginal Issues: Justice Issues," Government of New Brunswick, http://www2.gnb.ca/content/gnb/en /departments/aboriginal_affairs/publications/content/task_force.html#anchor 71985. ("New Brunswick remains the only province in Canada that does not benefit from the federal Court Worker Program [which] has had considerable success in reducing the alienation and intimidation Aboriginal people may experience when they enter the courtroom, and in providing post-sentencing services attuned to Aboriginal experience.")

Newfoundland and Labrador: Newfoundland and Labrador Legal Aid Commission, "Annual Report 2009-10," Newfoundland and Labrador Department of Justice, http://www.legalaid.nl.ca/publications.html, 11-12. See also "Innu-Aimun Legal Terms (Criminal Law) Kaueshinitunanit Aimuna Mushuau Dialect," Newfoundland and Labrador Department of Justice, http://www.justice.gov .nl.ca/just/publications/legal_mus_crim.pdf.

Northwest Territories: "Community Justice," Northwest Territories – Department of Justice, http://www.justice.gov.nt.ca/CommunityJustice/CommunityJustice.shtml.

Nova Scotia: Don Clairmont and Jane McMillan, "Directions In Mi'kmaq Justice: An Evaluation of the Mi'kmaq Justice Institute and Its Aftermath," http://www .gov.ns.ca/just/publications/docs/TFexesum.pdf.

Nunavut: "Department of Justice," Government of Nunavut, http://www.justice. gov.nu.ca/apps/authoring/dspPage.aspx?page=home.

Ontario: "Aboriginal Justice Strategy," Ontario Ministry of the Attorney General, http://www.attorneygeneral.jus.gov.on.ca/english/aboriginal_justice_strategy /default.asp.

Prince Edward Island: "Aboriginal Justice Program," Mi'kmaq Confederacy of Prince Edward Island, http://www.mcpei.ca/node/18.

Quebec: "Justice for and by the Aboriginals," Justice Quebec, http://www.justice .gouv.qc.ca/english/publications/rapports/coutu-f-a.htm. See also "Native Para-Judicial Services of Quebec," http://www.spaq.qc.ca.

Saskatchewan: "Aboriginal Courtworker Program," Government of Saskatchewan, http://www.justice.gov.sk.ca/aboriginalcourtworkerprogram. See also "Aboriginal Resource Officer Program," Government of Saskatchewan, http://www.justice .gov.sk.ca/Default.aspx?DN=8003d87c-449d-44c6-9fd1-3f59a442316f; "Location of Aboriginal Justice Strategy Programs in Canada: Saskatchewan," Department of Justice Canada, http://www.justice.gc.ca/eng/pi/ajs-sja/map3-carte3/sask.html; "Policy and Planning," Federation of Saskatchewan Indian Nations, http://www .fsin.com/index.php/policy-a-planning.html.

Yukon: "Aboriginal Law Group," Department of Justice – Government of Yukon, http://www.justice.gov.yk.ca/prog/ls/.

62 *"Gladue* (Aboriginal Persons) Court Ontario Court of Justice – Old City Hall Fact Sheet," ALST, http://www.aboriginallegal.ca/docs/apc_factsheet.htm.

63 Susan Goldberg, "Judging for the Twenty-First Century: A Problem Solving Approach" (2004), 37 [unpublished manuscript, on file with the National Judicial Institute].

64 Ibid.

65 The examples here are drawn from sentencing reports on file from the National Judicial Institute.

66 *Gladue.*

67 Roach, *"Gladue:* The Judicial and Political Reception," 365.

68 Ibid.

69 *Gladue,* para 79.

70 See Comack and Balfour, *"Racializing Violent Crime,"* 106-8.

71 In a decision following *Gladue,* the Supreme Court of Canada reasoned that proportionality requires that "in the final analysis, the overarching duty of a sentencing judge is to draw upon all the legitimate principles of sentencing to determine a 'just and appropriate' sentence which reflects the gravity of the offence committed and the moral blameworthiness of the offender." *R v Proulx,* 2000 SCC 1, [2000] 1 SCR 163 at para 61.

72 Anderson, "Governing Aboriginal Justice in Canada," 303.

73 Kent Roach, "One Step Forward, Two Steps Back: *Gladue* at Ten and in the Courts of Appeal," *Criminal Law Quarterly* 54 (2009): 474.

74 Ibid, 477. The notion that for more "serious offences" the sentences for Aboriginal and non-Aboriginal offenders would likely be similar or the same was further reaffirmed in the case *R v Wells,* 2000 SCC 10, [2000] 1 SCR 207. Roach suggests that *Wells* "continued the trend of ambiguity with respect to the application of *Gladue* in serious cases." Roach, "One Step Forward," 478.

75 Roach, "One Step Forward," 504.

76 Alana Klein, *"Gladue* in Quebec," *Criminal Law Quarterly* 54 (2009): 509.

77 *R v Ipeelee,* 2012 SCC 13, [2012] 1 SCR 433.

78 Ibid.

79 *Criminal Code*, s 742.1. A conditional sentence is a sentence of less than two years that is served in the community subject to the conditions prescribed in the order. A conditional sentence is not available where the offence provides for a mandatory minimum term of imprisonment, such as in the case of murder. A conditional sentence may be ordered where the court is satisfied that serving the sentence in the community would not endanger the safety of the community and would be consistent with the fundamental purpose and principles of sentencing in sections 718 to 718.2 of the *Criminal Code*.

80 Roach, "*Gladue:* The Judicial and Political Reception, " 369.

81 In *Gladue*, the Court outlined at length that the parliamentary intent behind Bill C-41 (which amended the *Criminal Code* and resulted in the addition of section 718.2[e]) was to directly address the overincarceration of Aboriginal peoples.

82 Roach, "*Gladue:* The Judicial and Political Reception," 370.

83 See Anderson, "Governing Aboriginal Justice in Canada," 303; George Pavlich, *Justice Fragmented: Mediating Community Disputes under Postmodern Conditions* (London: Routledge, 1996).

84 Roach, "One Step Forward," 481. *R v Morris*, 2006 SCC 59, [2006] 2 SCR 915.

85 Roach, "One Step Forward," 481.

86 See Office of the Correctional Investigator of Canada, "Backgrounder: Aboriginal Inmates" (16 October 2006), http://www.oci-bec.gc.ca/cnt/rpt/annrpt/annrpt2005 2006info-eng.aspx.

87 Samuel Perreault, "The Incarceration of Aboriginal People in Adult Correctional Services," Juristat 29, no 3 (2009): 5, http://www.statcan.gc.ca/pub/85-002-x/2009003 /article/10903-eng.pdf.

88 Ibid.

89 Williams analyzes the outcomes of cases involving Aboriginal women in Canada 2005-06. See Toni Williams, "Punishing Women: The Promise and Perils of Contextualized Sentencing for Aboriginal Women in Canada," *Cleveland State Law Review* 55 (2007): 286.

90 Philip Stenning and Julian V Roberts, "Empty Promises: Parliament, the Supreme Court, and the Sentencing of Aboriginal Offenders," *Saskatchewan Law Review* 64 (2001): 137-68.

91 Jonathan Rudin and Kent Roach, "Colloquy on 'Empty Promises: Parliament, the Supreme Court, and the Sentencing of Aboriginal Offenders' – 'Broken Promises: A Response to Stenning and Roberts'‴ Empty Promises,'" *Saskatchewan Law Review* 65 (2002): 16.

92 Rudin and Roach, "Broken Promises," 1, 3.

93 Roach, "One Step Forward," 472.

94 *Gladue*, para 12.

95 Ibid, para 11.

96 For examples and examinations of historical debates surrounding colonial constructions of Aboriginal identity in Canada, see Renisa Mawani, "Genealogies of the

Land: Aboriginality, Law, and Territory in Vancouver's Stanley Park," *Social and Legal Studies* 14, no 3 (2005): 315-39; C Pewewardy, "Will the 'Real' Indians Please Stand Up," *Multicultural Review* 7, no 2 (1998): 36-42; Patricia Monture-Angus, *Thunder in My Soul: A Mohawk Woman Speaks* (Halifax, NS: Fernwood Publishing, 1995); Bradford Morse and John Gokas, "Do the Métis Fall within Section 91(24) of the Constitution Act of 1867?" (Ottawa: Royal Commission on Aboriginal Peoples, 1993); Wendy Moss, "The Canadian State and Indian Women: The Struggle for Sex Equality under the Indian Act," in Caroline Andrews and Sandra Rodgers, eds, *Women and the Canadian State* (Montreal and Kingston: McGill-Queens University Press, 1997), 79-88.

97 The few articles that do consider the impact of the *Gladue* decision on Aboriginal women are the following. Lash, "Case Comment"; Josephine Savarese, "Gladue Was a Woman: The Importance of Gender in Restorative-based Sentencing," in Elizabeth Elliot and Robert Gordon, eds, *New Directions in Restorative Justice: Issues, Practice, Evaluation* (Vancouver: Willan Publishing, 2005), 134-50; Angela Cameron, "*R. v. Gladue*: Sentencing and Gendered Implications of Colonialism," in John D Whyte, ed, *Moving towards Justice: Legal Traditions and Aboriginal Justice* (Saskatoon, SK: Purich Press, 2008), 160-80.

98 *Gladue*, para 8.

99 Pate, "Aboriginal Women and Their Over-Representation in Prisons."

100 "Submission of the Canadian Association of Elizabeth Fry Societies to the Standing Committee on Justice, Human Rights, Public Safety and Emergency Preparedness (39th Parliament) Regarding Bill C-10: An Act to Amend the Criminal Code (Minimum Penalties for Offences Involving Firearms" (November 2006), Elizabeth Fry Societies, http://www.elizabethfry.ca/billC-10/billC-10-nov06.pdf.

101 Sherene H Razack, "Gendered Racial Violence," in Razack, *Race, Space and the Law*, 142.

102 *Gladue*, para 9.

103 Razack, "Gendered Racial Violence."

104 The naturalizing of sexual violence against Aboriginal women in the project of nation building has been well documented. For other examples, see Andrea Smith, *Sexual Violence and the American Indian Genocide* (Cambridge, MA: South End Press, 2005).

105 Sherene H Razack, *Looking White People in the Eye: Gender, Race and Culture in Courtrooms and Classrooms* (Toronto: University of Toronto Press, 2001), 40.

106 Wendy Brown, *States of Injury: Power and Freedom in Late Modernity* (Princeton, NJ: Princeton University Press, 1995), 13.

107 *Gladue*, para 61.

Chapter 4: Racial Injustice and Righting Historical Wrongs

1 *R v Hamilton*, [2003] OJ no 532.

2 *R v Gladue*, [1999] 1 SCR 668 [*Gladue*]. *Criminal Code*, RSC 1985, c C-46.

3 *R v Hamilton*, [2004] OJ no 3252 at para 99 (Ont CA) (QL) [*Hamilton* (Ont CA)].
4 *Hamilton* (Ont CA), para 60. See Richard Weisman, "Showing Remorse: Reflections on the Gap between Expression and Attribution in Cases of Wrongful Conviction," *Canadian Journal of Criminology and Criminal Justice* 46, no 2 (2004): 121-38; Chris Anderson, "Governing Aboriginal Justice in Canada: Constructing Responsible Individuals and Communities through 'Tradition,'" *Crime, Law and Social Change* 31, no 4 (1999): 303-26.
5 *Hamilton* (Ont CA), para 185.
6 *Immigration and Refugee Protection Act*, SC 2001, c 27.
7 *Hamilton* (Ont CA), para 69.
8 Ibid, paras 235-37.
9 *Her Majesty the Queen v. Marsha Alisjie Hamilton and Donna Rosemarie Mason*, proceeding transcripts from Ontario Superior Court of Justice, volume 1 (24 January 2003) (Neil Armstrong, Security Investigators Air Canada), 362, 365, 367 [*Hamilton and Mason* 2003].
10 Ibid, 368 [emphasis added].
11 Ibid, 362, 365, 367 [emphasis added].
12 Sonia N Lawrence and Toni Williams, "'Swallowed Up': Drug Couriers at the Borders of Canadian Sentencing," *University of Toronto Law Journal* 56, no 4 (2006): 301.
13 Furthermore, "legislative debates in the 1920s contain lurid anecdotes about predatory Chinese traffickers. Moreover, law enforcement targeted the Chinese population and judges meted out harsh sentences to Chinese men convicted of supplying drugs to white people. As the much smaller black population in Canada also became identified with illicit drug use, it too began to figure disproportionately among persons sentenced for drug offences." Lawrence and Williams, "'Swallowed Up,'" 301-2.
14 Ibid.
15 *Hamilton* (Ont CA), para 35.
16 Julia Sudbury, "'Mules,' 'Yardies' and Other Folk Devils: Mapping Cross-Border Imprisonment in Britain," in Julia Sudbury, ed, *Global Lockdown: Race, Gender and the Prison-Industrial Complex* (London: Routledge, 2005), 170.
17 *Hamilton* (Ont CA), para 35.
18 Lawrence and Williams, "'Swallowed Up,'" 306.
19 *Hamilton and Mason* 2003, transcripts (Edward Royle), 679.
20 Avtar Brah, *Cartographies of Diaspora* (London: Routledge, 1995), 105.
21 David M Tanovich, "Race, Sentencing and the 'War on Drugs,'" *Criminal Reports* 22 (2004): 45-56. Government of Ontario, *Report of the Commission on Systemic Racism in the Criminal Ontario Justice System* (Toronto: Queen's Printer, 1995).
22 Deterrence refers to the sentencing principle concerning the attempt to prevent or control potential criminal behaviour and actions through the sentencing paradigm of punishment and retribution.
23 *Hamilton* (Ont CA), para 153.

24 Ibid, para 163.
25 Ibid, para 152.
26 *Hamilton and Mason* 2003, transcripts (Edward Royle), 655, 656 [emphasis added].
27 Ibid, 657 [emphasis added].
28 Ibid.
29 Ibid, 658 [emphasis added].
30 Sherene H Razack, *Looking White People in the Eye: Gender, Race and Culture in Courtrooms and Classrooms* (Toronto: University of Toronto Press, 2001), 60.
31 Justice Hill, as noted in *US v Belanger*, [2003] OJ no 5862 (SCJ) (QL) [*Belanger*].
32 A subsequent decision concerning Justice Hill's potential bias and impartiality provides a summary of the secondary source material that he entered into *Hamilton*. See *Belanger*, para 10.
33 *Her Majesty the Queen v. Marsha Alisjie Hamilton and Donna Rosemarie Mason*, proceeding transcripts from Ontario Superior Court of Justice (12 November 2002), 16, 17, 18 (Justice Casey Hill).
34 When I presented this work at a workshop in a US context, a participant declared: "This judge is a hero," for his insertion of materials related to systemic racism and the criminal justice system.
35 *Belanger*, para 16.
36 Ibid.
37 *Hamilton* (Ont CA), para 33.
38 Tanovich, "Race, Sentencing and the 'War on Drugs,'" 45-56.
39 Richard Rorty in Kirstie McClure, "Difference, Diversity, and the Limits of Toleration," *Political Theory* 18, no 3 (1990): 361.
40 Ibid.
41 Sherene H Razack, *Dark Threats and White Knights: The Somalia Affair, Peacekeeping and the New Imperialism* (Toronto: University of Toronto Press, 2004), 14.
42 *Hamilton and Mason* 2003 (Justice Casey Hill), 898, 900, 901.
43 Ibid (J. North), 897.
44 Ibid (Justice Casey Hill), 897.
45 *R v Borde* set out this legal precedent borrowing at length from Government of Ontario, *Report of the Commission on Systemic Racism*. *R v Borde*, [2003] 172 CCC 225 at paras 18-24 (Ont CA) [*Borde*].
46 *Hamilton* (Ont CA), para 185.
47 *Canadian Charter of Rights and Freedoms*, Part 1 of the *Constitution Act, 1982*, being Schedule B to the *Canada Act 1982* (UK), 1982, c 11.
48 *Hamilton* (Ont CA), para 224.
49 Ibid, para 188.
50 Ibid, para 192.
51 Elazar Barkan, *The Guilt of Nations: Restitution and Negotiating Historical Injustices* (New York: Norton, 2000), xxvi.
52 *Hamilton* (Ont CA), paras 194-96.

53 The appeal decision is consolidated, and, in addition to *Hamilton*, it includes *R v Spencer*. Tracey-Ann Spencer, also a black woman who pleaded guilty to cocaine importation, received a college education and had full-time employment as a nurse. In the Crown's facta and in the oral argument at the appeal hearing, it was argued that these factors (education and employment status) did not render Spencer as deserving of a "reduced" sentence. *R v Spencer*, [2003] OJ no 1052 (QL) [*Spencer*].

54 *Hamilton* (Ont CA), para 198.

55 Lawrence and Williams, "'Swallowed Up,'" 326.

56 Ibid, 288.

57 Ibid, 326, 331.

58 *Hamilton* (Ont CA), para 179.

59 Margaret Parsons and Marie Chen, "In a World of Equality, Can Judges Stay Colour Blind?" *Toronto Star*, 3 March 2003, A21.

60 Philip Smith, "Unjust Sentence," *Globe and Mail*, 14 February 2003, A18.

61 "Justice Is Blind, Not Colour Blind," Editorial, *Toronto Star*, 24 February 2003, A22.

62 For more examples of scholars that examine the colonial foundation of the myth of Canada as a white settler society, see Sherene H Razack, "'Simple Logic:' Race, the Identity Documents Rule and the Story of a Nation Besieged and Betrayed," *Journal of Law and Social Policy* 15 (2002): 199-220; Kay Anderson, "Thinking 'Postnationally': Dialogue across Multicultural, Indigenous and Settler Spaces," *Annals of the Association of American Geographers* 90, no 2 (2001): 381-91.

63 *Hamilton* (Ont CA), para 7.

64 "Sentencing by Race," Editorial, *National Post*, 5 August 2004, A15.

65 *Hamilton* (Ont CA), para 72 [emphasis added].

66 Spencer was sentenced to imprisonment for two years less a day, which was to be served on a conditional basis. The terms of Spencer's conditional sentence included that she report to her order supervisor on a consistent basis, that she was permitted to be outside of her home for medical services, that she was allowed travel time and attendance at her place of employment, that she was given a four-hour occasion per week where she was permitted to purchase food and clothing, and she was permitted to attend religious services. Any other reason for being outside of her home was to be pre-approved by her order supervisor. The Crown requested that Spencer be sentenced to a term of four to five years. *Spencer*, para 86.

67 As noted in the Ontario Court of Appeal decision, "purity adjusted weight" is a technical phrase for measuring drug possession and is determined by multiplying the weight of the drug by the purity stated as a percentage. See *Hamilton* (Ont CA), para 27.

68 Ibid (Factum for the Appellant).

69 Ibid, para 9.

70 Ibid, paras 42, 44.

71 Ibid, para 47.

72 Ibid, para 4.

73 Lawrence and Williams, "'Swallowed Up,'" 315.

74 *R v Brown*, [2002] OJ no 295 (QL); *R v Parks* (1994), 84 CCC (3d) 353; *Gladue*; *R v S(RD)* (1997), 118 CCC (3d) 353 (SCC); *R v Richards* (1999), 26 CR (5th) 286.

75 Aboriginal Justice Implementation Commission, *Report of the Aboriginal Justice Inquiry of Manitoba*, November 1999, http://www.ajic.mb.ca/volume.html; Commission of Inquiry into Matters Relating to the Death of Neil Stonechild, *Final Report* (2004), http://www.stonechildinquiry.ca.

76 Royal Commission on Aboriginal Peoples, *Bridging the Cultural Divide: A Report on Aboriginal People and Criminal Justice in Canada* (Ottawa: Minister of Supply and Services, 1996).

77 For examples, see *Aboriginal Peoples and the Justice System* (Ottawa: Minister of Supplies and Services, 1993); Government of Ontario, *Report of the Commission on Systemic Racism*; Law Commission of Canada, *Transforming Relationships through Participatory Justice* (Toronto: Law Commission of Canada, 2003), 18; Office of the Correctional Investigator, "Backgrounder: Aboriginal Inmates" (20 February 2010), http://www.oci-bec.gc.ca/rpt/annrpt/annrpt20052006info-eng.aspx.

78 For examples, see Michael Jackson, "Locking Up Natives in Canada," *UBC Law Review* 23 (1989): 215-16; Robynne Neugebauer, ed, *Criminal Injustice: Racism in the Criminal Justice System* (Toronto: Canadian Scholars Press, 2000); Wendy Chan and Kiran Mirchandani, eds, *Crimes of Colour: Racialization and the Criminal Justice System in Canada* (Peterborough, ON: Broadview Press, 2002).

79 *Hamilton* (Ont CA), para 55 (Factum for the Appellant).

80 Ibid, para 57.

81 *Borde*.

82 Ibid, para 2.

83 Ibid, para 27 (Crown's facta) [emphasis added].

84 Ibid, para 428 [emphasis in original].

85 *Hamilton* (Ont CA), para 65 (Factum for the Appellant).

86 Ibid, para 67.

87 Ibid, para 70.

88 Ibid, para 73.

89 Ibid, para 75.

90 Lawrence and Williams, "'Swallowed Up,'" 326.

91 Ibid, 326, n 179.

92 *Opium and Drug Act*, SC 1911, c 17, as amended by SC 1920, c 31; SC 1921, c 42; SC 1922, c 36; RS 1923, c 22; RSC 1927, c 144; RS 1929, c 49.

93 *Hamilton* (Ont CA), para 80 (Factum for the Appellant).

94 The Crown further suggested that Justice Hill "erred in drawing the conclusion that over-representation in the penitentiary system alone justified a sentencing discount." Ibid, paras 86, 93.

95 Ibid, para 89.

96 Ibid, para 80.

97 Lawrence and Williams, "'Swallowed Up,'" 326.

98 Ibid, 327.

99 Ibid.

100 Ibid, 326-27.

101 See Jennifer Keck, "Remembering Kimberly Rogers," Canadian Council of Social Development, *Perception* 25, no 3/4 (2002), http://www.ccsd.ca/perception/2534/kimberly.htm.

102 *Hamilton* (Ont CA), para 97 (Factum for the Appellant, 12 January 2004).

103 Furthermore, the Crown argued that Spencer was *"singularly unworthy of credit due to delay,"* because of the fact that she was charged with two additional crimes while she awaited her sentencing hearing Ibid, para 105 [emphasis added].

104 Lawrence and Williams, "'Swallowed Up,'" 322. See *R v Johnston*, [2003] OJ no 4210 (Ont Sup Ct J) (QL) [*Johnston*].

105 *Johnston*.

106 *Hamilton* (Ont CA), para 109 (Factum for the Appellant).

107 Ibid, para 27.

108 The Crown argued that Justice Hill employed a mathematical formula for assessing the "purity adjusted weight" that was not consistent with Ontario Court of Appeal precedent in *R v Cunningham* and *R v Madden*. The "purity adjusted weight" has direct implications for sentencing guidelines as they are organized in the *Criminal Code*. See *Hamilton* (Ont CA), paras 109-16 (Factum for the Appellant, 12 January 2004). See also *R v Cunningham* (1996), 27 OR (3d) 786 (Ont CA); *R v Madden* (1996), 27 OR (3d) (Ont CA).

109 Lawrence and Williams, "'Swallowed Up,'" 305; *R v Smith*, [1987] 1 SCR 1045.

110 *Hamilton* (Ont CA), para 117 (Factum for the Appellant).

111 Ibid.

112 Ibid, para 137.

113 Julia Sudbury, "'Mules,' 'Yardies,' and Other Folk Devils," 175.

114 Susan C Boyd, *From Witches to Crack Moms: Women, Drug Law and Policy* (Durham, NC: Carolina Academic Press, 2004); Laura E Gomez, *Misconceiving Mothers: Legislators, Prosecutors and the Politics of Prenatal Drug Exposure* (Philadelphia, PA: Temple University Press, 1997).

115 *Hamilton* (Ont CA), para 138 (Factum for the Appellant).

116 *Baker v Canada (Minister of Citizenship and Immigration)*, [1999] 2 SCR 817 at para 2.

117 Lawrence and Williams, "'Swallowed Up,'" 299, n 49 [emphasis in original].

118 *Spencer*.

119 *Hamilton* (Ont CA), para 170 (Factum for the Appellant).

120 An organization is granted intervenor status at an appeal hearing when it is deemed by a judge (through a legal decision or motion) to have both a significant stake in

the proceedings (given the legal work of the organization) and "expert" knowledge relating to the specific legal questions at stake and the concomitant impact the issues may have on the particular communities that they represented.

121   *Hamilton* (Ont CA), para 10 (Factum of the Intervenor Native Women's Association of Canada (NWAC)).

122   Ibid, para22.

123   Ibid, para 9.

124   Ibid, para 11.

125   Ibid. *R v Proulx*, 2000 SCC 1, [2000] 1 SCR 61 [emphasis added].

126   *Hamilton* (Ont CA), para 20 (Factum of the Intervenor Native Women's Association of Canada (NWAC)).

127   Ibid.

128   Ibid, para 21.

129   Ibid, paras 19-33.

130   Importantly, the lawyer for the NWAC was the only person in Courtroom A of the Ontario Court of Appeal to stand before the panel and pronounce that what was at stake in the appeal hearing was how the sentencing process was going to deal with the ways in which "the legacy of colonialism is alive and well." From notes taken by the author at the appeal hearing.

131   *Hamilton* (Ont CA), para 7 (Factum of the Intervenor Aboriginal Legal Services of Toronto (ALST)).

132   *Gladue*, para 80 [emphasis in original].

133   *Hamilton* (Ont CA), para 12 (Factum of the Intervener ALST).

134   From *Hamilton* (Ont CA), para 15 (Factum of the Intervenor ALST). The commission on Systemic Racism in the Ontario Criminal Justice System was established in 1992 by the Ontario New Democratic Party to inquire into, and make recommendations about, the extent to which criminal justice practices, procedures, and policies in Ontario reflect systemic racism. The inquiry examined three major components of the criminal justice system: the police, courts, and correctional institutions. Government of Ontario, *Report of the Commission on Systemic Racism*.

135   *Hamilton* (Ont CA), para 33 (Factum of the Intervenor ALST).

136   Ibid, para 33.

137   Ibid, para 36.

138   Ibid, paras 39-55.

139   Ibid, para 2 (Factum of the Intervenors the African Canadian Legal Clinic (ACLC), the Congress of Black Women (Ontario Region) (CBW), and the Jamaican Canadian Association (JCA)).

140   The ACLC points to immigration policies in the early 1900s that barred "any immigrant belonging to the Negro race, which race is deemed unsuitable to the climate and requirements of Canada." Ibid, para 4.

141   Ibid, para 24.

142   Ibid, para 5.

143 Ibid, paras 20, 21.
144 Ibid, para 33.
145 Ibid, para 42.
146 Ibid, para 52.
147 Lawrence and Williams, "'Swallowed Up,'" 322.
148 *Spencer.*
149 Ibid, paras 30-32.
150 Ibid, para 47.
151 Patricia Hill Collins, *Black Feminist Thought: Knowledge, Consciousness and the Politics of Empowerment* (New York: Routledge, 1999), 277.
152 *Hamilton* (Ont CA), paras 54, 55 (Factum of the Intervenors ACLC, CBW, JCA).
153 *Immigration and Refugee Protection Act.*
154 *Hamilton* (Ont CA), para 59.
155 Ibid, para 2.
156 Ibid, para 1.
157 Ibid, para 3 [emphasis added].
158 Ibid, para 65.
159 Ibid, para 77.
160 Ibid.
161 Government of Ontario, *Report of the Commission on Systemic Racism*, 65, 69, 75. See also Angela Davis, "Incarceration and the Imbalance of Power," in *Invisible Punishment*, eds, M Mauer and M Chesney-Lind (New York: New Press, 2002), 61-78.
162 Sudbury, "'Mules,' 'Yardies,' and Other Folk Devils," 175; Government of Ontario, *Report of the Commission on Systemic Racism.*
163 I reproduce here the Ontario Court of Appeal's rationale for not imposing harsher sentences: "The ultimate question is, however, should these respondents be sent to jail now? They have served close to seventeen months of their conditional sentences. There is no suggestion that they have not complied with the terms of those sentences or that they have committed any further offences. This court has recognized both the need to give offenders credit for conditional sentences being served pending appeal and the added hardship occasioned by imposing sentences of imprisonment on appeal. The hardship is readily apparent in these cases. Had the respondents received the appropriate sentences at trial, they would have been released from custody on parole many months ago, and this sad episode in their lives would have been a bad memory by now. This was a significant appeal for the administration of justice. The decision of the trial judge raised important issues that required the attention of this court. Appeals take time. Lives go on. Things change. These human realities cannot be ignored when the Court of Appeal is called upon to impose sentences well after the event. The administration of justice would not be served by incarcerating the respondents for a few months at this time. *They have served significant, albeit, inadequate sentences.* To impose now, what would have been a fit sentence at trial, would work an undue hardship on the respondents. The

administration of justice is best served by allowing the respondents to complete their conditional sentences." *Hamilton* (Ont CA), paras 165, 166.

164   Kent Roach and Jonathan Rudin, "*Gladue:* The Judicial and Political Reception of a Promising Decision," *Canadian Journal of Criminology* 42, no 3 (2000): 355-88.

165   *Hamilton* (Ont CA), paras 3, 31 (Factum of the Intervenor ALST).

166   Ibid, para 99.

167   *Spencer* was heard with the *Hamilton* appeal.

168   *Hamilton* (Ont CA), para 99.

169   As noted in previous chapters, the Supreme Court of Canada held in *Gladue* that despite the fact that Gladue lived off the reserve, suggesting her potential distance from her "authentic" Aboriginal heritage, she was entitled to benefit from section 718.2(e) in order to fulfil Parliament's mandate to rectify the overincarceration of "all offenders, with particular attention to the circumstances of aboriginal offenders." *Gladue,* para 46.

170   *Hamilton* (Ont CA), para 2 (Factum of the Intervenors ACLC, CBW, JCA).

171   See *Gladue,* para 46; see also Patricia Hughes and Mary Jane Mossman, "Re-Thinking Access to Criminal Justice in Canada: A Critical Review of Needs and Responses," *Windsor Review of Legal and Social Issues* 13, no 1 (2002): 1-131.

172   *Hamilton* (Ont CA), para 100.

173   Ibid, para 104.

174   Lawrence and Williams further explain: The appeal court decision "describes cocaine importation as a crime that 'has always been considered among the most serious crimes known to Canadian law; cocaine is linked to 'social and economic harm ... throughout the Canadian community' ... These statements create the impression that cocaine importation has always been illegal in Canada and that it has always been harshly punished. Both claims are manifestly untrue, since cocaine was not subject to criminal prohibition until 1911 and the move to harsh penalties began only in the 1920's ... these statements, once they appear in cases, become truths that bind the legal system through the mechanism of precedent. Questioning whether the harms of cocaine have been exaggerated, exacerbated by criminalization, or even dramatized in order to target certain racial or ethnic groups becomes very difficult." Lawrence and Williams, "'Swallowed Up,'" 319-20.

175   See Renee Pelletier, "The Nullification of Section 718.2(e): Aggravating Aboriginal Over-Representation in Canadian Prisons," *Osgoode Hall Law Journal* 39 (2001): 469-89.

176   *Hamilton* (Ont CA), para 147.

177   Kenneth Nunn, "Race, Crime and the Pool of Surplus Criminality: Or Why the 'War on Drugs' Was a 'War on Blacks,'" *Journal of Gender Race and Justice* 6 (2002): 381.

178   Government of Ontario, *Report of the Commission on Systemic,* 69.

179   Boyd, *From Witches to Crack Moms.*

180   However, not all crimes with violent consequences are labelled serious and result in prison sentences. In the instance of corporate crimes, such as the violation of environmental or work place regulations that have resulted in the deaths of hundreds of people, a comparable logic has not followed. The direct, adverse, and often violent health effects of "white collar" crimes do not result in the more serious designation at sentencing. On the contrary, these crimes are distinguished as less serious or quasi-criminal. See Harry Glasbeek, *Wealth by Stealth: Corporate Crime, Corporate Law, and the Perversion of Democracy* (Toronto: Between the Lines, 2002).

Conclusion

1   House of Commons, "Bill C-10: An Act to Amend the Criminal Code (Minimum Penalties for Offences Involving Firearms) and to Make a Consequential Amendment to Another Act," Legislative Summary (22 February 2007), http://www.parl .gc.ca/About/Parliament/LegislativeSummaries/bills_ls.asp?lang=E&ls=c10&Parl =39&Ses=1&source=library_prb.

2   Alison Crawford, "Prison Watchdog Probes Spike in Number of Black Inmates," *CBC News*, 15 December 2011, http://www.cbc.ca/news/canada/story/2011/12/14 /crawford-black-prison.html.

3   *Criminal Code*, RSC 1985, c C-46.

4   Jonathan Rudin, "Addressing Aboriginal Overrepresentation Post-*Gladue:* A Realistic Assessment of How Social Change Occurs," *Criminal Justice Quarterly* 54 (2009): 447-69.

5   *R v Ipeelee*, [2009] 99 OR (3d) 419 [*Ipeelee*]; *R v Gladue*, [1999] 1 SCR 668 [*Gladue*].

6   *Gladue*, para 50. See also Lydia Guo, "R. v. Ipeelee: Correction, Conviction, and Culture," *The Court* (1 April 2012), http://www.thecourt.ca/2012/04/01/r-v-ipeelee -correction-conviction-and-culture/.

7   *Ipeelee*.

8   Ibid.

9   Ibid.

10   Ibid.

11   *R v Ipeelee*, 2001 NWTSC 33, [2001] NWTJ no 30 at paras 6, 11-21 (QL).

12   *Ipeelee*. The case was appealed to the Ontario Court of Appeal on the grounds that "(1) the sentence is demonstrably unfit; (2) the sentencing judge misapprehended the evidence relating to breaches that led to suspension of the appellant's release; (3) the appellant should have received enhanced credit for pre-sentence custody; and (4) the appellant's aboriginal status was not adequately considered."

13   Ibid, para 3.

14   Ibid.

15   Ibid, para 92.

16   Ibid, para 21

17   Ibid, para 27.

18 Ibid, para 61.
19 Erin Metzler, Duty Counsel, Legal Aid Ontario (presentation at the Third National Conference on Aboriginal Criminal Justice Post-*Gladue*, Toronto, 30 April 2011); *Gladue*, para 50.
20 *R v Abel*, 2008 BCSC 1731, [2008] BCJ no 2460 at para 28 (QL).
21 Examples of this trend can be found in the following cases: *R v Sisco*, 2008 ONCJ 12, 76 WCB (2d) 210, [2008] OJ no 157 (QL); *R v Casemore*, 2009 SKQB 306, 336 SaskR 110, [2009] SJ no 440 (QL); *R v Hunter*, 180 SaskR 47, [1999] SJ no 355 (QL); *R v McDougall*, 2009 MBQB 299, [2009] MJ no 400 (QL); *R v Fobister*, [2009] OJ no 2576 (QL); *R v Keenatch*, 2009 SKPC 72, [2009] SJ no 395 (QL); *R v Whiskeyjack*, 2008 ONCA 800, 93 OR (3d) 743. [2008] OJ no 4755 (QL); *R v Niganobe*, 72 MVR (5th) 280, [2008] OJ no 4181 (QL); *R v Plain*, 77 WCB (2d) 566, [2008] OJ no 2188 (QL); *R v Betsidea*, 2007 NWTSC 85, 75 WCB (2d) 462, [2007] NWTJ no 90 (QL). This list is not exhaustive.
22 These observations were made by Jonathan Rudin (Program Director, Aboriginal Legal Services), Judy L. Mungovan (Counsel, Aboriginal Justice Leadership Team, Criminal Law Division, Ministry of Attorney General [Ontario]), Erin Winocour (Assistant Crown Attorney, Criminal Law Policy Division, Ministry of Attorney General [Ontario] at the Second National Conference on Aboriginal Criminal Justice Post-*Gladue* (Toronto, Ontario, April, 24, 2010).
23 *Ipeelee*.
24 Ibid.
25 Adrian Humphreys, "Aboriginal Sentences Reduced over 'Shameful' Lack of Background Reports," *National Post*, 17 May 2012, http://news.nationalpost .com/2012/05/17/aboriginal-sentences-reduced-over-shameful-lack-of-background -reports/; Kirk Makin, "Judges Must Weigh Cultural Factors in Native Sentencing, Court Rules," *Globe and Mail*, 23 March 2012, http://www.theglobeandmail.com /news/national/judges-must-weigh-cultural-factors-in-native-sentencing-court -rules/article535585/.
26 For examples, see *R v Cardinal*, 2009 ABPC 296, CELR (3d) 146, [2009] AJ no 1083 at para 2746 (QL); *R v Ray*, 79 WCB (2d) 556, [2008] OJ no 4185 at para 30 (QL) [*Ray*]; *R v Meawasige*, 2008 ONCJ 122, 77 WCB (2d) 207, [2008] OJ no 1085 at para 27 (QL); *Craigan*; *R v Gelenzoski*, [2006] AJ no 1009 at para 14 (QL); *Nickerson*; *R v FL*, [2002] OTC 347, [2002] OJ no 1989 at para 17 (QL) [*FL*]; *R v Auger*, 2000 ABQB 450, [2000] 10 WWR 329, [2000] AJ no 784 at para 62 (QL) [*Auger*]; *R v Caissey*, 2008 ONCJ 716, [2008] OJ no 5472 at para 2 (QL) [*Caissey*].
27 *Craigan*.
28 *FL*.
29 *Ray*.
30 *Auger*.
31 *Caissey*.

32 *R v Smith*, 2008 ONCJ 628, [2008] OJ no 4867 at para 53 (QL). See also *R v Bachmier*, 2005 ONCJ 36, 63 WCB (2d) 606, [2005] OJ no 496 at para 21 (QL).

33 *R v Collins*, 2001 ONCA 182, [2011] OJ no 978 at para 32 (QL). See also Erin Metzler (Duty Counsel, Legal Aid Ontario), "*Gladue* before the Courts (2010-2011)" (paper presented at the Third National Conference on Aboriginal Criminal Justice Post-*Gladue*, Toronto, 30 April 2011).

34 *Julian*; *R v Yee*, 2006 SKPC 31, 278 SaskR 75, [2006] SJ no 226 at para 14 (QL); *R v Kootoo*, [2000] NuJ no 10 at para 26 (QL).

35 *Caissey*.

36 Examples of this trend can be found in the following cases: *R v Natomagan*, 2010 SKPC 7, [2010] SJ no 45 (QL); *R v Zarpa*, 2009 NLTD 175, [2009] NJ no 309 (QL); *R v Jacobish*, 2008 NLTD 149, 279 Nfld & PEIR 45, [2008] NJ no 254 (QL); *R v Jacobish*, 2008 NLTD 148, 279 Nfld & PEIR 331, [2008] NJ no 255 (QL); *R v Maracle*, 2008 ONCJ 711, [2008] OJ no 5500 (QL); *R v Phillips*, 2005 ONCJ 498, 68 WCB (2d) 472, [2005] OJ no 5852 (QL); *R v Keeash*, [2003] OJ no 3413 (QL); *R v Kejick*, [2001] OJ no 5077 (QL); *R v Rowell*, 2001 BCCA 512, 158 BCAC 184, [2001] BCJ no 1837 (QL); *R v T.K.*, [2001] OJ no 5070 (QL). This list is not exhaustive.

37 Examples of this trend can be found in the following cases: *R v Green*, 2010 ONCJ 84, [2010] OJ no 1069 (QL); *R v Guimond*, 2010 MBQB 1, [2010] MJ no 19 (QL); *R v Stevens*, 2009 NSPC 46, 282 NSR (2d) 314, [2009] NSJ no 449 (QL); *R v Constant*, 2009 SKPC 80, [2009] SJ no 358 (QL); *R v Quash*, 2009 YKTC 54, [2009] YJ no 72 (QL); *R v Gregoire*, 2009 NLTD 21, 284 Nfld & PEIR 290, [2009] NJ no 37 (QL); *R v Morning Bird*, 2008 ABCA 419, 440 AR 396, [2008] AJ no 1373 (QL); *R v Silversmith*, 77 MVR (5th) 54, [2008] OJ no 4646 (QL); *R v Wilson*, 2008 ABQB 588, 79 WCB (2d) 765, [2008] AJ no 1086 (QL); *R v Brooks*, 2008 NSPC 58, [2008] NSJ no 519 (QL). This list is not exhaustive.

38 Michel Foucault, *Discipline and Punish: The Birth of the Prison* (New York: Vintage Books, 1977), 21.

39 Michel Foucualt, *Ethics, Subjectivity, Truth*, edited by Paul Rabinow (New York: New Press, 1994), 73.

40 Paige Raibmon, *Authentic Indians: Episodes of Encounter from the Late Nineteenth-Century Northwest Coast* (Durham, NC: Duke University Press, 2005), 206.

41 Ibid, 207.

42 Elazar Barkan, *The Guilt of Nations: Restitution and Negotiating Historical Injustices* (Baltimore, MD: Johns Hopkins University Press, 2000), xxviii.

43 Elizabeth A Povinelli, *The Cunning of Recognition: Indigenous Alterities and the Making of Australian Multiculturalism* (Durham, NC; Duke University Press, 2002), 38.

44 Povinelli, *Cunning of Recognition*, 39 [emphasis in original].

45 Hannah Arendt, *Responsibility and Judgement*, edited by Jerome Kohn (New York: Schocken Books, 2003), 14.

46 Michel-Rolph Trouillot, "Abortive Rituals: Historical Apologies in the Global Era," *Interventions* 2, no 2 (2000): 174.

47   Ibid.
48   Farid Abdel-Nour, "National Responsibility," *Political Theory* 31, no 5 (2003): 703 [emphasis in original].
49   Honorable Allan Rock (Minister of Justice and the Attorney General of Canada) moved for leave to introduce Bill C-41, *An Act to Amend the Criminal Code (Sentencing) and Other Acts as a Consequence Thereof. House of Commons Debates* 35th Parliament, 1st Session, No 84 (13 June 1994) at 1155 (Hon Allan Rock).
50   Abdel-Nour, "National Responsibility," 713.

Bibliography

Abdel-Nour, Farid. "National Responsibility." *Political Theory* 31, no 5 (2003): 693-719.

Aboriginal Justice Implementation Commission. "Report of the Aboriginal Justice Inquiry of Manitoba," November 1999, http://www.ajic.mb.ca/volume.html.

"Aboriginal Justice Initiatives." Manitoba Department of Justice, http://www.gov.mb.ca/justice/aboriginal/index.html.

"Aboriginal Justice Program." Mi'kmaq Confederacy of Prince Edward Island, http://www.mcpei.ca/node/18.

"Aboriginal Justice Programs and Services." Justice BC, http://www.justicebc.ca/en/cjis/understanding/aboriginal/programs.html.

"Aboriginal Justice Strategy." Department of Justice Canada, http://www.justice.gc.ca/eng/pi/ajs-sja/index.html.

"Aboriginal Justice Strategy." Ontario Ministry of the Attorney General, http://www.attorneygeneral.jus.gov.on.ca/english/aboriginal_justice_strategy/default.asp.

"Aboriginal Law Group." Department of Justice, Government of Yukon, http://www.justice.gov.yk.ca/prog/ls/.

"Aboriginal Legal Services of Toronto." Aboriginal Legal Services of Toronto, http://www.aboriginallegal.ca/.

Aboriginal Peoples and the Justice System: Report from the National Round Table on Aboriginal Justice Issues. Ottawa: Minister of Supplies and Services, 1993.

Acorn, Annalise. *Compulsory Compassion: A Critique of Restorative Justice.* Vancouver: UBC Press, 2004.

Adams, Michael, and Amy Langstaff. *Unlikely Utopia: The Surprising Triumph of Canadian Pluralism.* Toronto: Viking Press, 2007.

Adjin-Tettey, Elizabeth. "Sentencing Aboriginal Offenders: Balancing Offenders' Needs, the Interests of Victims and Society and the Decolonization of Aboriginal Peoples." *Canadian Journal of Women and the Law* 19, no 1 (2007): 179-216.

Ahmed, Sara. "Affective Economies." *Social Text* 22, no 2 (2004): 117-39.

Alfred, Taiaiake. "Sovereignty." In Philip J. Deloria and Neal Salisbury, eds, *A Companion to American Indian History*, 460-74. New York: Blackwell Publishers, 2004.

Amadiume, Ifi, and Abdullahi An-Na'im. *The Politics of Memory: Truth, Healing and Social Justice*. New York: Zed Books, 2000.

Anderson, Chris. "Governing Aboriginal Justice in Canada: Constructing Responsible Individuals and Communities through 'Tradition.'" *Crime, Law and Social Change* 31 (1999): 303-26.

Anderson, Kay. "Thinking 'Postnationally:' Dialogue across Multicultural, Indigenous and Settler Spaces." *Annals of the Association of American Geographers* 90, no 2 (2000): 381-91.

–. *Vancouver's Chinatown: Racial Discourse in Canada 1875-1980*. Montreal and Kingston: McGill-Queen's University Press, 1991.

"Apology to Interned Italian-Canadians Questioned." *CBC News*, 6 May 2010, http://www.cbc.ca/canada/ottawa/story/2010/05/06/internment-ww2-italian-candians-apology.html.

Appiah, Kwame Anthony. "Race." In Frank Lentricchia and Tom McLaughlin, eds, *Critical Terms for Literary Study*, 275-87. Chicago: University of Chicago Press, 1990.

Arendt, Hannah. *Responsibility and Judgment*. Edited by Jerome Kohn. New York: Schocken Books, 2003.

Asad, Talal. "Ethnographic Representation, Statistics and Modern Power." *Social Research* 61, no 1 (1994): 55-88.

Auty, Kate. "Koori Court Victoria: Magistrates Court (Koori Court) Act 2002." Paper presented at the Law and Society Conference, Chicago, 27-30 May 2004.

Backhouse, Constance. *Colour-Coded: A Legal History of Racism in Canada, 1900-1950*. Toronto: University of Toronto Press, 1999.

Bannerji, Himani. *The Dark Side of the Nation: Essays on Multiculturalism, Nationalism and Gender*. Toronto: Canadian Scholars Press, 2000.

Barkan, Elazar. *The Guilt of Nations: Restitution and Negotiating Historical Injustices*. New York: Norton, 2000.

Barkan, Elazar, and Alexander Karn. *Taking Wrongs Seriously: Apologies and Reconciliation*. Stanford, CA: Stanford University Press, 2006.

Bergson, Henri. *Matter and Memory*. Translated by NM Paul and WS Palmer. New York: Zone Books, 1988.

Berlant, Lauren. *The Anatomy of National Fantasy: Hawthorne, Utopia and Everyday Life*. Chicago: University of Chicago Press, 1991.

Best, Stephen, and Saidiya Hartman. "Fugitive Justice." *Representations* 92 (2005): 1-15.

Bhabha, Homi K. "'Race' Time and the Revision of Modernity." In Les Back and Jon Solomos, ed, *Theories of Race and Racism: A Reader*, 354-72. London: Routledge, 2000.

–. *The Location of Culture*. London: Routledge, 1994.

Biolsi, Thomas. *Deadliest Enemies: Law and Race Relations on and off Rosebud Reservation*. Minneapolis, MN: University of Minnesota Press, 2007.

Borrows, John. *Recovering Canada: The Resurgence of Indigenous Law*. Toronto: University of Toronto Press, 2002.

Boyd, Susan C. *From Witches to Crack Moms: Women, Drug Law and Policy*. Durham, NC: Carolina Academic Press, 2004.

Brah, Avtar. *Cartographies of Diaspora*. London: Routledge, 1995.

Braithwaite, John. "Restorative Justice: Assessing Optimistic and Pessimistic Accounts." In M Tonry, ed, *Crime and Justice: A Review of Research*, 1-127. Chicago: University of Chicago Press, 1999.

Brooks, Roy L. *When Sorry Isn't Enough: The Controversy over Apologies and Reparations for Human Injustice*. New York: New York University Press, 1999.

Brown, Wendy. *States of Injury: Power and Freedom in Late Modernity*. Princeton, NJ: Princeton University Press, 1995.

–. "Suffering Rights as Paradoxes." *Constellations* 7, no 2 (2000): 230-41.

Bushie, Berma. "Community Holistic Circle Healing." *International Institute for Restorative Practices*, 1999, http://www.iirp.edu/article_detail.php?article_id=NDc0.

Cairns, Alan. "Coming to Terms with the Past." In John Torpey, ed, *Politics and the Past: On Repairing Historical Injustice*, 63-90. New York: Rowman and Littlefield, 2003.

–. "The Canadian Constitutional Experiment." *Dalhousie Law Journal* 9 (1984-85): 87-114.

Cameron, Angela. "*R. v. Gladue:* Sentencing and Gendered Implications of Colonialism." In John D Whyte, *Moving towards Justice: Legal Traditions and Aboriginal Justice*, 160-80. Saskatoon, SK: Purich Press, 2008.

–. "Stopping the Violence: Canadian Feminist Debates on Restorative Justice and Intimate Violence." *Theoretical Criminology* 10, no 1 (2006): 49-66.

Canada. *House of Commons Debates*, 35th Parliament, 1st Session, No 84, 13 June 1994, 084.

–. *House of Commons Debates*, 41st Parliament, 1st Session, No 62, 16 October 2006, 062.

"Canada's Expression of Sorrow." Editorial. *Globe and Mail*, 12 June 2008, A16.

Chan, Wendy, and Kiran Mirchandani, eds. *Crimes of Colour: Racialization and the Criminal Justice System in Canada*. Peterborough, ON: Broadview Press, 2002.

Clairmont, Don, and Jane McMillan. "Directions in Mi'kmaq Justice: An Evaluation of the Mi'kmaq Justice Institute and Its Aftermath," 2001, http://www.gov.ns.ca/just/publications/docs/tfexesum.pdf.

Cohen, Stanley. "State Crimes of Previous Regimes: Knowledge, Accountability, and the Policing of the Past." *Law and Social Inquiry* 20 (1995): 7-50.

Collins, Patricia Hill. *Black Feminist Thought: Knowledge, Consciousness and the Politics of Empowerment.* New York: Routledge, 1999.

Comack, Elizabeth, and Gillian Balfour. "Racializing Violent Crime." In Elizabeth Comack and Gillian Balfour, eds, *The Power to Criminalize: Violence, Inequality and the Law*, 78-109. Black Point, NS: Fernwood Publishing, 2004.

Comaroff, Jean, and John L Comaroff. "Introduction." In Jean Comaroff and John L Comaroff, eds, *Law and Disorder in the Postcolony*, 1-56. Chicago: University of Chicago Press, 2006.

"Community Dumps Sewage into Arctic Fjord after Flood." *Globe and Mail*, 12 June 2008, A7.

"Community Justice." Northwest Territories – Department of Justice, February 2011, http://www.justice.gov.nt.ca/CommunityJustice/CommunityJustice.shtml.

Cooper, Afua. *The Hanging of Angelique: The Untold Story of Canadian Slavery and the Burning of Old Montreal.* Toronto: Harper Collins, 2006.

Cooper, Frederick, and Ann Laura Stoler. "Between Metropole and Colony: Rethinking a Research Agenda." In Frederick Cooper and Ann Laura Stoler, eds, *Tensions of Empire: Colonial Cultures in a Bourgeois World*, 1-58. Berkeley, CA: University of California Press, 1997.

–, eds. *Tensions of Empire: Colonial Cultures in a Bourgeois World.* Berkeley, CA: University of California Press, 1997.

Council for Aboriginal Reconciliation. "Final Report of the Royal Commission into Aboriginal Deaths in Custody," 1998, Indigenous Law Resources, http://www.austlii.edu.au/au/other/IndigLRes/rciadic/.

Cowlishaw, Gillian. *Blackfellas, Whitefellas and the Hidden Injuries of Race.* Oxford: Blackwell Publishers, 2004.

–. "Disappointing Indigenous People: Violence and the Refusal to Help." *Public Culture* 15, no 1 (2003): 103-25.

Crawford, Alison. "Prison Watchdog Probes Spike in Number of Black Inmates." *CBC News*, 15 December 2011, http://www.cbc.ca/news/canada/story/2011/12/14/crawford-black-prison.html.

Cunliffe, Emma, and Angela Cameron. "Writing the Circle: Judicially Convened Sentencing Circles and the Textual Organization of Criminal Justice." *Canadian Journal of Women and the Law* 19, no 1 (2007): 1-35.

Daubney, David. *Taking Responsibility: Report of the Standing Committee on Justice and Solicitor General on Its Review of Sentencing, Conditional Release and Related Aspects of Corrections.* Ottawa: Canadian Government Publishing Centre, 1988.

Daubney, David, and Gordon Perry. "An Overview of Bill C-41." In Julian V Roberts and David P Cole, eds, *Making Sense of Sentencing*, 31-47. Toronto: University of Toronto Press, 1999.

Davis, Angela. *Are Prisons Obsolete?* New York: Seven Stories Press, 2003.

–. "Incarceration and the Imbalance of Power." In M Mauer and M Chesney-Lind, eds, *Invisible Punishment*, 61-78. New York: New Press, 2002.

Fiske, Jo-Anne, and Betty Patrick. *Cis Dideen Kat, When the Plumes Rise: The Way of the Lake Babine Nation.* Vancouver: UBC Press, 2000.

Forti, Simona. "The Biopolitics of Souls: Racism, Nazism, and Plato." *Political Theory* 34, no 9 (2006): 9-32.

Foucault, Michel. *Discipline and Punish: The Birth of the Prison.* New York: Vintage Books, 1977.

–. *The History of Sexuality: An Introduction*, volume 1. New York: Vintage, 1978.

–. *Ethics, Subjectivity, Truth.* Edited by Paul Rabinow. New York: New Press, 1994.

–. *The History of Sexuality*, volume 1. New York: Vintage Books, 1990.

–. *"Society Must Be Defended": Lectures at the College de France 1975–1976.* Edited by Mauro Bertani et al. New York: Picador, 1997.

Furniss, Elizabeth. *The Burden of History: Colonialism and the Frontier Myth in a Rural Canadian Community.* Vancouver: UBC Press, 1999.

Gibney, Mark, Rhoda E Howard-Hassmann, Jean-Marc Coicaud, and Niklaus Steiner, eds. *The Age of Apology.* Philadelphia, PA: University of Philadelphia Press, 2008.

Gilroy, Paul. *Against Race: Imagining Political Culture beyond the Color Line.* Cambridge, MA: Harvard University Press, 2000.

"Gladue (Aboriginal Persons) Court." Aboriginal Legal Services of Toronto, http://www.aboriginallegal.ca/gladue.php.

"Gladue (Aboriginal Persons) Court Ontario Court of Justice – Old City Hall Fact Sheet," 3 October 2001, http://www.aboriginallegal.ca/docs/apc_factsheet.htm.

Glasbeek, Harry. *Wealth by Stealth: Corporate Crime, Corporate Law, and the Perversion of Democracy.* Toronto: Between the Lines, 2002.

Goldberg, David. *Racist Culture.* Cambridge, MA: Blackwell Publishers, 1993.

–. *The Racial State.* Oxford: Blackwell Publishers, 2002.

–. *The Threat of Race: Reflections on Racial Neoliberalism.* Oxford: Blackwell Publishers, 2008.

Goldberg, Susan. *Judging for the Twenty-First Century: A Problem Solving Approach.* Unpublished manuscript, on file with the National Judicial Institute, 2004.

Gomez, Laura E. *Misconceiving Mothers: Legislators, Prosecutors and the Politics of Prenatal Drug Exposure.* Philadelphia, PA: Temple University Press, 1997.

Gordon, Colin. "Governmental Rationality: An Introduction." In Graham Burchell, Colin Gordon, and Peter Miller, eds, *The Foucault Effect: Studies in Governmentality*, 1-52. Chicago, IL: University of Chicago Press, 1991.

Government of Alberta. "Aboriginal Justice," 2011, Alberta Justice and Solicitor General, http://justice.alberta.ca/programs_services/aboriginal/Pages/default.aspx.

Government of Nunavut. "Department of Justice," 2011, http://www.justice.gov.nu.ca/apps/authoring/dspPage.aspx?page=home.

Government of Ontario. *Report of the Commission on Systemic Racism in the Ontario Criminal Justice System.* Toronto: Queen's Printer, 1995.

Government of Saskatchewan. "Aboriginal Courtworker Program," 2007, http://www.justice.govsk.ca/aboriginalcourtworkerprogram.

–. "Aboriginal Resource Officer Program," 2007, http://www.justice.gov.sk.ca/Default.aspx?DN=8003d87c-449d-44c6-9fd1-3f59a442316f.

Govier, Trudy, and Wilhelm Verwoerd. "Trust and the Problem of National Reconciliation." *Philosophy of the Social Sciences* 32 (2002): 178-205.

Green, Joyce. "From Stonechild to Social Cohesion: Anti-Racist Challenges for Saskatchewan." Paper presented to the Canadian Political Science Association, London, ON, 2-4 June 2005, http://www.cpsa-acsp.ca/papers-2005/Greene.pdf.

Green, Ross. *Justice in Aboriginal Communities: Sentencing Alternatives*. Saskatoon, SK: Purich Publishing, 1998.

–. "Treat *Gladue* as a Call to Action." *Lawyers Weekly* 42 (2000): 12.

Guo, Lydia. "*R. v. Ipeelee*: Correction, Conviction, and Culture." *The Court*, 1 April 2012, http://www.thecourt.ca/2012/04/01/r-v-ipeelee-correction-conviction-and-culture/.

Hall, Stuart. "Gramsci's Relevance to the Study of Race and Ethnicity." In D Morley and H Chen, eds, *Stuart Hall: Critical Dialogues in Cultural Studies*, 411-40. London: Routledge, 1996.

"Harper Apologizes in B.C. for 1914 *Komagata Maru* Incident." *CBC News*, 3 August 2008, http://www.cbc.ca/news/canada/british-columbia/story/2008/08/03/harper-apology.html.

Harris, Mark. "From Australian Courts to Aboriginal Courts in Australia: Bridging the Gap?" *Current Issues in Criminal Justice* 16 (2004): 26-41.

Haslip, Susan. "Aboriginal Sentencing Reform in Canada – Prospects for Success: Standing Tall with Both Feet Planted Firmly in the Air." *Murdoch University Electronic Journal of Law* 7, no 1 (2000), http://www.murdoch.edu.au/elaw/issues/v7n1/haslip71nf.html.

Hayner, Priscilla B. *Unspeakable Truths: Facing the Challenges of Truth Commissions*. London: Routledge, 2002.

"Health Canada Apologizes for Body Bags." *CBC News*, 17 September 2009, http://www.cbc.ca/news/canada/manitoba/story/2009/09/17/mb-body-bags-butler-jones-manitoba.html.

Henry, Frances. "Review of the Report of the Commission on Systemic Racism in the Ontario Criminal Justice System." *Windsor Yearbook of Access to Justice* 15 (1996): 230-35.

Her Majesty the Queen v. Marsha Alisjie Hamilton and Donna Rosemarie Mason. Proceeding transcripts from Ontario Superior Court of Justice, volume 1.

Hesse, Barnor. "Racialized Modernity: An Analytics of White Mythologies." *Racial Studies* 30, no 4 (2007): 643-63.

"Highlights from the Report of the Royal Commission on Aboriginal Peoples." Indian and Northern Affairs Canada, 15 September 2010, http://www.aadnc-aandc.gc.ca/eng/1100100014597.

House of Commons. "Bill C-10: An Act to Amend the Criminal Code (Minimum Penalties for Offences Involving Firearms) and to Make a Consequential Amendment to Another Act." Legislative Summary (10 May 2006), http://www.parl.gc.ca/About/Parliament/LegislativeSummaries/bills_ls.asp?ls=c10&source=library_prb&Parl=39&Ses=1&Language=E.

–. Standing Committee on Justice and Legal Affairs. "Respecting Bill C-41: An Act to Amend the Criminal Code (Sentencing) and Other Acts in Consequence Thereof." In *Minutes of Proceedings*, No 62 (17 November 1994).

–. Standing Committee on Justice and Legal Affairs. "Respecting Bill C-41: An Act to Amend the Criminal Code (Sentencing) and Other Acts in Consequence Thereof." In *Minutes of Proceedings*, No 75 (7 February 1995).

–. Standing Committee on Justice and Legal Affairs. "Respecting Bill C-41: An Act to Amend the Criminal Code (Sentencing) and Other Acts in Consequence Thereof." In *Minutes of Proceedings*, No 79 (14 February 1995).

–. Standing Committee on Justice and Legal Affairs. "Respecting Bill C-41: An Act to Amend the Criminal Code (Sentencing) and Other Acts in Consequence Thereof." In *Minutes of Proceedings*, No 85 (28 February 1995).

Hughes, Patricia, and Mary Jane Mossman. "Re-Thinking Access to Criminal Justice in Canada: A Critical Review of Needs and Responses." *Windsor Review of Legal and Social Issues* 13, no 1 (2002): 1-131.

Humphreys, Adrian. "Aboriginal Sentences Reduced over 'Shameful' Lack of Background Reports." *National Post*, 17 May 2012, http://news.nationalpost.com/2012/05/17/aboriginal-sentences-reduced-over-shameful-lack-of-background-reports/.

Hussain, Nasser. "Towards a Jurisprudence of Emergency." *Law and Critique* 10, no 3 (1999): 93-115.

The Implications of Restorative Justice for Aboriginal Women and Children Survivors of Violence: A Comparative Overview of Five Communities in British Columbia. Vancouver: Aboriginal Women's Action Network, 2001.

"Innu-Aimun Legal Terms (Criminal Law) Kaueshinitunanit Aimuna Mushuau Dialect." Newfoundland and Labrador Department of Justice, 2007, http://www.justice.gov.nl.ca/just/publications/legal_mus_crim.pdf.

"Inuit Get Federal Apology for Relocation." *CBC News*, 18 August 2010, http://www.cbc.ca/news/canada/north/story/2010/08/18/apology-inuit-relocation.html.

"Ipperwash Report Released." *Maclean's*, 31 May 2007, http://www.macleans.ca/canada/national/article.jsp?content=20070531_165856_1396.

Ivison, Duncan. "The Technical and the Political: Discourse of Race, Reasons of State." *Social and Legal Studies* 7, no 4 (1998): 561-66.

Jackson, Michael. "Locking Up Natives in Canada." *UBC Law Review* 23 (1989): 215-300.

James, Matt. "Recognition, Redistribution and Redress: The Case of the 'Chinese Head Tax,'" *Canadian Journal of Political Science* 37, no 4 (2004): 883-902.

Jamie T. Gladue v. Queen, Transcripts from the Supreme Court Proceedings (VHS recording), 10 December 1998.

"Justice for and by the Aboriginals." Justice Quebec, 2003, http://www.justice.gouvqc.ca/english/publications/rapports/coutu-f-a.htm.

"Justice Is Blind, Not Colour Blind." Editorial. *Toronto Star*, 24 February 2003, A22.

Keck, Jennifer. "Remembering Kimberly Rogers." Canadian Council of Social Development. *Perception* 25, no 3/4 (2002), http://www.ccsd.ca/perception/2534/kimberly.htm.

Kelm, Mary-Ellen. *Colonizing Bodies: Aboriginal Health and Healing in British Columbia 1900-50*. Vancouver: UBC Press, 1998.

Klein, Alana. "*Gladue* in Quebec." *Criminal Law Quarterly* 54 (2009): 506-28.

Kymlicka, Will. *Multicultural Citizenship: A Liberal Theory of Minority Rights*. Oxford: Oxford University Press, 1995.

–. *Multicultural Odysseys: Navigating the New International Politics of Diversity*. Oxford: Oxford University Press, 2007.

Kymlicka, Will, and Bashir Bashir. *The Politics of Reconciliation in Multicultural Societies*. Oxford: Oxford University Press, 2008.

LaPrairie, Carol. "Community Types, Crime and Police Services on Canadian Indian Reserves." *Journal of Research in Crime and Delinquency* 25, no 4 (1988): 375-91.

–. "The Role of Sentencing in the Over-Representation of Aboriginal People in Correctional Institutions." *Canadian Journal of Criminology* 32 (1990): 429-40.

LaPrairie, Carol, and Jane Dickson-Gilmore. *Will the Circle Be Unbroken?: Aboriginal Communities, Restorative Justice and the Challenge of Conflict and Change*. Toronto: University of Toronto Press, 2005.

LaRocque, Emma. *Defeathering the Indian*. Agincourt, ON: Book Society of Canada, 1975.

–. "Re-examining Culturally Appropriate Models in Criminal Justice Applications." In M Asch, ed, *Aboriginal and Treaty Rights in Canada: Essays on Law, Equity, and Respect for Difference*, 75–96. Vancouver: UBC Press, 1997.

Laselva, Samuel V. *Foundations of Canadian Federalism: Paradoxes, Achievements and Tragedies of Nationhood*. Montreal and Kingston: McGill-Queen's University Press, 1996.

Lash, Jean. "Case Comment: *R. v. Gladue*." *Canadian Woman Studies* 20, no 3 (2000): 85-91.

Law Commission of Canada. *Transforming Relationships through Participatory Justice*. Toronto: Law Commission of Canada, 2003.

Lawrence, Sonia, and Toni Williams. "'Swallowed Up:' Drug Couriers at the Borders of Canadian Sentencing." *University of Toronto Law Journal* 56, no 4 (2006): 285-332.

Lerman, David. "Restoring Justice." *Tikkun: A Bimonthly Jewish and Interfaith Critique of Politics, Culture and Society* (September/October 1999), http://www.tikkun.org/article.php/sep1999_lerman.

Lewis, Gail. *"Race," Gender, Social Welfare: Encounters in a Postcolonial Society.* Cambridge: Polity Press, 2000.

"Life after Auschwitz." *CBC Archives,* July 2009, http://www.cbc.ca/archives /categories/war-conflict/second-world-war/life-after-auschwitz/topic-life-after -auschwitz.html.

Llewellyn, Jennifer J. "Restorative Justice in *Borde* and *Hamilton:* A Systemic Problem?" *Criminal Reports* 8 (2003): 308-16.

"Location of Aboriginal Justice Strategy Programs in Canada: Saskatchewan." Department of Justice Canada, 1 December 2011, http://www.justice.gc.ca/eng /pi/ajs-sja/map3-carte3/sask.html.

"A Long-Awaited Apology." *CBC Archives,* 11 June 2008, http://rc-archives.cbc.ca /programs/2345-15394/page/1/.

Luciuk, Lubomyr, ed. "Righting an Injustice: The Debate over Redress for Canada's First National Internment Operations," 1994, http://www.infoukes.com/history /internment/booklet02/.

Makin, Kirk. "Judges Must Weigh Cultural Factors in Native Sentencing, Court Rules." *Globe and Mail,* 23 March 2012, http://www.theglobeandmail.com/news /national/judges-must-weigh-cultural-factors-in-native-sentencing-court-rules /article535585/.

Manson, Allan, Patrick Healy, and Gary Trotter. *Sentencing and Penal Policy in Canada: Cases, Materials and Commentary.* Toronto: Emond Montgomery, 2000.

Marchetti, Elena, and Kathleen Daly. "Indigenous Courts and Justice Practices in Australia." Australian Institute of Criminology. National Library of Australia, May 2004, http://catalogue.nla.gov.au/Record/3311379.

Mawani, Renisa. "'Cleansing the Conscience of the People': Reading Head Tax Redress in Multicultural Canada." *Canadian Journal of Law and Society* 19, no 2 (2004): 127-51.

–. *Colonial Proximities: Crossracial Encounters and Juridical Truths in British Columbia, 1871-1921.* Vancouver: UBC Press, 2009.

–. "Genealogies of the Land: Aboriginality, Law, and Territory in Vancouver's Stanley Park." *Social and Legal Studies* 14, no 3 (2005): 315-39.

Mbembe, Achille. "Necropolitics." *Public Culture* 15, no 1 (2003): 11-40.

–. *On the Postcolony.* Berkeley, CA: University of California Press, 2001.

McAllister, Kirsten Emiko. *Terrain of Memory: A Japanese Canadian Memorial Project.* Vancouver: UBC Press, 2010.

McClintock, Anne. *Imperial Leather: Race, Gender and Sexuality in the Colonial Contest.* London: Routledge, 1995.

McClure, Kirstie M. "Difference, Diversity, and the Limit of Toleration." *Political Theory* 18, no 3 (1990): 361-91.

McGillivray, Anne, and Brenda Comasky. *Black Eyes All of the Time.* Toronto: University of Toronto Press, 1999.

Metzler, Erin. Duty Counsel, Legal Aid Ontario. Presentation to the Third National Conference on Aboriginal Criminal Justice Post-*Gladue*, Toronto, 30 April 2011.

Miller, Bruce G. *The Problem of Justice: Tradition and Law in the Coast Salish World.* Lincoln, NE: University of Nebraska Press, 2000.

Miller, David. *National Responsibility and Global Justice.* Oxford: Oxford University Press, 2007.

Minow, Martha. *Between Vengeance and Forgiveness: Facing History after Genocide and Mass Violence.* Boston, MA: Beacon Press, 1998.

Miyagawa, Mitch. "A Sorry State." *The Walrus* (December 2009): 22-30.

Monture-Okanee, Patricia A. Interview. *CBC National News*, 16 October 2006.

–. "Justice as Healing: Thinking about Change." Native Law Centre, 1995, http://www.usask.ca/nativelaw/publications/jah/1995/JAH_Thinking_Change.pdf.

Monture, Patricia. *Thunder in My Soul: A Mohawk Woman Speaks.* Halifax, NS: Fernwood Publishing, 1995.

Moran, Mayo, and David Dzyenhaus, eds. *Calling Power to Account: Law, Reparations and the Chinese Canadian Head Tax Case.* Toronto: University of Toronto Press, 2005.

Morse, Bradford, and John Gokas. "Do the Métis Fall within Section 91(24) of the Constitution Act of 1867?" Ottawa: Royal Commission on Aboriginal Peoples, 1993.

Moss, Wendy. "The Canadian State and Indian Women: The Struggle for Sex Equality under the Indian Act." In Caroline Andrews and Sandra Rodgers, eds, *Women and the Canadian State*, 79-88. Montreal and Kingston: McGill-Queens University Press, 1997.

Murdocca, Carmela. "National Responsibility and Systemic Racism in Criminal Sentencing: The Case of *R. v. Hamilton*." In Law Commission of Canada, ed, *The "Place" of Justice*, 67-94. Black Point, NS: Fernwood Publishing, 2006.

Napoleon, Val. "*Delgamuukw*: A Legal Straightjacket for Oral Histories?" *Canadian Journal of Law and Society* 20, no 2 (2005): 123-55.

Narayan, Uma. *Dislocating Cultures: Identities, Tradition and Third World Feminism.* London: Routledge, 1997.

Native Counselling Services of Alberta. *A Cost-Benefit Analysis of Hollow Water's Community Holistic Circle Healing.* Public Safety Canada, 2001, http://www.publicsafety.gc.ca/res/cor/apc/apc-20-eng.aspx.

"Native Para-Judicial Services of Quebec," 2006, http://www.spaq.qc.ca/.

Nelson, Jennifer. *Razing Africville: A Geography of Racism.* Toronto: University of Toronto Press, 2008.

Neugebauer, Robynne, ed. *Criminal Injustice: Racism in the Criminal Justice System.* Toronto: Canadian Scholars Press, 2000.

Newfoundland and Labrador Legal Aid Commission, "Annual Report 2009–10." Newfoundland and Labrador Department of Justice, 2010, http://www.legalaid.nl.ca/publications.html.

Niezen, Ronald. *The Rediscovered Self: Indigenous Identity and Cultural Justice.* Montreal and Kingston: McGill-Queen's University Press, 2009.

Nobles, Melissa. *The Politics of Official Apologies.* New York: Cambridge University Press, 2008.

"No Charges in Alleged Alberta Homeless Roundup." *Globe and Mail,* 12 June 2008, A7.

Nunn, Kenneth. "Race, Crime and the Pool of Surplus Criminality: Or Why the 'War on Drugs' Was a 'War on Blacks.'" *Journal of Gender Race and Justice* 6, no 381 (2002): 381-445.

Office of the Correctional Investigator. "Backgrounder: Aboriginal Inmates," 10 February 2010, http://www.oci-bec.gc.ca/rpt/annrpt/annrpt20052006info-eng.aspx.

Parsons, Margaret, and Marie Chen. "In a World of Equality, Can Judges Stay Colour Blind?" *Toronto Star,* 3 March 2003, A21.

Pate, Kate (Executive Director, Canadian Association of Elizabeth Fry Societies). "Aboriginal Women and Their Over-Representation in Prisons." Paper presented at the Third National Conference on Aboriginal Criminal Justice Post-*Gladue,* Osgoode Hall, York University, Toronto, 30 April 2011.

Pavlich, George. *Governing Paradoxes of Restorative Justice.* London: Glasshouse Press, 2005.

–. *Justice Fragmented: Mediating Community Disputes under Postmodern Conditions.* London: Routledge, 1996.

Payne, Leigh A. *Unsettling Accounts: Neither Truth Nor Reconciliation in Confessions of State Violence.* Durham, NC: Duke University Press, 2008.

Pelletier, Renee. "The Nullification of Section 718.2(e): Aggravating Aboriginal Over-Representation in Canadian Prisons." *Osgoode Hall Law Journal* 39 (2001): 469-89.

Perreault, Samuel. "The Incarceration of Aboriginal People in Adult Correctional Services." *Juristat* 29, no 3, Statistics Canada, July 2009, http://www.statcan.gc.ca/pub/85-002-x/2009003/article/10903-eng.pdf.

Pewewardy, C. "Will the 'Real' Indians Please Stand Up." *Multicultural Review* 7, no 2 (1998): 36-42.

"Policy and Planning." Federation of Saskatchewan Indian Nations, http://www.fsin.com/index.php/policy-a-planning.html.

Povinelli, Elizabeth A. *The Cunning of Recognition: Indigenous Alterities and the Making of Australian Multiculturalism.* Durham, NC: Duke University Press, 2002.

Pranis, Kay, Barry Stewart, and Mark Wedge. *Peacemaking Circles: From Crime to Community.* St Paul, MN: Living Justice Press, 2003.

Price, Steven, and Anupama Rao, eds. *Discipline and the Other Body: Correction, Corporeality and Colonialism.* Durham, NC: Duke University Press, 2006.

"Prime Minister Harper Offers Full Apology on Behalf of Canadians for the Indian Residential Schools System." Prime Minister of Canada Stephen Harper, http://pm.gc.ca/eng/media.asp?category=2&id=2149.

Ptacek, James, ed. *Restorative Justice and Violence against Women*. Oxford: Oxford University Press, 2010.

Quigley, Tim. "Are We Doing Anything about the Disproportionate Jailing of Aboriginal People?" *Criminal Law Quarterly* 42 (1999): 129-60.

Rabinow, Paul. *The Foucault Reader*. New York: Pantheon Books, 1984.

Raibmon, Paige. *Authentic Indians: Episodes of Encounter from the Late Nineteenth Century Northwest Coast*. Durham, NC: Duke University Press, 2005.

Razack, Sherene H. *Dark Threats and White Knights: The Somalia Affair, Peacekeeping and the New Imperialism*. Toronto: University of Toronto Press, 2004.

–. "Gendered Racial Violence and Spatialized Justice: The Murder of Pamela George." In Sherene Razack, ed, *Race, Space and the Law: Unmapping a White Settler Society*, 99-120. Toronto: Between the Lines, 2002.

–. "Introduction: When Place Becomes Race." In Sherene H. Razack, ed, *Race, Space and the Law: Unmapping a White Settler Society*, 1-20. Toronto: Between the Lines, 2002.

–. *Looking White People in the Eye: Gender, Race and Culture in Courtrooms and Classrooms*. Toronto: University of Toronto Press, 1998.

–. "Making Canada White: Law and the Policing of Bodies of Colour in the 1990s." *Canadian Journal of Law and Society* 14, no 1 (1990): 159-84.

–. "'Simple Logic': Race, The Identity Documents Rule and The Story of a Nation Besieged and Betrayed." *Journal of Law and Social Policy* 15 (2002): 199-220.

"RCMP Apologizes for B.C. Pepper Spray Incident." *CBC News*, 5 July 2007, http://www.cbc.ca/news/canada/british-columbia/story/2007/07/05/pepper-spray.html.

"Report of the Task Force on Aboriginal Issues: Justice Issues." Government of New Brunswick, 1999, http://www2.gnb.ca/content/gnb/en/departments/aboriginal_affairs/publications/content/task_force.html.

Richland, Justin B. *Arguing with Tradition: The Language of Law in the Hopi Tribal Court*. Chicago: University of Chicago Press, 2008.

Ricoeur, Paul. *Memory, History, Forgetting*. Translated by K Blamey and D Pellauer. Chicago: University of Chicago Press, 2004.

Roach, Kent. "One Step Forward, Two Steps Back: *Gladue* at Ten and in the Courts of Appeal." *Criminal Law Quarterly* 54 (2009): 470-505.

–. "Systemic Racism and Criminal Justice Policy." *Windsor Yearbook of Access to Justice* 15 (1995): 236-49.

Roach, Kent, and Jonathan Rudin. "*Gladue:* The Judicial and Political Reception of a Promising Decision." *Canadian Journal of Criminology* 42 (2000): 355-88.

Roberts, Julian V. "Sentencing Reform: The Canadian Approach." *Federal Sentencing Reporter* 9, no 5 (1997): 245-49.

Roberts, Julian V, and David P Cole. "Introduction to Sentencing and Parole." In Julian V Roberts and David P Cole, eds, *Making Sense of Sentencing*, 2-30. Toronto: University of Toronto Press, 1999.

–, eds. *Making Sense of Sentencing*. Toronto: University of Toronto Press, 1999.

Rose, Nikolas, and Peter Miller. "Political Power beyond the State: Problematics of Government." *British Journal of Sociology* 43, no 2 (1992): 172-205.

Royal Commission on Aboriginal Peoples. *Bridging the Cultural Divide: A Report on Aboriginal People and Criminal Justice in Canada*. Ottawa: Queen's Printer, 1996.

Rudin, Jonathan. "Addressing Aboriginal Overrepresentation Post-*Gladue*: A Realistic Assessment of How Social Change Occurs." *Criminal Law Quarterly* 54 (2009): 447-69.

–. "Justice, Race and Time." *Toronto Star*, 17 February 2003, A21.

Rudin, Jonathan, and Kent Roach. "Broken Promises: A Response to Stenning and Roberts' 'Empty Promises,' 'Colloquy on Empty Promises: Parliament, the Supreme Court, and the Sentencing of Aboriginal Offenders.'" *Saskatchewan Law Review* 65 (2002): 3-34.

Rudin, Jonathan, Judy L Mungovan, and Erin Winocour. Presentation at the Second National Conference on Aboriginal Criminal Justice Post-*Gladue*, Toronto, 24 April 2010.

R v Hamilton. Factum for the Appellant, 12 January 2004.

R v Hamilton. Factum of the Interveners the African Canadian Legal Clinic, the Congress of Black Women (Ontario Region), and the Jamaican Canadian Association, 12 January 2004.

R v Hamilton. Factum of the Intervener Native Women's Association of Canada, 12 January 2004.

Said, Edward. *Culture and Imperialism*. New York: Vintage, 1994.

Savarese, Josephine. "Gladue Was a Woman: The Importance of Gender in Restorative-based Sentencing." In Elizabeth Elliot and Robert Gordon, eds, *New Directions in Restorative Justice: Issues, Practice, Evaluation*, 135-50. Vancouver: Willan Publishing, 2005.

Sawatsky, Jarem. *The Ethic of Traditional Communities and the Spirit of Healing Justice: Studies from Hollow Water, the Iona Community and Plum Village*. London: Jessica Kingsley Publishers, 2009.

Schaap, Andrew. *Political Reconciliation*. London: Routledge, 2005.

–. "Power and Responsibility: Should We Spare the King's Head?" *Politics* 20, no 3 (2000): 129-35.

Scott, David. "Colonial Governmentality." *Social Text* 43 (1995): 191-220.

–. *Refashioning Futures: Criticism after Postcoloniality*. Princeton, NJ: Princeton University Press, 1999.

"Sentencing by Race." Editorial. *National Post*, 5 August 2004, A15.

The Sentencing Project. "Executive Summary: Does the Punishment Fit the Crime? Drug Users and Drunk Drivers, Questions of Race and Class," 1993, http://www.sentencingproject.org/search/search.cfm?search_string=%22Questions+of+Race+and+Class%22&submit=SEARCH.

Smith, Andrea. *Conquest: Sexual Violence and the American Indian Genocide.* Cambridge, MA: South End Press, 2005.

Smith, Philip. "Letter to the Editor: Unjust Sentence." *Globe and Mail,* 14 February 2003, A18.

Spivak, Gayatri. *Outside the Teaching Machine.* New York: Routledge, 1993.

Stenning, Philip, and Julian V Roberts. "Empty Promises: Parliament, the Supreme Court, and the Sentencing of Aboriginal Offenders." *Saskatchewan Law Review* 64 (2001): 137-68.

"Stolen Sisters: Helen Betty Osborne." Amnesty International, 4 October 2007, http://www.amnesty.ca/research/reports/no-more-stolen-sisters-the-need-for-a-comprehensive-response-to-discrimination-and-.

Stoler, Ann Laura, ed. *Haunted By Empire: Geographies of Intimacy in North American History.* Durham, NC: Duke University Press, 2006.

Stoler, Ann Laura. *Race and the Education of Desire: Foucault's History of Sexuality and the Colonial Order of Things.* Durham, NC: Duke University Press, 1995.

Strang, Heather, and John Braithwaite, eds. *Restorative Justice and Family Violence.* Cambridge: Cambridge University Press, 2002.

Stuart, Barry, and Kay Pranis, "Peacemaking Circles: Reflections on Principal Features and Primary Outcomes." In Dennis Sullivan and Larry Tifft, eds, *Handbook of Restorative Justice,* 121-33. New York: Routledge, 2006.

"Submission of the Canadian Association of Elizabeth Fry Societies to the Standing Committee on Justice, Human Rights, Public Safety and Emergency Preparedness (39th Parliament) Regarding Bill C-10: An Act to amend the Criminal Code (Minimum Penalties for Offences Involving Firearms)," November 2006, http://www.elizabethfry.ca/billC-10/billC-10-nov06.pdf.

Sudbury, Julia. "'Mules,' 'Yardies' and Other Folk Devils: Mapping Cross-Border Imprisonment in Britain." In Julia Sudbury, ed, *Global Lockdown: Race, Gender and the Prison-Industrial Complex,* 167-84. London: Routledge, 2005.

Tanovich, David M. *The Colour of Justice: Policing and Race in Canada.* Toronto: Irwin Law, 2006.

–. "Race, Sentencing and the 'War on Drugs.'" *Criminal Reports* 22 (2004): 45-56.

Thompson, Janna. "Apology, Historical Obligations and the Ethics of Memory." *Memory Studies* 2 no 2 (2009): 195-210.

–. "From Slaughter to Abduction: Coming to Terms with the Past in Australia," 2004, http://www.cappe.edu.au/docs/working-papers/Thompson6.pdf.

–. "Historical Responsibility and Liberal Societies." *Intergenerational Justice Review* 9 (2009): 13-18.

–. *Taking Responsibility for the Past: Reparation and Historical Injustice*. Oxford: Blackwell Publishers, 2002.

Tonry, Michael. "The Fragmentation of Sentencing and Corrections in America." National Institute of Justice, September 1999, http://www.ojp.usdoj.gov/nij /pubs-sum/175721.htm.

Torpey, John. *Making Whole What Has Been Smashed: On Reparation Politics*. Cambridge, MA: Harvard University Press, 2006.

–. *Politics of the Past: On Repairing Historical Injustices*. New York: Rowman and Littlefield, 2003.

Trouillot, Michel-Rolph. "Abortive Rituals: Historical Apologies in the Global Era." *Interventions* 2 no 2 (2000): 171-86.

Tuhiwai Smith, Linda. *Decolonizing Methodologies: Research and Indigenous Peoples*. London: Zed Books, 1999.

Turpel, Mary Ellen. "On the Question of Adapting the Canadian Criminal Justice System for Aboriginal Peoples: Don't Fence Me In." In Royal Commission on Aboriginal Peoples, ed, *Aboriginal Peoples and the Justice System: Report from the National Round Table on Aboriginal Justice Issues*, 166-67. Ottawa: Supply and Services, 1997.

Valverde, Mariana. "Practices of Citizenship and Scales of Governance." *New Criminal Law Review* 13, no 2 (2010): 216-40.

Van de Veen, Sherry L. *Some Canadian Problem Solving Court Processes*. Unpublished manuscript, on file with the National Judicial Institute, 2003.

Villa-Vicencio, Charles, and Erik Doxtader, "Introduction: Provocations at the End of Amnesty." In Charles Villa-Vicencio and Erik Doxtader, eds, *The Provocations of Amnesty: Memory, Justice and Impunity*, x-xx. Trenton, NJ: Africa World Press, 2004.

Walker, Margaret Urban. *What Is Reparative Justice?* Milwaukee, WI: Marquette University Press, 2011.

Walters, Mark D. "The Jurisprudence of Reconciliation: Aboriginal Rights in Canada." In Will Kymlicka and Bashir Bashir, eds, *The Politics of Reconciliation in Multicultural Societies*, 165-91. Oxford: Oxford University Press, 2008.

Weeden, Chris. *Feminist Practice and Poststructuralist Theory*. New York: Blackwell Publishers, 1987.

Weisman, Richard. "Showing Remorse: Reflections on the Gap Between Expression and Attribution in Cases of Wrongful Conviction." *Canadian Journal of Criminology and Criminal Justice* 46, no 2 (2004): 121-38.

Williams, Toni. "Punishing Women: The Promise and Perils of Contextualized Sentencing for Aboriginal Women in Canada." *Cleveland State Law Review* 55, no 3 (2007): 269-86.

Woolford, Andrew. *The Politics of Restorative Justice*. Toronto: Fernwood Publishing, 2009.

Wright Commission. "Commission of Inquiry into the Matters Relating to the Death of Neil Stonechild," 2004, http://www.stonechildinquiry.ca.

Cases Cited

Baker v Canada (Minister of Citizenship and Immigration), [1999] 2 SCR 817.
Delgamuukw v British Columbia, [1997] 3 SCR 1010.
R c Amitook, 2006 QCCQ 2705, [2006] QJ no 2951 (QL).
R c Idlout, 2009 QCCQ 5104, [2009] QJ no 5759 (QL).
R c JO, 2007 QCCQ 716, [2007] QJ no 920 (QL).
R c Papatie, 2009 QCCQ 4491, [2009] QJ no 8234 (QL).
R c Petiquay, 2006 QCCQ 506, [2006] QJ no 658 (QL).
R c Pootoogee, 2009 QCCQ 6605, [2009] QJ no 7164 (QL).
R c Volant, [2002] QJ no 71 (QL).
R v AAE, 2004 BCCA 220, 61 WCB (2d) 706, [2004] BCJ no 780 (QL).
R v Abel, 2008 BCSC 1731, [2008] BCJ no 2460 (QL).
R v Allan, [2008] OJ no 2794 (QL).
R v Auger, 2000 ABQB 450, [2000] 10 WWR 329, [2000] AJ no 784 (QL).
R v Bachmier, 2005 ONCJ 36, 63 WCB (2d) 606, [2005] OJ no 496 (QL).
R v Bansfield, 2008 ONCJ 383, 79 WCB (2d) 297, [2008] OJ no 3292 (QL).
R v Bardy, 2008 ONCJ 751, [2008] OJ no 5707 (QL).
R v Batisse, 2009 ONCA 114, 93 OR (3d) 643, [2009] OJ no 452 (QL).
R v Bernard, 1999 ABQB 524, 259 AR 171, [1999] AJ no 812 (QL).
R v Betsidea, 2007 NWTSC 85, 75 WCB (2d) 462, [2007] NWTJ no 90 (QL).
R v BL, 54 WCB (2d) 296, [2002] MJ no 240 (QL).
R v Borde, [2003] 172 CCC 225 (Ont CA) (QL).
R v Brittain, 2001 SKCA 125, 213 SaskR 218, [2001] SJ no 708 (QL).
R v Brizard, 68 WCB (2d) 556, [2006] OJ no 729 (QL).
R v Brooks, 2008 NSPC 58, [2008] NSJ no 519 (QL).
R v Brossault, 2009 BCSC 464, [2009] BCJ no 682 (QL).
R v Brown, [2002] OJ no 295 (QL).
R v Brown, [2009] OJ no 979 (QL).
R v Caissey, 2008 ONCJ 716, [2008] OJ no 5472 (QL).
R v Cardinal, 2009 ABPC 296, 46 CELR (3d) 146, [2009] AJ no 1083 (QL).
R v Carratt, 1999 SKQB 116, 185 SaskR 221, [1999] SJ no 626 (QL).
R v Casemore, 2009 SKQB 306, 336 SaskR 110, [2009] SJ no 440 (QL).
R v Collins, 2001 ONCA 182, [2011] OJ no 978 (QL).
R v Constant, 2009 SKPC 80, [2009] SJ no 358 (QL).
R v Craigan, 2007 BCPC 184, [2007] BCJ no 1279 (QL).
R v Cunningham (1996), 27 OR (3d) 786 (Ont CA).
R v Dantimo, [2009] OJ no 655 (QL).
R v Dayfoot, 2007 ONCJ 332, 74 WCB (2d) 298, [2007] OJ no 2869 (QL).
R v DB, 2003 BCPC 260, [2003] BCJ no 1735 (QL).

R v DBM, 2002 YKTC 81 [2002] YJ no 96 (QL).

R v Dorian, 57 WCB (2d) 362, [2003] OJ no 1415 (QL).

R v DRWC, 2004 ABQB 21, 351 AR 13, [2003] AJ no 1669 (QL).

R v Edwards, 2001 BCSC 688, 51 WCB (2d) 41, [2001] BCJ no 1062 (QL).

R v Elliott, 2006 ABPC 372, 42 MVR (5th) 66, [2006] AJ no 1686 (QL).

R v Esquega, [2009] OJ no 514 (QL).

R v FL, [2002] OTC 347, [2002] OJ no 1989 (QL).

R v Fobister, [2009] OJ no 2576 (QL).

R v Fox, 2001 ABCA 64, 277 AR 298, [2001] AJ no 268 (QL).

R v Gelenzoski, [2006] AJ no 1009 (QL).

R v Gladue, 1999 ABCA 279, 46 MVR (3d) 183, [1999] AJ no 1132 (QL).

R v Gladue, [1999] 1 SCR 668.

R v Gladue, [2006] AJ no 1196 (QL).

R v Green, 2010 ONCJ 84, [2010] OJ no 1069 (QL).

R v Gregoire, 2009 NLTD 21, 284 Nfld & PEIR 290, [2009] NJ no 37 (QL).

R v Guimond, 2010 MBQB 1, [2010] MJ no 19 (QL).

R v Hamilton, [2003] OJ no 532 (QL) (QL).

R v Hamilton, [2004] OJ no 3252 (Ont CA) (QL) (QL).

R v Healy, 1999 ABCA 220, 237 AR 195, [1999] AJ no 817 (QL).

R v Henhawk, 2009 ONCJ 142, [2009] OJ no 1365 (QL).

R v Hunter, 180 SaskR 47, [1999] SJ no 355 (QL).

R v Huxford, 2010 ONCJ 33, [2010] OJ no 482 (QL).

R v IDB, 2005 ABQB 421, [2005] AJ no 689 (QL).

R v Ipeelee, 2001 NWTSC 33, [2001] NWTJ (QL).

R v Ipeelee, [2009] 99 OR (3d) 419 (QL).

R v Ipeelee, [2009] OJ no 5402 (QL).

R v Ipeelee, 2012 SCC 13.

R v Jacobish, 2008 NLTD 149, 279 Nfld & PEIR 45, [2008] NJ no 254 (QL).

R v Jacobish, 2008 NLTD 148, 279 Nfld & PEIR 331, [2008] NJ no 255 (QL).

R v JKE, 2005 YKSC 61, 68 W.C.B. (2d) 604, [2005] YJ no 100 (QL).

R v John, 2004 SKCA 13, [2004] 7 WWR 643, [2004] SJ no 61 (QL).

R v Johnston, [2003] OJ no 4210 (QL).

R v Julian, 2006 NSPC 67, 251 NSR (2d) 44, [2006] NSJ no 545) (QL).

R v Kakekagamick, 69 WCB (2d) 157, [2006] OJ no 1449 (QL).

R v Keeash, [2003] OJ no 3413 (QL).

R v Keenatch, 2009 SKPC 72, [2009] SJ no 395 (QL).

R v Kejick, [2001] OJ no 5077 (QL).

R v Kelly, [1999] NWTJ no 122 (QL).

R v Knowlton, 2001 ABPC 163, 297 AR 264, [2001] AJ no 1176 (QL).

R v Kokopenace, [2008] OJ no 4582 (QL).

R v Kootenay, [2006] AJ no 950 (QL).

R v Kootoo, [2000] NuJ no 10 (QL).

R v Kwandibens, 2008 ONCJ 434, [2008] OJ no 3679 (QL).

R v Laliberte, 2000 SKCA 27, [2000] 4 WWR 491, [2000] SJ no 138 (QL).

R v Lampe, 2007 NLTD 116, 269 Nfld & PEIR 82, [2007] NJ no 228 (QL).

R v Lazore, 2008 ONCJ 578, [2008] OJ no 4545 (QL).

R v LC, 2001 YKYC 2, [2001] YJ no 42 (QL).

R v Logan, 125 OAC 152, 139 CCC (3d) 57, [1999] OJ no 3411 (QL).

R v Madden (1996), 27 OR (3d) (Ont CA).

R v Maracle, 2008 ONCJ 711, [2008] OJ no 5500 (QL).

R v Marchment, [2000] OJ no 3559 (QL).

R v Martin, 2004 NWTSC 15, [2004] NWTJ no 19 (QL).

R v McDougall, 2009 MBQB 299, [2009] MJ no 400 (QL).

R v Meawasige, 2008 ONCJ 122, 77 WCB (2d) 207, [2008] OJ no 1085 (QL).

R v Mills, 2002 BCCA 35, 162 BCAC 179, [2002] BCJ no 64 at para 15 (QL).

R v ML, 187 SaskR 195, [2000] SJ no 17 at para 49 (QL).

R v Monture, 2008 ONCJ 416, 75 MVR (5th) 197, [2008] OJ no 3648 (QL).

R v Morin, [1997] OJ no 2413 (QL).

R v Morning Bird, 2008 ABCA 419, 440 AR 396, [2008] AJ no 1373 (QL).

R v Morris, [2006] 2 SCR 915, 2006 SCC 59.

R v MP, 1999 OTC 153, [1999] OJ no 5375 (QL).

R v Natomagan, 2010 SKPC 7, [2010] SJ no 45 (QL).

R v Nickerson, 2006 BCSC 1390, [2006] BCJ no 2148 (QL).

R v Niganobe, 72 MVR (5th) 280, [2008] OJ no 4181 (QL).

R v Noltcho, 1999 SKQB 232, [1999] SJ no 833 (QL).

R v Obed, 2006 NLTD 155, 260 Nfld & PEIR 286, [2006] NJ no 284 (QL).

R v Pangman, 2001 MBCA 64, [2001] 8 WWR 10, [2001] MJ no 217 (QL).

R v Parks (1994), 84 CCC (3d) 353.

R v Peters, 2010 ONCA 30, 250 CCC (3d) 277, [2010] OJ no 128 (QL).

R v Phillips, 2005 ONCJ 498, 68 WCB (2d) 472, [2005] OJ no 5852 (QL).

R v PJO, 2008 ABPC 112, [2008] AJ no 442 (QL).

R v Plain, 77 WCB (2d) 566, [2008] OJ no 2188 (QL).

R v Poker, 2006 NLTD 154, 261 Nfld & PEIR 1, [2006] NJ no 285 (QL).

R v Prevost, 79 WCB (2d) 78, [2008] OJ no 3609 (QL).

R v Proulx, 2000 SCC 1, [2000] 1 SCR 61.

R v Quash, 2009 YKTC 54, [2009] YJ no 72 (QL).

R v Ray, 79 WCB (2d) 556, [2008] OJ no 4185 (QL).

R v Richards (1999), 26 CR (5th) 286.

R v Ross, [2000] SJ no 561 (QL).

R v Rowell, 2001 BCCA 512, 158 BCAC 184, [2001] BCJ no 1837 (QL).

R v S(RD) (1997), 118 CCC (3d) 353 (SCC).

R v S.C., 2001 BCPC 112, [2001] BCJ no 2206 (QL).

R v Silversmith, 77 MVR (5th) 54, [2008] OJ no 4646 (QL).

R v Sisco, 2008 ONCJ 12, 76 WCB (2d) 210, [2008] OJ no 157 (QL).

R v Skani, 2002 ABQB 1097, 331 AR 50, [2002] AJ no 1579 (QL).

R v SM, 2004 SKQB 358, 253 SaskR 80, [2004] SJ no 572 (QL).

R v Small-Buffalo, 2009 ABQB 353, [2009] 9 WWR 516, [2009] AJ no 647 (QL).

R v Smith, 2008 ONCJ 628, [2008] OJ no 4867 (QL).

R v SMW, 2003 BCPC 379, [2003] BCJ no 2511 (QL).

R v Spencer, [2003] OJ no 1052 .

R. v Spencer, [2004] 72 OR (3d) 47, 241 DLR (4th) 542, 186 CCC (3d) 181.

R v Stevens, 2009 NSPC 46, 282 NSR (2d) 314, [2009] NSJ no 449 (QL).

R v Sutherland, 2010 ONCJ 103, [2010] OJ no 1188 (QL).

R v TDP, 2004 SKPC 57, 250 SaskR 3, [2004] SJ no 254 (QL).

R v Teepell, [2009] OJ no 3989 (QL).

R v T.K., [2001] OJ no 5070 (QL).

R v Travers, 16 MVR (4th) 113, [2001] MJ no 250 (QL).

R v Wells, 2000 SCC 10, [2000] 1 SCR 207, [2000] SCJ no 11 (QL).

R v Wells, [2000] 1 SCR 207, 141 CCC (3d) 368.

R v Whiskeyjack, 2008 ONCA 800, 93 OR (3d) 743, [2008] OJ no 4755 (QL).

R v Wilson, 2001 BCSC 1653, 52 WCB (2d) 214, [2001] BCJ no 2546 (QL).

R v Wilson, 2008 ABQB 588, 79 WCB (2d) 765, [2008] AJ no 1086 (QL).

R v Wilson, 2009 ABCA 257, 457 AR 373, [2009] AJ no 781 (QL).

R v WJL, 2005 BCPC 572, [2005] BCJ no 2733 (QL).

R v WLQ, 2005 SKQB 10, 259 SaskR 103, [2005] SJ no 13 (QL).

R v Yee, 2006 SKPC 31, 278 SaskR 75, [2006] SJ no 226 (QL).

R v Zarpa, 2009 NLTD 175, [2009] NJ no 309 (QL).

US v Belanger, [2003] OJ no 5862 (QL).

Index

reconciliation politics, 13; and section 718.2(e), 14, 24, 77, 132, 164, 181-82; in sentencing, 3, 130-33, 164, 168
National Responsibility and Global Injustice (Miller), 13
nationalism: and criminal law, ix, 60-61; inclusion of Aboriginal spokespersons, 36; as linked to racism, 52, 53, 193*n*66; multiculturalism, 25 (*see also* multiculturalism); as racial and cultural narrative, 118, 125, 132, 134-35, 143, 167, 169; white settler-colonialism, 34, 53, 182 (*see also* white settler societies)
Native Women's Association of Canada (NWAC), 115, 150-53, 167, 218*n*130
Neil Stonechild Inquiry, 45
New Democratic Party of Ontario, 45, 218*n*134
North, John, 122, 126

Office of the Correctional Investigator, 38, 107
Ontario Court of Appeal, 7, 25, 76, 105, 115, 136, 144, 157, 160, 162-63, 168, 177, 219*n*163, 220*n*174; *Borde,* 138-39, 153 (*see also R. v Borde*); *Gladue,* 105, 162-64 (see also *R. v Gladue*); *Hamilton,* 7, 114-15, 135, 165, 167, 215*n*67 (*see also R. v Hamilton*); *Ipeelee,* 174, 221*n*12, (*see also R. v Ipeelee*); *R. v Collins,* 177, *R v. Spencer,* 158. *See also* African Canadian Legal Clinic (ACLC); Hill, Justice Casey
Ontario Review Board, 8
Ontario Superior Court of Justice, 24-25, 114, 126, 134-36
Opium Act, 118, 143
Osborne, Helen Betty, 43
overincarceration, 3-7; of Aboriginal people, 1, 6, 35, 45, 77, 107, 189*n*28;

of Aborginal women, ix, 9; of African Canadians in Ontario jails, 153, 165-67; ameliorated by community justice, 62; Bill C-41, 60, 211*n*81; of black Canadians, 75, 155; of black women, 127, 147 (*see also* black women); as connected to colonialism and historical injustice, 40-41, 44-45, 48, 75-76, 85, 136, 167; as continuing to rise despite provisions, 107-8, 112, 171; legislative intent and effects of section 718.2(e), 1 3, 5-6, 24, 29, 55-56, 58, 83, 96, 100, 108, 111-12, 114, 138 (*see also* restorative justice); material reality vs discursive politics, 78; overrepresentation of indigenous and racialized people in prisons, viii, ix, 8, 76, 172, 175; of racialized communities in Canada, 75; as a result of "culture clash," 40; as a result of socio-economic disadvantage, 40, 128; as a result of systemic racism, 63, 113 (*see also* systemic racism); taking national responsibility for, 13, 61-65, 71-72, 184; as tied to cultural difference, 36-38, 42-43, 62, 84-85, 90 (*see also* cultural difference). *See also* systemic racism

Parliament, 8, 24, 38, 58-59, 67, 75, 84, 96, 106; introduction of Bill-C41, 7; parliamentary committee, 4; parliamentary debates, vii, 2, 73, 724; parliamentary intent, 83, 90, 97, 138, 141, 211*n*81
Parsons, Margaret, 134. *See also* African Canadian Legal Clinic (ACLC)
Parti Québécois, 60, 75
patriarchy, 34, 63, 69, 107
Pauktuutit, 1- 4, 16, 22, 31, 64-70, 72, 187*n*3, 203*n*25. *See also* Standing

Donn Short
"Don't Be So Gay!" Queers, Bullying, and Making Schools Safe (2013)

Melissa Munn and Chris Bruckert
On the Outside: From Lengthy Imprisonment to Lasting Freedom (2013)

Emmett Macfarlane
*Governing from the Bench: The Supreme Court of Canada
and the Judicial Role* (2013)

Ron Ellis
Unjust by Design: The Administrative Justice System in Canada (2013)

David R. Boyd
*The Right to a Healthy Environment: Revitalizing Canada's
Constitution* (2012)

David Milward
*Aboriginal Justice and the Charter: Realizing a Culturally Sensitive
Interpretation of Legal Rights* (2012)

Shelley A.M. Gavigan
*Hunger, Horses, and Government Men: Criminal Law on the Aboriginal
Plains, 1870-1905* (2012)

Steven Bittle
*Still Dying for a Living: Corporate Criminal Liability after the Westray
Mine Disaster* (2012)

Jacqueline D. Krikorian
International Trade Law and Domestic Policy: Canada, the United States, and the WTO (2012)

Michael Boudreau
City of Order: Crime and Society in Halifax, 1918-35 (2012)

David R. Boyd
The Environmental Rights Revolution: A Global Study of Constitutions, Human Rights, and the Environment (2012)

Lesley Erickson
Westward Bound: Sex, Violence, the Law, and the Making of a Settler Society (2011)

Elaine Craig
Troubling Sex: Towards a Legal Theory of Sexual Integrity (2011)

Laura DeVries
Conflict in Caledonia: Aboriginal Land Rights and the Rule of Law (2011)

Jocelyn Downie and Jennifer J. Llewellyn (eds.)
Being Relational: Reflections on Relational Theory and Health Law (2011)

Grace Li Xiu Woo
Ghost Dancing with Colonialism: Decolonization and Indigenous Rights at the Supreme Court of Canada (2011)

Fiona Kelly
Transforming Law's Family: The Legal Recognition of Planned Lesbian Motherhood (2011)

Colleen Bell
The Freedom of Security: Governing Canada in the Age of Counter-Terrorism (2011)

James B. Kelly and Christopher P. Manfredi (eds.)
Contested Constitutionalism: Reflections on the Canadian Charter of Rights and Freedoms (2009)

Catherine Bell and Robert K. Paterson (eds.)
Protection of First Nations Cultural Heritage: Laws, Policy, and Reform (2008)

Hamar Foster, Benjamin L. Berger, and A.R. Buck (eds.)
The Grand Experiment: Law and Legal Culture in British Settler Societies (2008)

Richard J. Moon (ed.)
Law and Religious Pluralism in Canada (2008)

Catherine Bell and Val Napoleon (eds.)
First Nations Cultural Heritage and Law: Case Studies, Voices, and Perspectives (2008)

Douglas C. Harris
Landing Native Fisheries: Indian Reserves and Fishing Rights in British Columbia, 1849-1925 (2008)

Peggy J. Blair
Lament for a First Nation: The Williams Treaties of Southern Ontario (2008)

Lori G. Beaman
Defining Harm: Religious Freedom and the Limits of the Law (2007)

Stephen Tierney (ed.)
Multiculturalism and the Canadian Constitution (2007)

Julie Macfarlane
The New Lawyer: How Settlement Is Transforming the Practice of Law (2007)

Randy K. Lippert
Sanctuary, Sovereignty, Sacrifice: Canadian Sanctuary Incidents, Power, and Law (2005)

James B. Kelly
Governing with the Charter: Legislative and Judicial Activism and Framers' Intent (2005)

Dianne Pothier and Richard Devlin (eds.)
Critical Disability Theory: Essays in Philosophy, Politics, Policy, and Law (2005)

Susan G. Drummond
Mapping Marriage Law in Spanish Gitano Communities (2005)

Louis A. Knafla and Jonathan Swainger (eds.)
Laws and Societies in the Canadian Prairie West, 1670-1940 (2005)

Ikechi Mgbeoji
Global Biopiracy: Patents, Plants, and Indigenous Knowledge (2005)

Florian Sauvageau, David Schneiderman, and David Taras, with Ruth Klinkhammer and Pierre Trudel
The Last Word: Media Coverage of the Supreme Court of Canada (2005)

Gerald Kernerman
Multicultural Nationalism: Civilizing Difference, Constituting Community (2005)

Pamela A. Jordan
Defending Rights in Russia: Lawyers, the State, and Legal Reform in the Post-Soviet Era (2005)

Anna Pratt
Securing Borders: Detention and Deportation in Canada (2005)

Kirsten Johnson Kramar
Unwilling Mothers, Unwanted Babies: Infanticide in Canada (2005)

W.A. Bogart
Good Government? Good Citizens? Courts, Politics, and Markets in a Changing Canada (2005)

Catherine Dauvergne
Humanitarianism, Identity, and Nation: Migration Laws in Canada and Australia (2005)

Michael Lee Ross
First Nations Sacred Sites in Canada's Courts (2005)

Andrew Woolford
Between Justice and Certainty: Treaty Making in British Columbia (2005)

John McLaren, Andrew Buck, and Nancy Wright (eds.)
Despotic Dominion: Property Rights in British Settler Societies (2004)

Georges Campeau
From UI to EI: Waging War on the Welfare State (2004)

Alvin J. Esau
The Courts and the Colonies: The Litigation of Hutterite Church Disputes (2004)

Christopher N. Kendall
Gay Male Pornography: An Issue of Sex Discrimination (2004)

Roy B. Flemming
Tournament of Appeals: Granting Judicial Review in Canada (2004)

Constance Backhouse and Nancy L. Backhouse
The Heiress vs the Establishment: Mrs. Campbell's Campaign for Legal Justice (2004)

Christopher P. Manfredi
Feminist Activism in the Supreme Court: Legal Mobilization and the Women's Legal Education and Action Fund (2004)

Annalise Acorn
Compulsory Compassion: A Critique of Restorative Justice (2004)

Jonathan Swainger and Constance Backhouse (eds.)
People and Place: Historical Influences on Legal Culture (2003)

Jim Phillips and Rosemary Gartner
Murdering Holiness: The Trials of Franz Creffield and George Mitchell (2003)

David R. Boyd
Unnatural Law: Rethinking Canadian Environmental Law and Policy (2003)

Ikechi Mgbeoji
Collective Insecurity: The Liberian Crisis, Unilateralism, and Global Order (2003)

Rebecca Johnson
Taxing Choices: The Intersection of Class, Gender, Parenthood, and the Law (2002)

John McLaren, Robert Menzies, and Dorothy E. Chunn (eds.)
Regulating Lives: Historical Essays on the State, Society, the Individual, and the Law (2002)

Joan Brockman
Gender in the Legal Profession: Fitting or Breaking the Mould (2001)

Printed and bound in Canada by Friesens

Set in Myriad and Sabon by Artegraphica Design Co. Ltd.

Copy editor: Stacy Belden

Proofreader: Shirarose Wilensky